DEVIANT SCIENCE

DEVIANT SCIENCE
The Case of Parapsychology

James McClenon

University of Pennsylvania Press

PHILADELPHIA

Design by Design For Publishing, Bob Nance

Library of Congress Cataloging in Publication Data

McClenon, James.
  Deviant science.
  Bibliography: p.
  Includes index.
  1. Psychical research. I. Title.
BF1040.M326   1984   133.8   83–14680
ISBN 0–8122–1178–2 (pbk.)

Printed in the United States of America

Contents

Figures

Tables

Abbreviations

AAAS	American Association for the Advancement of Science
APA	American Psychological Association
ASPR	American Society for Psychical Research
CCA	Committee on Council Affairs
CIA	Central Intelligence Agency
CSFR	Committee for Scientific Freedom and Responsibility
CSICOP	Committee for the Scientific Investigation of Claims of the Paranormal
DIA	Defense Intelligence Agency
ESP	Extra-sensory Perception
FRNM	Foundation for Research on the Nature of Man
FCC	Federal Communications Commission
IEEE	Institute of Electrical and Electronic Engineers
JFK	John F. Kennedy University
NSF	National Science Foundation
PA	Parapsychological Association
PF	Parapsychology Foundation
PMIR	Psi-mediated Instrumental Response
PRF	Psychical Research Foundation
SPR	Society for Psychical Research
SRI	SRI International (formerly Stanford Research Institute)

Acknowledgments

In a work such as this one, in which over a hundred individuals were formally interviewed and even more contributed information informally, it is impossible to acknowledge personally all contributions. I would like to express my appreciation to both the proponents and critics of parapsychology who helped me gather information about this field. I would also like to thank the many professors and scientists who helped by expressing their opinions on this realm of inquiry. Some helped a great deal through their critiques of earlier versions of this book: Richard H. Brown (chair of my dissertation committee), George Ritzer, Jennie McIntyre, Harvey Greisman, James Glass, Stanley Krippner, Gertrude Schmeidler, Michaelson Maher, Michael Thailbourne, Marcello Truzzi, Catherine Borras, and the two anonymous readers obtained through the University of Pennsylvania Press deserve particular thanks. I wish to acknowledge the following individuals, whose writings proved highly valuable in my theoretical formulations: Richard H. Brown, Harry Collins, Trevor Pinch, Thomas Kuhn, Marcello Truzzi, Brian and S. Lynne Mackenzie, M. J. Mulkay, D. Scott Rogo, Paul Allison, Ron Westrum, Seymour Mauskopf, and Michael McVaugh. Others should be thanked for their efforts in helping me acquire information: David Phillips, William Braud, Maydelle Stewart, Rhea White, George Hansen, Rex Stanford, Dorothy Pope, Howard Zimmerman, Theodore Rockwell, John Timmerman, J. Richard Greenwell, Grover Krantz, Stanley Krippner, Douglas Dean, Catherine Borras, K. Ramakrishna Rao, James Randi, Ray Hyman, Paul Kurtz, John Ringle. Pat Woodall should be commended for her typing of this manuscript again and again. David Sweet and the copyeditor Robert Brown are thanked for their editorial assistance.

1

Introduction

The Problem

Over a century has passed since scientists first began investigating claims about phenomena labeled as paranormal. Why have these claims remained unresolved for so long? Scientific efforts concerning them have not led to any consensus on the facticity or ontological status of the various alleged phenomena, nor does there seem to be a tendency toward consensus. However, stable social patterns have evolved surrounding a small number of scientists investigating the paranormal and the larger scientific community.

As defined by those within the field, parapsychology is "The branch of science that deals with psi communication, i.e., behavioral or personal exchanges with the environment which are extrasensorimotor—not dependent on the senses and muscles" (*Journal of Parapsychology*, Glossary, 1982). The claims of some parapsychologists to have found evidence supporting the existence of psi continue to create controversy within the scientific community. Indeed, some scientists even deny that such investigations fall within the realm of science at all.

None of the major theoretical orientations within the sociology of science can explain the stability of social conditions surrounding parapsychology. Griffith and Mullins (1972) argue convincingly that most scientific specialties maintain only loose networks of organization and communication. Whenever a "radical conceptual reorganization" seems possible within a field, "coherent social groups" are likely to form. Griffith and Mullins (1972) studied various groups in this category (quantum mechanics, the "phage group" in biology, the algebraists, operant conditioning, audition research, and ethnomethodology) and found remarkably similar social characteristics and patterns of development. Allison (1973) found that the field of parapsychology closely resembled these coherent groups socially and developmentally, but noted some unusual features. Coherent groups in science generally have only comparatively brief life-spans, typically ten to fifteen years, after which they are either absorbed into mainstream science or die out (Griffith and Mullins, 1972). Parapsychology involves a coherent social group, which has existed since J. B. Rhine established it as a research paradigm in 1934. The propensity for long-term survival of this "coherent social group" constitutes a puzzle within the sociology of science. Parapsychology has neither died out nor has it been absorbed into mainstream science. The field has gained a degree of scientific legitimacy, having been granted affiliate status with the American Association for the Advancement of Science in 1969, but even this affiliation has been challenged from time to time.

This current study involves the social processes by which legitimacy is granted or denied new forms of scientific inquiry. Parapsychology, a field on the margins of legitimacy, is used as an example.

The Theoretical Orientation

It is often thought that scientific research is immune to "nonscientific" forces. A more relativistic sociology of science developed by Kuhn, Lakatos, Feyerabend, Mulkay, Pinch, and H. M. Collins, exposes social components that contribute to scientific progress. This study draws from these individuals' theoretical orientations and extends them in order to develop a framework explaining the social phenomena surrounding the field of parapsychology. These social phenomena can be understood through an analysis that uses theories of deviant behavior as well as analyses of scientism, that is, the study of the ideological aspects of science. Scientism can be defined as the body of ideas used by scientists to legitimate their practices. By necessity, this ideology is somewhat covert, implicit, and latent since science is assumed to be "free from presuppositions" except for the supposition that the rules of logic and method are valid (Weber, 1962).

Although philosophers of science are unable to agree on the precise nature of scientism, the sociologist can study it through observing the attitudes and actions of scientists and noting the means by which these attitudes and actions are rationalized.

Science is defined by the methodology through which it generates knowledge. This methodology is based on various metaphysical assumptions that have evolved with the historical development of science. Science is perceived as rational in that its findings derive from reason, inference, and logic in evaluating special forms of observation. Because the use of reason by a community of scientists involves a process of argumentation, science, to a degree, must be defined in a sociological manner. Scientific knowledge derives from a process of argumentation with rhetorical and political aspects. The social definition of science tends to depend on scientists in powerful positions who interpret the ideas (scientism) used to legitimate the practices of science. Scientism should not be considered a negative aspect of science but an ever-changing tool used to conduct science as a collective endeavor. It is necessary in maintaining the boundaries of the scientific community.

One aspect of maintaining boundaries is deciding whether any specific anomaly should be allowed into the scientific process. Various anomalistic phenomena fail to meet scientistic criteria and are rejected. They have been granted such low ontological status that investigations of such anomalies are not published in scientific literature. Scientists engage in a rhetorical and political process that labels various systems of belief regarding these anomalies as deviant. Scientists who continue their research in rejected anomalies are stigmatized. These scientists can create a stable relationship with orthodox science by increasing their adherence to scientific ideology, and will tend to do so after being labeled deviant. Social stability occurs when such "deviant" scientists receive support from the public and maintain (or increase) their adherence to scientific methodology, thereby indirectly supporting the very ideology that labels them as deviant.

Parapsychology as Science

It is often maintained that parapsychology is a cult or is concerned with the occult (e.g., Boring, 1966; Rawcliffe, 1959; Szasz, 1957). This assumption is incorrect. Allison, who began his sociological investigation of parapsychology as a skeptic, seems almost surprised when he states, "Whatever one's beliefs about the existence of the phenomena they claim to study, parapsychologists cannot be easily dismissed as charlatans. The productive researchers are predominantly academics with Ph.D.'s in psychology or the natural sciences. To all outward appearances, they maintain rigorous standards, both technical and professional. Moreover, they have accumulated a body of evidence concerning the existence and nature of psi which is undeniably impressive, if not always fully convincing" (Allison, 1973:3). He also notes, "In short, professional parapsychologists have many characteristics in common with research workers in most scientific specialisms. A careful reading of the two experimental journals will indicate that parapsychologists also practice a highly technical, rigorous, and quantitative methodology. In fact, if one knew nothing of parapsychological terminology, it would be difficult to distinguish the *Journal of Parapsychology* from say, *The Journal of Experimental Psychology*" (Allison, 1979:277).

This apparent scientific orientation of parapsychological research is a product of over a century of interaction between those who investigated alleged phenomena and those hostile to investigations that had positive results. It is possible to trace a loose chain of events involving science and unusual claims beginning with Mesmerism (1770s through early 1850s) and continuing through the Spiritualistic movement (1848 through 1900s), to the founding of the Society for Psychical Research (SPR) in 1882 in England.

Before the eighteenth century, the investigation of any phenomena considered paranormal was delegated to Church officials whose goal was to determine whether such events were due to demonic forces, God's grace, or an illusion on the part of the experiencing individual. The interpretation of psychic experience by these officials changed during the Middle Ages. Between 1215 and the early 1400s, associating with demons was considered an illusion by Church officials. Later, in 1484, Pope Innocent VIII issued a bull affirming the reality of witchcraft and authorizing the Holy Inquisition to punish those who practiced it (Currie, 1968).

The rise of a scientific ideology led to a dialectic between science and what might be termed the "parapsychological tradition." With the growing importance of science during the eighteenth century, psychic experience was considered a topic for scientific inquiry.

Science assumes that knowledge will be generated through any valid scientific investigation no matter what the anomaly being investigated. This assumption contains a paradox. Because science exists as a community of individuals with finite resources, inquiries that do not seem particularly fruitful are restricted. Labeling some scientific activities as deviant has this effect and also unifies the scientific community. The parapsychological tradition constitutes a form of deviant science, an idea that will be developed more fully later in this chapter.

Franz Anton Mesmer's hypnotically oriented therapeutic procedures in the middle of the eighteenth century initiated the development of Mesmerism, considered by its proponents to be scientific. Science had evolved politically to the degree that instead of Church officials becoming involved, a scientific committee in Paris investigated Mesmer, denouncing him in 1784 (although a later French government commission reversed this original judgment; Rogo, 1975). Hundreds of denunciations of Mesmerism as quackery, fraud, and chicanery can be found in early Victorian medical journals (Parssinen, 1979).

The Spiritualistic movement, which was launched by the unexplained rapping sounds surrounding Margaret and Kate Fox in 1847, also generated scientific investigation and controversy. An early Spiritualist investigation, although granted minor importance by modern parapsychologists, illustrates the tension between science and the parapsychological tradition. Robert Hare, emeritus professor of chemistry at the University of Pennsylvania (and inventor of the oxy-hydrogen blowpipe), constructed a mechanism for measuring a hypothetical "psychic force." He conducted (in his own words), "an experiment made with the greatest care and precision, which proved the existence of a power independent of any possible or conceivable mortal agency" (Hare, 1856:431 and quoted by Nicol, 1977:307). Yet, in 1855 when he submitted a preliminary report to the president of the American Association for the Advancement of Science (AAAS), "the standing committee resolved that the subject did not fall within the objects of the Association" (Nicol, 1977:307).

The "scientific" investigation of mediums during the Spiritualist era revealed that these individuals frequently cheated. D. D. Home (1833–1886) is often mentioned as a notable exception. Home's demonstrations took place in adequate light; he sat among the observers; he allowed investigation by numerous researchers yet was never found to commit fraud. The sheer quantity of ostensible phenomena overwhelms the imagination. It was reported that fire-balls wandered over the room and through solid objects, spirits appeared as dim shapes, flowers fell from the ceiling, spirit hands appeared, furniture moved around as though it were weightless, and Home himself floated around like a balloon (Medhurst et al., 1972).

Various famous scientists showed interest in psychic phenomena. Alfred Russell Wallace, who developed the theory of evolution inde-pendently of Charles Darwin, became a supporter of the Spiritualistic movement in 1865 and began proselytizing his fellow scientists (Kottler, 1974). William Crookes's investigations in 1870 captured the attention of major scientists like Rayleigh, Barrett, and Galton, directing them toward the field. Although Crookes pioneered the study of electrical discharge in gases and the development of vacuum tubes, nothing he discovered about "psychic forces" was accepted. Crookes improved on Robert Hare's method for measuring the so-called psychic force, and constructed various apparatus for testing Home's psychic ability, intending to preclude fraud. Although Crookes never gave up his belief in psychic phenomena, which was supported by his experimental results, he could not convince his skeptical colleagues. He eventually gave up his psychic investigations, returned to orthodox scientific research, and received the Order of Merit and a knighthood (Palfreman, 1979). Crookes's interaction with his skeptical fellow scientists led to methodological progress in psychical research, a tightening up of experimental conditions, and the use of mechanical instruments (Gauld, 1968). This era was char-acterized by the general tendency of skeptical scientists to criticize vigorously psychical research while refraining from becoming deeply involved with the activity themselves, a pattern that persists.

The formation of the SPR in 1882 could be viewed as a "manifes-tation and formalization among the upper class of a broad-based intel-lectual/and religious movement" (Allison, 1973:27). The expressed purpose was "making an organized and systematic attempt to inves-tigate the large group of phenomena designated by such terms as mesmeric, psychical, and spiritualistic" (SPR, 1882:3–6). The written output of the SPR was enormous. Between 1882 and 1890, it published 11,000 pages of journals and proceedings and 4,000 pages of books (Gauld, 1968:313). The SPR was remarkable for its ability to attract well-known people. "In 1887 its Council Members and Honorary Members included a past Prime Minister (Gladstone—

elected on Myers' proposal . . .), and a future Prime Minister (Arthur Balfour); eight [fellows of the Royal Society]—Wallace, Couch, Adams, Lord Rayleigh, Oliver Lodge, A. MacAlister, J. Venn, Balfour Stewart and J. J. Thomson; two bishops; and Tennyson and Ruskin, two of the outstanding literary figures of the day" (Gauld, 1968:140).

Scientific criticism seems to have resulted in a tightening of investigative methodology and an intellectual division between factions within the SPR. The conflict ended in 1887 with the mass resignation of most of the spiritualists, an event that did not stem the SPR's success in recruiting new members. Membership mushroomed from 150 in 1883 to 946 in 1900 (Allison, 1973:27).

Psychical research in America proceeded sporadically. The American Society for Psychical Research (ASPR), founded in 1884, did not attract as renowned a group of individuals (except for William James) as did the SPR. Strangely enough, this may have allowed a closer affiliation between psychical research and the university system since psychic research created less commotion. Under the auspices of Stanford University, John Edgar Coover, a man quite skeptical of claims of the paranormal, conducted a psychic research experiment that used statistical analysis and control groups in testing for psi. In a massive volume, Coover (1917) concluded that there was no evidence for the existence of mental telepathy. Coover demonstrated his bias against the reality of psi by arbitrarily setting the statistical criterion for evidence of it at an inordinately high level (he chose the odds against chance at 50,000 to 1, whereas 100 to 1 is generally considered statistically significant in most scientific experiments). Parapsychologists have pointed out that although there were no significant differences between Coover's experimental and control groups, both groups scored significantly higher than the scoring rate expected by chance to the degree that the result would occur by chance only three times out of a thousand experiments ($p < .003$). One might suggest that Coover's experimental and control groups were manifesting clairvoyance (Rhine, 1937:21; Schmeidler and McConnell, 1958). The results of Coover's work were considered a setback for psychical research because they were frequently cited by skeptics who doubted the existence of psi.

Other telepathy experiments were conducted demonstrating the possibility of psi on various occasions (by Ochorowicz, Gurney, Thaw, Dessoir), but skeptical scientists could not be certain that sensory cueing or fraud could be precluded as possible explanations for the experimental results. The SPR researchers found that some of their subjects used sensory cueing in early experiments (Cerullo, 1982).

In 1920, G. Heymans, M. J. F. W. Brugmans, and A. A. Weinberg conducted a series of tests at Groningen University, Holland, with the intention of precluding sensory cueing and fraud (Brugmans, 1922; Murphy, 1961:56–62; Schouten and Kelly et al., 1968; Zorab, 1976). The prepared apparatus included an acoustically sealed window in a second-level floor, which allowed the researchers to observe a subject making target choices. Specially prepared curtains and boards also prevented sensory cueing. Target squares were picked by a random selection process. A primitive physiological apparatus reported the active/passive state of awareness of the subject. A. Van Dam, a student who was said to be a gifted telepath, had come to the attention of Professor Heymans, who organized this experiment. The Groningen experiments with Van Dam are notable for the care with which they were carried out (demonstrating methodological progress in psychical research), for the amazing level of success the series had in demonstrating psi (the probability of the results having occurred by chance is less than one in 79 quintillion), and for the finding of a state of mind correlated with the demonstration of psi. Van Dam's success rate was highly correlated with his "feeling of passivity" as measured by the galvanometerlike apparatus (Rogo, 1975).

Parapsychologists often cite this experiment as being one of the first to support the existence of psi (e.g., Beloff, 1980). This is not to say that skeptics were unable to criticize the experimental methodology that was used or that they were compelled to accept the hypothesis that psi is real. This is far from the case. In this particular experiment criticism focused on the method of selecting targets and the possibility that sensory cueing might explain the experimental results (the experiment's apparatus no longer exists). It is beyond the scope of this present study to review the validity of any particular parapsychological experiment. The reader should be cautioned that no set of arguments regarding the psi hypothesis is compelling for all scientific observers. The major rhetorical strategies used by proponents and their critics are reviewed in chapter 3. For positive reviews of the experimental research associated with the field of parapsychology, see Wolman (1977) or Rogo (1975). For more skeptical reviews, see Zusne and Jones (1982), Marks and Kammann (1980), and Hansel (1966).

➤ Modern psychic research can be said to have begun with J. B. Rhine's research in the Psychology Department at Duke University. In 1934, Rhine used the now-famous ESP cards (which contain a star, cross, square, circle, or wavy lines) to test subjects for paranormal perception. Beginning with a series of pilot experiments, Rhine found various college students who seemed to have ability in guessing the correct symbol on the specially designed five-suit deck. Proceeding cautiously, Rhine kept tightening the experimental procedures, searching for more and more ways to make fraud impossible. He invited skeptics to criticize his work and gave space to them in the newly created *Journal of Parapsychology*. Rhine's (1937) book, *New Frontiers of the Mind*, raised a storm of criticism, though much of the protest was silenced when Burton Camp, president of the Institute of Mathematical Statistics, affirmed that the statistical procedures used by Rhine were valid and correct (Mauskopf and McVaugh, 1979). As with all controversial research, critics are able to point out what they believe to be methodological flaws in the experimental design and analysis (Hansel, 1966).

➤ J. B. Rhine and J. G. Pratt carried out thousands of experiments of this type under varying conditions (Pratt, Rhine, et al., 1940). They claimed that some individuals did indeed possess a paranormal perceptual ability and that it was possible to obtain a high degree of improbability by continued testing of a gifted subject.

Rhine's major endeavor is generally considered to be the establishment of the parapsychological paradigm. Although others had previously used statistical methods, Rhine introduced a set of standardized procedures that included the attempt to eliminate sensory cues, the recording of results, and the interpretation of data. Rhine also founded and organized parapsychology as an ongoing social and scientific endeavor. He established its base of resources and its patterns of recruitment and training. Between 1935 and 1947, twenty-one students worked with Rhine at his Duke University Parapsychological Laboratory, though only a few were active at any one time (Rhine, 1968). During the 1930s and 1940s, research turned toward demonstrating various other psychic abilities besides ESP. Rhine claimed to have demonstrated the existence of psychokinesis, the direct influence of the mind on material objects. He also reported evidence demonstrating precognition, the ability to predict randomly generated events in the future.

Rhine's research attracted the attention of various outside scientists who also began devoting their research efforts to the field: R. A. McConnell (University of Pittsburgh), Gertrude Schmeidler (City University of New York), and Ian Stevenson (University of Virginia). By 1983, over a dozen parapsychological research "centers" existed in the United States with approximately thirty full-time researchers.

Parapsychology has very stable organizations. Of the fifteen parapsychology organizations described by White (1973), fourteen still existed in 1983 and the researcher associated with the one that closed is directing a new center at a different location. Of the ten periodicals White described in 1973, eight still exist and the other two are merely in a new form with different names. The membership of the Parapsychological Association (PA) was 126 in 1958, 205 in 1970, 279 in 1980 (White, 1982), and 306 in 1983. Howard Zimmerman (1982), the executive secretary of the PA, notes, "The growth has been slow, primarily because so many applicants do not meet Council's entrance requirements. On the other hand, turnover is almost nil. Once they get in, few choose to sever the relationship." The membership of the ASPR also shows an increase. It had 867 members in 1962, 2,141 in 1970, and 2,161 in 1977. The membership of the SPR (in England) remained fairly constant during this period: 1,094 in 1960, 1,175 in 1970, and 1,094 in 1977 (White, 1982).

This brief historical overview of the development of modern parapsychology reveals a sciencelike social structure within the field. This should not be surprising. The social and methodological aspects of parapsychology have evolved through the efforts of legitimate scientists (recruited generally from other fields) and can be seen as a reflection of and a response to the evaluation of the scientific community. Parapsychologists require for themselves much tighter methodological controls than do sociologists or psychologists. For example, they require researchers to label clearly as post hoc any observations made after an experiment has been completed. Their social organization resembles orthodox science in that parapsychologists seek recognition from their peers by publishing in parapsychological journals (for example, *Journal of Parapsychology, The Journal of the American Society for Psychical Research, European Journal of Parapsychology*) and by presenting papers at annual professional conferences (for example, the PA and its regional affiliate, the Southeast Regional Parapsychological Association).

Although widespread scientific resistance to parapsychology still exists, various "milestones" toward scientific legitimation have been passed, such as (1) the election of the PA to the AAAS on December 30, 1969 (Dean, 1970; Freedland, 1972); (2) the publication of various parapsychological research findings in highly reputable journals (three major examples exist, although most parapsychologists do not consider them representative of the field: Duane and Behrendt, 1965; Puthoff and Targ, 1976; Targ and Puthoff, 1974); (3) beginning in 1940, the listing of articles on parapsychology in *Psychological Abstracts*; (4) the offering by colleges and universities of courses in parapsychology (Rhine, 1972, lists eleven such courses, and the ASPR [1980] lists over 50); and (5) the inclusion in the 1968 *International Encyclopedia of the Social Sciences* of a fourteen-page article on parapsychology (written by Gertrude Schmeidler, a past president of the PA).

Parapsychology as Deviance

If parapsychologists seem from all outward appearances to be scientists, why is the field not a fully legitimate science? Why do many scientists oppose the very suggestion that parapsychological phenomena might be a valid subject of inquiry? Why does a certain segment of the academic community (8 percent in Wagner and Monnet's [1979] sample) consider the investigation of ESP not to be a legitimate scientific undertaking?

The answer lies in the deviant role that parapsychologists play in relation to science. Deviance can be defined as "those acts, attributes, and beliefs which, when performed or made known about an actor, elicit an evaluative social sanction or sanctions from an observer" (Scarpitti and McFarlane, 1975:5). The acts that parapsychologists engage in include conducting research in anomalies with low ontological status. Parapsychologists hold beliefs (or are assumed to hold beliefs) that violate some of the metaphysical foundations of science. Some scientists assume that because science is successful, its causal ontology is therefore comprehensively adequate. They impose sanctions on parapsychologists for violating these metaphysical assumptions by demanding higher degrees of exactitude and greater methodological rigor from the field. They portray as incompetent those parapsychologists who find evidence to support psi. This prevents parapsychologists from using orthodox funding, receiving fair treatment on tenure and promotion, or publishing their research in orthodox scientific journals. Individuals who report their psychic experiences also may be stigmatized. Their sanity and honesty are often questioned; they are considered to be unusual; and they sometimes question their own mental stability as a result of this stigma.

Two basic demands often set forth as a requirement for parapsychology's legitimization are (1) a repeatable experiment, and (2) a theoretical orientation integrating parapsychology within mainstream science. Although these demands seem appropriate even to some parapsychologists, their validity is derived from the assumption that psi violates the metaphysical foundations of science. Psi is deemed extraordinary. Therefore extraordinary demands are required of the field in order that it might gain legitimacy. These demands are selectively applied to deviant sciences like parapsychology as part of the process of deviant labeling.

The requirement of, and search for, a "repeatable" experiment is often presented by critics and among parapsychologists themselves (e.g., *CIBA Foundation Symposium on Extra-Sensory Perception,* 1956) as necessary. Although research replicability is sought by laboratory researchers in all fields, there should be no need for a completely repeatable experiment to make any field legitimate. If psychology or sociology were stripped of all their "nonrepeatable" experiments, they would be restricted to only their most simplistic and absurdly commonsensical formulations. Astronomy or geology are so little oriented toward experimentation that the criterion of replication is hardly applicable to them, yet these fields are still considered legitimate. The factor that is desired is the ability to predict the phenomena being investigated; this quality indicates the usefulness or maturity of a science rather than its legitimacy.

It should be recognized that there are degrees of replicability. Some forms of inquiry produce higher levels of replicability than others. Physics has numerous experiments that are highly replicable (and others that are not). Biology, sociology, psychology, and parapsychology often must depend on statistical replications, with long-term research programs, to shed light on specific questions. The problem within parapsychology is not that its researchers find that no level of replicability exists. If that were the case, then consensus could be reached. The problem stems from the fact that the thousands of published research articles on psi seem to indicate that some phenomena *do* exist. Allison's (1973) questionnaire results from PA members revealed that they felt the most important reason explaining other scientists' resistance to the work of parapsychologists was that "scientists are simply unfamiliar with the present evidence for psi." As is found in all other statistically oriented sciences, analysis of long-term lines of research reveals various trends demonstrating a degree of replicability. Honorton (1978) compiled a list of all psi experiments that used Schmidt's type of random event generator. Thirty-five out of fifty-four experiments achieved a .05 level of significance. Studies that used meditation, hypnosis, and Ganzfeld stimulation (a form of sensory restriction) also acheived a replication rate above 50 percent (Rao, 1980). Certain patterns have also emerged showing qualities related to successful ESP subjects. For example, believers in ESP tend to score higher than disbelievers (Palmer, 1978). Well-adjusted subjects score better than neurotic subjects (Kanthamani and Rao, 1973); extraverted individuals score better than introverted ones (Humphrey, 1951); and success in ESP scoring tends to decline within a run, within the experiment, and during the course of the individual's career as a subject (Thouless, 1963).

A degree of replicability also has been demonstrated by various gifted subjects who have cooperated fully with scientific investigators. William Delmore (Kanthamani and Kelly, 1974; Kelly and Kanthamani, 1972; Kelly, Kanthamani, Child, and Young, 1975), Pavel Stepanik (Pratt, Keil, Stevenson, 1970; Pratt, 1973) and Ingo Swann (Puthoff and Targ, 1976; Swann, 1975) have fairly consistently produced evidence of psi under laboratory conditions. This is not to say that psi can be produced on demand. No research subject claims or demonstrates this ability.

It should not be assumed that all parapsychologists believe in the existence of psi or that all have found evidence for its existence. Allison (1973) found among his parapsychological respondents that 4 percent of those who engaged in experimental research during the last ten years never found any parapsychological effects and 19 percent have more failures than successes in eliciting evidence of psi.

All in all, 77 percent of Allison's sample of the PA stated that their experiments demonstrated the probability that psi occurred (achieved statistical significance at the .05 level) about 50 percent of the time or better. The problem is not that they failed to produce any evidence for the phenomenon they investigated, but that the phenomenon has been labeled "extraordinary," requiring an "extraordinary" proof. Consequently, the present level of replicability is considered insufficient. Refusing to accept these scientists' claims constitutes an aspect of labeling them as deviant since they are regarded by some as either incompetent or fraudulent.

Numerous theories exist that seek to explain the phenomena that parapsychologists investigate. Determining the validity or utility of these theories is an aspect of the scientific process. Certainly a single major theoretical orientation should not be required for a field to gain legitimacy. Various fields, such as sociology, have numerous theoretical orientations yet are still considered legitimate. A brief review of the theories that have been developed within parapsychology illustrates that the field does not lack theoretical orientations. It would seem that the deviant status ascribed to the field has caused these orientations to be deemed scientifically unsatisfactory. Some of them are considered quite promising by many parapsychologists who have used them to generate testable hypotheses.

One theoretical orientation often used to generate hypotheses is that ESP works like a signal lost in the "noise" of normal human consciousness. The experiments that have been conducted to test hypotheses derived from this theory tend to support it. States of mind in which the "noise" of normal human consciousness is reduced (for example, hypnosis, Ganzfeld stimulation, deep relaxation, meditation, sensory deprivation) seem conducive to psi (Palmer, 1978). On the other hand, normal electromagnetic radiation has been dismissed as a possible psi information carrier since experiments with Faraday cages (and other shielding), which effectively block normal electromagnetic radiation, fail to block the telepathy effect (see Vasiliev, 1963). Furthermore, some parapsychologists believe that the telepathy or ESP "signal" fails to attenuate with distance.

Parapsychologically oriented physicists have developed mathematical models of psi that are derived from quantum mechanics (Schmidt, 1975a, b, 1978; E. H. Walker, 1975). These models are empirically testable and various experiments have been conducted using hypotheses derived from them.

Both physical and nonphysical theories explaining telepathy have been developed (Ryzl, 1970). Physical theories suggest that short electromagnetic radiation, gravity waves, neutrinos, tachyons, or psitrons may act as transmitters of information. Stanford (1978) has developed a "conformance model" for psi that has stimulated a great deal of research (Braud, 1980). In this model, psi is explained as "changes in the ordering of a relatively unordered system in relationship to a relatively ordered system with a disposition" (Stanford, 1977a:17).

Nonphysical theories often take the form of philosophical orientations rather than mechanistic models. LeShan (1969, 1974) presents the idea of a "clairvoyant reality" in which psi is not unusual, time is not a reality, and there is a unity in all things. The writings of the ancient Hindu Patanjali (Prabhavananda and Isherwood, 1953, is merely one translation) present guidelines for the development of siddhis (psychic powers), which coincide with LeShan's concept. These orientations might be considered as mind-sets that are claimed to be conducive to psi rather than scientific theories. If these philosophical orientations were deemed better "theories" than the more mechanistic orientations, then they would pose a paradox for science in its present state. Chapter 2 will note that the scientistic orientation grants higher status to physical theories than it does to nonphysical theories.

Among phenomena studied by parapsychologists, precognition seems to violate the laws of physics the most. While physical theories generally do not deal with precognition, nonphysical theories do. Targ (1972) suggests that information on a forthcoming event is carried by precursor waves. He notes that laws of physics do not necessarily forbid transmitting information from the future to the present. It would seem then that quantum mechanical models of psi developed by physicists who are interested in parapsychology attempt to bridge the gap between physical and nonphysical theories of psi.

Parapsychologists point out that numerous other psychological phenomena are studied without the benefit of full theoretical explanation (for example, learning, memory, hypnosis, etc.). B. F. Skinner treated learning like a black box. The stimulus goes in; the response comes out. The mechanism need not be understood in order for scientific research to continue. One parapsychologist I interviewed said: "In this sense, ESP is exactly analogous to learning. In learning, the stimulus is shown to the subject and the subject responds; in ESP the stimulus is not shown to the subject and the subject responds to it—taken in this positivistic way, ESP is no more of a threat to science than is learning or gravitation. We see effects; we don't know yet how they're produced."

It should be noted that the very same process that prevents parapsychology from being granted full legitimacy also prevents the social and behavioral sciences from achieving high status among the sciences. Scientistic criteria place the theories of sociology and psychology in a lower position than the theories of physics (Whyte, 1956). The experimental results generated by these fields are less replicable than many of those within physics. Yet, these fields are granted greater legitimacy than parapsychology. The differentiating factor between parapsychology and the other social sciences is the "extraordinary" quality of the anomaly that psi represents. Chapter 2 will explore the relationship between "extraordinarity" and scientism.

Some philosophers make the doubtful claim that a clear distinction between science and nonscience is possible. They assert that scientific claims are verifiable only through empirical observation and that these claims must contain the element of "falsifiability" in order for them to be scientific. For a summary of these formulations, see Hempel (1950) or Ashby (1967). Yet, the meaningfulness of a statement and the degree to which it is verifiable or falsifiable is established by a consensus among scientists (Overington, 1979). Scientific laws, themselves, are general statements that are not actually verifiable or falsifiable by particular observations. It would seem that an understanding of the means by which science is demarcated from nonscience may lie more within sociological theory than within the philosophy of science.

The Mertonian Model of the Sociology of Science

Merton, generally considered the father of American sociology of science, began his pioneering work with his doctoral dissertation (Merton, 1938/1970), in which he explored the relationship between Puritanism and the development of science. Although his theoretical formulation has been vigorously criticized (Hall, 1963; Sklair, 1972), it stands much like Weber's theory of the Protestant ethic and the rise of capitalism, empirically undemonstrated yet logically interesting. "The Puritan ethic, as an ideal-typical expression of the value-attitudes basic to ascetic Protestantism generally, so canalized the interests of seventeenth-century Englishmen as to constitute one important *element* in the enhanced cultivation of science. The deep-rooted religious *interests* of the day demanded in their forceful implications the systematic, rational, and empirical study of Nature for the glorification of God in His works and for the control of the corrupt world" (Merton, 1957:574).

Merton notes a point-to-point correlation between the principles of Puritanism and the attributes, goals, and results of science. Science is pictured as having many of the same sources as capitalism, and as embodying the "rationality" of the Western world. Calvinists supported the ability to reason, utilitarianism, and works that were helpful to the larger community.

The realization that, as early as the seventeenth century, science had an ideological foundation can help us understand how the scientific community devises boundaries to define science. The ideological foundations of science are derived from the same Calvinist, Puritan roots that Merton hypothesizes contributed to the evolution of science. Deviant science can be viewed as a form of heresay that is in disharmony with these ideological foundations.

This ideology can also be viewed as supporting the institutional values (or norms) that Merton (1942) hypothesized to exist in modern science. *Universalism* emphasized that particular characteristics of individual scientists (race, class, origin, religion) were irrelevant to the validity of scientific work. *Communalism* is the principle that scientific knowledge should be made available to the entire scientific community. *Disinterestedness* is the requirement that scientists not distort their findings to serve their own ends but serve the interest of the larger scientific community. *Organized skepticism* refers to the responsibility of scientists to evaluate critically their own and others' work. Although Merton's arguments concerning the norms of science have been weakened by his critics (e.g., Barnes and Dolby, 1970; Downey, 1967; Sklair, 1972), it would seem that some social norms must exist to aid in distinguishing between a scientist and a nonscientist. These norms may be applicable at only one point in time, in certain fields of science, or remain only tacit and implicit.

In all probability, parapsychologists do not violate Merton's norms more than other scientists (Allison, 1973; Collins and Pinch, 1979). Scientists frequently assume that parapsychologists violate these norms, but this assumption is merely an aspect of the process labeling them as deviant. Collins and Pinch (1979) note, "In the construction of the paranormal, nothing unscientific is happening." The cause of parapsychology's stigma must be due to violation of other norms.

Mitroff's (1974) empirical study of a group of Apollo moon scientists reveals that science contains both norms and counternorms. Mitroff supports Merton's and Barber's concept of sociological ambivalence. This concept states that social institutions reflect potentially conflicting sets of norms. Mitroff observed scientists maintaining deep emotional commitments to their ideas, engaging in solitary behavior, and participating in organized dogmatism. These forms of behavior seem derived from what Mitroff terms the "counternorms" of science. They are associated with the personal character of science, as opposed to the Mertonian norms that are rooted in the impersonal character of science. Mitroff argues that the sociologically ambivalent character of science seems necessary for the ultimate rationality of science and that counternorms may be dominant for ill-structured problems.

Mitroff does not claim that Mertonian norms are never used by scientists to differentiate science from nonscience. In fact, one of his scientist-respondents accuses a colleague of not being "a true scientist" owing to his adherence to counternorms. Certainly the Mertonian norms have a degree of status within Western science. One of the Mertonian norms (universalism) is formally recognized as a criterion for affiliation with the AAAS (McDaniel and Borras, 1979) and the other norms are often referred to as valid and just.

Mitroff's (1974) formulations involving counternorms could shed light on the issue, as Mitroff suggests that counternorms might be more often used in "ambiguous" areas. But even the label of "ambiguity" is culturally specific. The problem of demonstrating psi by employing Rhine's methodology is not ambiguous, nor should Rhine's statistically oriented paradigm lead to ambiguity since "the statistical analysis is essentially valid" (Camp, 1938). The research in this field should lead toward a consensus, yet this has not occurred nor does it seem likely to occur. Although Mitroff's idea of counternorms is valuable in understanding the process of labeling parapsychologists as deviant, the concept does not explain the "ambiguity" associated with parapsychology.

Merton portrays the growth of science as due to the scientists' institutionally reinforced drive to achieve professional peer recognition. This recognition is gained almost exclusively by making a new scientific discovery. The reward system is governed by scientific norms and is self-contained within science. Merton's investigation into disputes over priority of discovery reveals that these conflicts are frequent and intense (Merton, 1973). This observation supports his model of the system of rewards and motivation in science.

The parapsychologist can be viewed as adapting to a disjunction between institutionalized means (methods of gaining a desired end) and cultural goals. Although seeking the accepted goal of scientific recognition, the deviant scientist is using an innovative means in the hope of attaining that goal. This form of deviant behavior is encouraged, in a way, by the scientific milieu that overemphasizes the goal of success and underemphasizes the use of accepted means. The concept of the functions of deviant science will be discussed more fully later in this chapter. This present description parallels Merton's (1968) anomie theory of deviant behavior, which he does not incorporate into his sociology of science.

The role of Merton's norms in the reward system of science is not always clear. Although science as a whole may be damaged by violations of Mertonian norms, some individual scientists are not penalized. Merton's examples of science in Nazi Germany and the Soviet Union illustrate this point. Merton is correct in viewing the exchange system for the scientific profession as different from that of other professions. The scientist as pure researcher has no "clients" comparable to the lawyer's clients or the physician's patients. The scientific community has no formal "code of ethics" pertaining to the responsibilities of scientists to nonscientific sponsors, comparable to the codes of ethics of the legal or medical professions. The scientist produces knowledge that is evaluated by his colleagues, who determine his status as a scientist. This tendency for science to exist as a closed community, not dependent on clients, increases the importance of understanding the hidden norms or ideology that exist within science.

Merton's model for the sociology of science does not explain the process of deviance labeling involved in parapsychology's failure to attain legitimacy. Some observers believe that disputes over priority do not exist in parapsychology (Allison, 1973), and that the reward system within the field differs from that of more established fields. "Discoveries" made by the psychical researcher are not granted recognition but instead draw negative sanctions from other scientists. Adherence to Merton's norms has not given parapsychology legitimacy. It would seem that other norms come into play which lead to parapsychology's deviant label.

Merton's original formulations on the relationship between Puritanism and science may be pertinent. The historically evolved, metaphysical foundation of modern science gives it unspecified norms that Merton did not recognize. Science in each age rests on certain assumptions, usually implicit and unquestioned by scientists of the time. A basic assumption of modern science derived from the Puritan ethic is a widespread, instinctive conviction in the existence of an order of things, and, in particular, of an order in nature. This belief is easily extended into the assumption that natural laws are mechanistic and "inviolable" and, hence, parapsychology as a science is absurd since its task is to explain violations of natural "law."

Broad (1978) suggests that certain "basic limiting principles" exist which restrict ways we obtain knowledge about, and interact with, the world. For example, we can use only sensory means to determine our exterior reality; we have only inferential knowledge about the future; our muscles are the only means of affecting the physical world; mental events occur only in conjunction with brain events. Extending Broad's philosophical formulations, it might be suggested that the assumption of "basic limiting principles" constitutes a form of scientific norm that parapsychologists violate (or attempt to violate) through their research.

The historical evolution of science in the West has led to a tacit and implicit ideology that legitimates the practice of science. One aspect of this ideology, the basic limiting principles, constitutes a norm that parapsychologists claim to violate in an attempt to gain recognition. Although Merton's (1968) theoretical orientations can explain deviant science as a mode of adaptation to a disjunction between institutionalized means and cultural goals within some segments of science, his model for the sociology of science is weak in hypothesizing how norms may change over time. Thomas Kuhn has developed a paradigm that is oriented toward explaining these changes as revolutions within science.

The Kuhnian Paradigm

Thomas Kuhn's book *The Structure of Scientific Revolutions* (1962/1970a) opened up a range of problems that had previously been avoided. Kuhn thinks the bulk of conventional research, or "normal science," consists of producing expected solutions to prescribed problems according to standardized procedures. This "puzzle solving" is not oriented toward the pursuit of novelty of fact or theory, but merely fills in puzzles generated by existing theories. Although Kuhn (1970a) uses a variety of terms for the standardized procedures and "mindset" utilized (for example, dogma, theory, exemplar), the term most valued is "paradigm." Paradigms are the "universally recognized scientific achievements that for a time provide model problems and solutions to a community of practitioners" (p. viii). They include law, theory, application, and instrumentation. A paradigm is rarely an object of replication. "Like an accepted judicial decision in the common law, it is an object for future articulation and specification under new or more stringent conditions" (p. 23). Paradigms are necessary in science so that the discipline and focus required for the pursuit of normal science can be attained. In the "normal" science process, "anomalies" or phenomena that violate the paradigm assumptions sometimes occur. These are generally ignored unless a crisis occurs causing more and more scientists to devote attention to the anomalies previously discovered. Eventually, a new paradigm may evolve containing a theoretical explanation for the anomalies that produce crisis. In the stage of revolutionary science, scientists must choose between paradigms, since their cognitive exclusiveness does not allow an individual to entertain both with respect to the same field. Eventually, the new paradigm may replace the old. Kuhn points out that crises in the history of science, although frequent, are often resolved within the ruling paradigm, thus avoiding a revolutionary upheaval. Kuhn's idea of a structure of scientific revolutions can be summarized as follows: A paradigm leads to normal science. Normal science produces anomalies. Anomalies bring about crises, which in turn produce revolution. New paradigms can emerge from scientific revolution. Normal science guided by a new paradigm is the eventual outcome.

Problems with defining the term "paradigm" weaken Kuhn's explanatory power. "At the very outset, the explanatory value of the notion of a paradigm is suspect: for the truth of the thesis that shared paradigms are (or are behind) the common factors guiding scientific research appears to be guaranteed, not so much by a close examination of actual historical cases, however scholarly, as by the breadth of definition of the term 'paradigm' " (Shapere, 1964:385) Masterman (1970) has classified twenty-one different definitions (falling into metaphysical, social, and construct categories) of the word "paradigm" as used by Kuhn, but these many definitions should not defeat him. Kuhn believes paradigms are open to "direct inspection" (Kuhn, 1962:44), and historians can "agree in their *identification* of a paradigm without agreeing on, or even attempting to produce, a full *interpretation* or *rationalization* of it" (p. 44). Yet at the same time, paradigms seem by nature to be tacit and implicit and, therefore, not open to direct inspection. It would seem that paradigms can only be defined by their social effect, much as "normal" behavior is defined by the forms of behavior labeled as "deviant."

Kuhn's inability to explain the political and rhetorical process involved in paradigm shifts prevents his theory from presenting a sociological explanation for scientific change. The logical tendency of Kuhn's original position is that scientific replacement is not cumulative; it is merely change, since Kuhn believes that "the competition between paradigms is not the sort of battle that can be resolved by proofs" (p. 147) but is more like a "conversion experience" (p. 150). This very aspect of scientific revolutions causes M. D. King to criticize the paradigm orientation:

It does not present a convincing analysis of the internal structure of scientific revolutions; indeed, it concedes that they are intrinsically unanalyzable events by likening them to gestalt-switches or acts of religious conversion. As a consequence, Kuhn does not succeed in developing a sociological theory of scientific change. He fails to do so because from the outset he separated scientific growth into distinct phases. In periods of "normal" science, scientists' basic commitments—conceptual, methodological, technical—are virtually constant. During the interval of "extraordinary" science, there is a complete switch-around in these commitments. (King, 1971:31)

Other critiques of Kuhn revolve about the difficulties in distinguishing normal and revolutionary science or even whether normal science exists (Feyerabend, 1970b). Some critics point out that various historical cases do not fit Kuhn's theoretical pattern (Heidelberger, 1980; Greene, 1980).

Numerous parapsychologists feel that their field has revolutionary potential (Allison, 1973) and, hence, fits clearly into the Kuhnian scheme. This belief springs in part from the lack of clarity in Kuhn's original formulations and from a general belief among parapsychologists that paranormal phenomena constitute Kuhnian anomalies. This orientation fails to consider the special social treatment given to the phenomena that parapsychologists investigate. All anomalies do not have equal ontological status.

Kuhn's method of determining the difference between science and nonscience fails to explain the political and rhetorical processes involved in labeling deviance. In his analysis of the differences between his orientation and that of Karl Popper, he points to the puzzle-solving tradition in all sciences as a form of demarcation (Kuhn, 1970b). His critics (e.g., Feyerabend, 1970b) point out that such varied occupations as theology and bank robbery also involve puzzle-solving traditions. Kuhn's (1970c) "Reflections on My Critics" summarizes four conditions for a mature scientific field:

First is Sir [Karl Popper's] demarcation criterion without which no field is potentially a science: for some range of natural phenomena concrete predictions must emerge from the practice of the field. Second, for some interesting subclass of phenomena, whatever passes for predictive success must be constantly achieved. . . . Third, predictive techniques must have roots in a theory which, however metaphysical, simultaneously justifies them, explains their limited success and suggests means for their improvement in both precision and scope. Finally, the improvement of predictive technique must be a challenging task, demanding on occasions the very highest measure of talent and devotion. (Kuhn, 1970c:245, 246)

This form of demarcation seems irrelevant to emerging fields. It parallels closely the demand from parapsychology's critics to have a repeatable experiment and a major theoretical orientation. Although parapsychologists may claim (1) to be able to make concrete predictions emerging from the practice of the field, (2) to have achieved a limited degree of predictive success, (3) to have theories justifying this success, and (4) to find the improvement of this predictive technique a challenging task, they are still attacked by critics. Social factors determine the degree to which an observer deems parapsychology to have complied with Kuhn's criteria.

The social treatment of the PA illustrates this point. The PA applied for affiliation with the AAAS in 1961 but was rejected "on grounds that at present, parapsychology is not firmly or generally accepted as a science" (AAAS minutes, 1961). It was again rejected in 1963.

Although parapsychology made no startling advances toward a repeatable experiment or a major theoretical orientation, it was granted affiliation on December 30, 1969 (Dean, 1970). This affiliation seems to have been granted as a result of intense lobbying activity on behalf of Douglas Dean of the PA and a last-minute speech of advocacy by Margaret Mead immediately before the voting. This example illustrates the need to include processes associated with the sociology of knowledge within the sociology of science. Determining whether a group meets the tacit and implicit criteria required to be regarded as a science is a rhetorical and political process.

Mulkay's Contributions to the Sociology of Science

Mulkay (1972a, b) adds deviance labeling to his model of the sociology of science and clarifies the role of scientific revolution within science. He feels Kuhn's weakness lies in the fact that the cycle from normal to revolutionary to normal is not the predominant pattern. Rather than one form of scientific innovation, Mulkay presents five types:

1. Information gained through normal science.
2. Ideas developed in the course of gradual redefinitions.
3. Notions occurring as a result of movement of researchers between existing areas of research.
4. Developments from the investigation of new areas of ignorance.
5. Conception introduced in the course of revolutionary upheaval.

In this theoretical orientation, revolutions are reduced to only one of the types of innovation. It would appear that many of Kuhn's revolutions are merely innovations because their impact is somewhat limited (Mulkay, 1969).

Mulkay suggests that scientific discovery and innovation can be viewed as a special type of social deviance since the paradigm is a special type of cognitive norm. He states that the desire for social recognition is the motivating factor in innovation. Scientists are attracted to the problems that offer the most social rewards, and because they desire recognition, they must consider more risky investigations. Mulkay agrees with Whitley's (1972:81) observations: "It may well be that cognitively 'marginal' scientists may be more innovative than 'integrated' ones just as the romantic myth of the artist starving in his garret suggests that the socially marginal artist produces 'greater' art than the pampered literary lion." This does not mean that all starving artists or fringe-area scientists become great, but that in them is the capacity for great innovation. Although Gieryn and Hirsh (1983) list many case studies confirming the hypothesis that marginality is related to scientific innovation, their own examination of X-ray astronomy during its formulative years (1960–1975) fails to support it. They suggest that the concept of marginality is too ambiguous to be useful as a conceptual tool in regard to studies of sources of scientific innovation.

Even though this may be the case, Mulkay's (1972a) theoretical orientation presents testable hypotheses regarding status within science and sources of scientific innovation. He predicts that scientific "members of high status are less likely to deviate from more important norms than from less central norms" (p. 49).

In enduring groups, high levels of recognition usually depend on comformity to certain central norms. If this is true in science, then *radical* innovation, that is, repudiation of basic cognitive norms, would involve considerable risk even for those in high rank. (Mulkay, 1972a: 49)

The acceptance of radical innovation jeopardizes the earlier contributions of high status scientists and "thereby threatens the very standards on which their eminence depends" (p. 49). "We would expect such scientists to develop strong mental sets and a reduced ability to perceive anomalies" (p. 50). This hypothesis is peripherally supported by data presented in chapter 5.

These theoretical orientations, coupled with Mulkay's (1979) observation of a "cultural interpretation in science," allows a reformulation of Kuhn's paradigm. Scientific innovation occurs as part of a scientific/cultural process within science. Scientists innovate through normal scientific activity, redefining existing ideas, moving between existing fields, exploring new unknown areas, and revolutionary upheavals. Scientists tend to reject aspects of this innovative process that clash with the scientific/cultural Zeitgeist.

The orientations that have evolved within the "relativistic" sociology of science are also highly pertinent to this present study. For example, Collins and Pinch (1982) have developed a radical Kuhnian position in which border realms of inquiry need not be labeled as pseudoscience but considered as potential scientific revolutions. Their research reveals the rhetorical and social aspect of science in which replicability is a product of, rather than an explanation for, scientific "knowledge." "Scientific authority is socially negotiated and socially sanctioned" (Collins and Pinch, 1982:178).

The theoretical orientation developed in this present study accepts Collins and Pinch's (1982) radical Kuhnian position but draws upon the theories of deviant behavior to explain the longevity of parapsychology. In that deviant behavior fulfills certain functions for the community which labels it as such, this present study draws different conclusions from those of Collins and Pinch (1982) regarding deviant science's potential for the future. For example, Collins and Pinch (1982:184) feel that paranormal metal-bending investigations were "almost certain . . . to fade away as just another fad." They validly assert that this does not affect their sociological conclusions. This present study would suggest that since such investigations function as a form of deviant behavior within science, they will, more than likely, survive. The form that such investigations take will reflect the methods used to label these realms of inquiry as deviant. For example, although the intrusion of conjurers masquerading as metal benders (as occurred in 1983) may change the nature of this type of research, it would seem that as long as individuals claim to bend metal paranormally, some scientists will attempt to verify their claims. These researchers will be forced to be more cautious than those observed by Collins and Pinch (1982). (For an interesting case which illustrates this point and which occurred after the publication of Collins and Pinch's [1982] book, see Broad, 1983).

In order to develop the idea of deviant science as a lasting endeavor, an ideology must be described that science uses in labeling some realms of inquiry as deviant. This ideology will be referred to as "scientism."

A Theoretical Orientation Using the Concept of Scientism

Scientism, the ideas that legitimate the practices of science, is a concept that has been used by theorists in the past to critique the modern mind-set. Whyte (1956:23) defines scientism as the practical aspect of what he terms the "Social Ethic." It is "the promise that with the same techniques that have worked in the physical sciences we can eventually create an exact science of man." Hayek (1952) describes scientism as based on three fallacies: objectivism, collectivism, and historicism. Scientism can be viewed as an attempt to dispense with subjective knowledge. Voegelin (1948:462) divides scientism into three components: "(1) the assumption that the mathematized science of natural phenomena is a model science to which all other sciences ought to conform; (2) that all realms of being are accessible to the methods of the sciences of phenomena; and (3) that all reality which is not accessible to sciences of phenomena is either irrelevant or, in the more radical form of the dogma, illusionary."

The notion of a unified science of man has been around for centuries. Philosophers such as Erasmus, Descartes, Hobbes, Saint-Simon, and Auguste Comte have expressed aspects of the scientistic orientation. The core of modern scientism maintains that there is a unitary scientific method that generates value-free knowledge and that the standards of exactness and certainty in the physical sciences are the only explanatory models for this knowledge. Scientism defines rationality as predictive effectiveness and instrumental efficiency.

Modern societies tend to invoke science to support and justify the interests of dominant social elites. Those critical of social inequality often view scientism negatively. Shroyer (1970) feels scientism is the "fundamental false consciousness of our epoch." Scientism mystifies the social function of science, creates a crisis in man's knowledge of himself, and works against "a broader mode of rationalization that would maximize the participation and individuation of affected people" (Shroyer, 1970).

This study should not be considered a critique of scientism. Because the methodology of science is an inherent part of scientism and because this study attempts to fall within the sociology of science, this study itself can be considered scientistic to the degree that sociology is scientific. It gains legitimacy from this ideological affiliation.

Rather than viewing scientism as a kind of cancerous outgrowth of science that restricts the development of "true" human knowledge, this present study regards it as an inherent aspect of science. Because science is an endeavor undertaken by a community of practitioners, scientism is a necessity. This concept can be used to explain the longevity of parapsychology through theories derived from the study of deviant behavior.

Scientific knowledge has some aspects that are equivalent to legal knowledge. Collins and Pinch (1982:178) note that "scientists are experts in the natural world in the same way as lawyers are experts on the law." Kuhn (1962:23) also notes a parallel situation: he considers scientific paradigms as "like an accepted judicial decision in the common law," in that they are continuously the object of "further articulation." This parallel can be extended to explain the functions of labeling some realms of inquiry as deviant. Certain aspects of, and actions within, science involve courtlike judgments. Some activities are labeled as deviant through "common law" decisions. Scientists whose research is rejected are vaguely equivalent both to the members of society who are judged to be "guilty" of some misdeed and to the lawyers who defend these individuals.

Emile Durkheim (1895/1938) noted that crime and its punishment have various functions benefiting the society in which they occur. This can explain the fact that all societies label some forms of behavior as deviant (although there is a lack of consistency as to which types of behavior actually are labeled as such). The social purpose of punishments is actually a form of ritual enacted for the benefit of society. Rituals involve a common emotion that creates a symbolic belief which binds people closer to their group.

Unifying a group through ritual procedures is what R. Collins (1982:vi) terms "non-obvious sociology":

. . . the human power of reasoning is based on nonrational foundations, . . . human society is held together not by rational agreements but by deeper emotional processes that produce social bonds of trust among particular kinds of people. Society is made up of groups. These groups are often in conflict with each other; but each group can operate only to the extent that each group is held together. That requires some nonrational mechanism producing common emotions and ideals.

R. Collins (1982:vii) points out that rituals are one way of generating this deeper emotional process:

. . . rituals are little social machines that create groups and attach them to emotionally significant social symbols.

This occurs since rituals, or standardized ceremonial behavior, carried out by a group of people,

creates a symbolic belief that binds people closer to the group. Carrying out rituals over and over again is what serves to keep the group tied together. (p. 110)

Court cases create a ritual process which involves solemn proceedings, elaborate etiquette, and specially trained actors. Lawyers attempt to stir up collective sentiment in order to sway the judge and jury through a controlled process of argumentation. Through this process, the law becomes real and "justice" is carried out. Equivalently, it is through the ritualized process of presentation and publication of scientific reports that science becomes real and that "scientific knowledge" is created.

Durkheim (1938) argues that without crime there would be no punishment rituals. The rules could not be acted out and the public would not be made aware of them. Social stagnation would result and/or the group would fall apart. For this reason, Durkheim argues, even a society of saints would label some of its community as deviant. Certain forms of behavior that were considered to be "less-than-perfectly-saintly" would be labeled as wrong and would be punished. This would be necessary for the group to maintain cohesiveness and to inform group members of the types of behavior that are wrong. Durkheim's theory has gained a degree of acceptance among sociologists. Kai T. Erikson (1966) has applied it to his study of the Puritans in colonial America. Even among this highly religious group, "crime waves" were noted that seemed to fulfill functions for the group.

Science also has rituals, which are similar to court proceedings (though less public). Research must be evaluated before it can be presented before the greater scientific community. Procedures involving journal editors, standard forms of discourse, argumentation by referees, and so on create a process of judgment which generates "scientific knowledge." Some forms of research are judged unworthy and are rejected. Certain "common law" standards have evolved to guide these evaluations.

This equivalency can even be extended to describe some forms of both political and scientific revolution. R. Collins's (1982:116) description of successful communities of criminals can be considered equivalent to successful Kuhnian revolutions in science:

Look at what happens when crime becomes more and more successful. Individual criminals can do only so much. They are much more effective at stealing, embezzling, or whatever if they are organized. Individual thieves give way to gangs, and gangs to organized crime syndicates. But notice, organized crime now becomes a little society of its own. It creates its own hierarchy, its own rules, and it attempts to enforce these rules upon its own members. Organized crime tends toward regularity and normalcy. It begins to deplore unnecessary violence and strife. The more successful it is, the more it approximates an ordinary business. The very success of crime, then, tends to make it more law-abiding and less criminal. . . . The state arose from a type of criminality but was forced to create a morality just to survive.

Science can be considered a form of innovation that parallels crime. We might echo Collins's (1982) last sentences with regard to scientific revolutions of the past: The very success of some scientists meant that they had to take responsibility for maintaining social order around them. The more successful a scientific ideology becomes the more its proponents turn into enforcers of laws. Science arose from a type of innovation but was forced to create deviant sciences just to survive.

The theoretical model developed by this study has the purpose of explaining the historical continuity of parapsychology (see figure 1-1). This model views the ideological aspects of science as derived from a "mega-paradigm" that has evolved historically. This mega-paradigm is tacit and implicit and, therefore, is not open to direct inspection. It reveals itself through the generation of ideas that legitimate the practices of science. These ideas are particularly valued by elite elements within science since it is the task of these individuals to implement policies derived from these ideologies. Part of the process of demarcating science from nonscience involves judging the ontological status of anomalous phenomena. Some anomalies fail to meet scientistic criteria. The investigation of such phenomena is not allowed to enter into the cultural process of science. Phenomena that are considered "extraordinary" (or that have "extraordinary" explanations) and that involve research methodologies that lack experimentation or that fail to gain the appearance of high rates of replication are especially suitable for rejection by those adhering to the scientistic ideology. Some of these anomalies might be said to violate "basic limiting principles" that constitute tacit norms of science; consequently, they are rejected.

Investigators who are interested in the rejected anomaly are labeled as deviant. Once a phenomenon has been rejected, its proponents must cope with the stigma of believing in something whose ontological status is in doubt. When this form of labeling as deviant occurs within the scientific community, the behavior of seeking the deviant experience (demonstrating the existence of the anomaly) is

The Theoretical Model

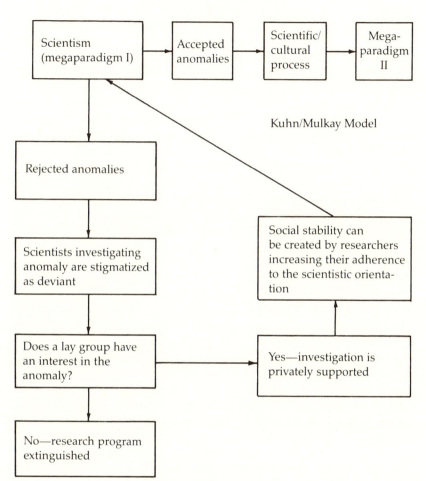

Figure 1-1.

often extinguished. The scientist who has been labeled as deviant frequently finds that his or her sources of funding no longer exist, that chances for promotion and tenure have diminished, and that avenues for publication of research results are being denied. These results might be considered aspects of primary deviance.

The forms of behavior that evolve from the original deviant act (the investigation of a rejected anomaly) tend to consolidate the stigmatized individual's role as a deviant. The scientist who has been stigmatized may continue his or her research if he or she receives support from a lay individual or group, a practice that tends to strengthen the scientist's stigma. When many individuals have had the same unusual experience, groups can use the rejected anomaly as a means of social organization. They support scientific research with the goal of devising explanations for the anomaly in question, thereby reducing the stigma associated with its experience. Sometimes they harbor a latent goal of overthrowing (or embarrassing) those harboring the scientistic ideology. This activity is frequently associated with interaction with nonscientific media, which also contributes to increased censure for the deviant scientist. These aspects might be considered the results of secondary deviance.

Scientists investigating the rejected anomaly sometimes attempt to gain legitimacy through increasing their adherence to the scientific methodology. This allows a stable social situation to occur in that the deviant scientist can attain a limited degree of acceptance. Some elements of the research conducted by the scientist who has been labeled as deviant may coincide with the scientistic orientation. These elements may be granted legitimacy by the scientific community even as the process of labeling the scientist as deviant continues. The process of labeling particular investigators as deviant supports the scientistic orientation and creates a demarcation between what is considered "science" and realms of inquiry that are labeled as "nonscience."

This orientation supports the propositions of Dentler and Erikson. Groups tend to induce, sustain, and permit deviant behavior. Deviant behavior functions in enduring groups to help maintain group equilibrium. Groups will resist the trend toward alienation of a member whose behavior is deviant (Dentler and Erikson, 1959). These propositions help explain the long-term stable relationship that exists between science and parapsychology since the latter can be viewed as a "deviant science."

The study also uses theories of deviant behavior associated with labeling and stigma. The behavior of individuals labeled as deviant is affected by their acceptance of the deviant social status and by efforts at adjustment. This is basically an interactionist perspective. This orientation also helps to explain the stability of social relationships between parapsychology and science.

The theoretical orientation in this present study can be explained in three propositions:

Proposition 1: *An ideology has evolved from the metaphysical foundations of science that serves as a guide to scientists in differentiating between anomalies that are rejected from anomalies that are allowed to affect the cultural process of science.*

Assumptions made by scientists during the start of the seventeenth century were important in the development of a scientific ideology. It was assumed that the physical world could only be completely understood through the application of mathematics and that only measurable qualities were valuable to science. These assumptions led to the belief in experimental methodology and the importance of replicability. A "parapsychological tradition" exists which constitutes a continuing reaction against the exclusion of uniquely mental qualities. Since this tradition exists as a form of "counterideology" to scientism, its proponents turn their attention to anomalies that seem to violate the assumptions inherent within science. These individuals are labeled as deviant by the scientistic community and must locate support from lay individuals or groups if long-term research efforts are to be undertaken. A discussion of the historical background of science and parapsychology as well as example cases illustrating accepted and rejected anomalies is contained in chapter 2. This discussion supports the proposition by illustrating the connection between scientism and the acceptance or rejection of anomalies.

Proposition 2: *Scientists engage in a rhetorical and political process by labeling certain belief systems as deviant.*

Science can be viewed as a process in which qualified speakers use rhetorical strategies to present arguments before scientific audiences through journals and scientific meetings (Overington, 1977). The labeling of selected belief systems as deviant makes the rhetorical aspect of science more apparent than it is within "normal" science.

Investigating these rhetorical aspects requires analyzing the philosophical and polemical statements of parapsychologists and their critics contained in the journals concerned with this field (such as *Journal of Parapsychology, European Journal of Parapsychology, Journal of The American Society for Psychical Research, The Zetetic Scholar*), books published by proponents of both sides, letters exchanged between proponents of the two sides, and verbal communications of proponents observed through a participant observation study. Theodore Rockwell (an individual who has collected a large and complete library of documents of this type) consented to let me use his library for my analysis. I also used past sociological analyses which I found valuable for this aspect of the study (especially Collins and Pinch, 1978).

The rhetorical aspect of the conflict between parapsychologists and their critics is discussed in chapter 3. This analysis reveals a typical pattern of conflict in which actual argumentation occurs on only a few specific points. The successful labeling of parapsychologists as deviant (a major critical strategy) contributes to the power of critics.

The political aspects of the deviance-labeling process were investigated and revealed through the reconstruction and analysis of example cases that demonstrate success or failure of paraspychology in its quest for legitimization. Four sample cases were selected and are discussed in chapter 4: 1. The argument between J. B. Rhine and various psychologists over the validity of his statistical methodology. Information about this argument is reported by Mauskopf and McVaugh (1979), and was also gained by interviewing parapsychologists who had firsthand experience or were familiar with it. 2. The political struggles of parapsychology for legitimate status within AAAS. This case was investigated by talking with various individuals who have followed this struggle closely, and by reading the files of the AAAS, written reports (for example, Dean, 1970), private correspondence (contained in the files of Howard Zimmerman, executive secretary of the PA), and media reports. 3. The struggle of various parapsychologists to create a professorship in parapsychology at the University of California at Santa Barbara. This case was investigated by interviewing individuals who were closely involved with the struggle, and by reading the final report that was presented to the regents of the University of California at Santa Barbara. 4. The attempts of an organization (many of whose members are critical of parapsychology) to curb and control media presentations of claims of the paranormal. This case was investigated by interviewing various individuals who closely followed this issue and by reading media reports. This case involves a complaint filed with the Federal Communications Commission by the Committee for the Scientific Investigation into Claims of the Paranormal regarding media coverage of psychic phenomena.

In order to gain a greater understanding of the rhetorical and political process of science, I mailed a questionnaire (see Appendix A) to 497 elite Council members and selected section committee representatives of the AAAS. These individuals constitute a population of the "administrative elite" within American science. Since elite scientists might be expected to demonstrate greater adherence to the scientistic ideology, it was predicted that they would be more skeptical of parapsychologists' claims than would average scientists. This prediction was accurate and the questionnaire results are reported in chapter 5. The questionnaire also revealed a relation between belief in ESP and personal experience of anomalous phenomena. Skepticism was associated with a priori assumptions regarding ESP as would be predicted by the theoretical model.

Proposition 3: *Scientists labeled as deviant can create a stable relationship with orthodox science by increasing their adherence to the scientific orientation, and will tend to do so in response to being labeled as deviant.*

Research on this proposition required the use of past studies of parapsychologists (for example, Allison, 1973; McConnell and Clark, 1980). It also required interviews with professional parapsychologists (interview format is contained in Appendix D) and a participant observation study of parapsychology.

Research centers were selected for investigation by requesting a list of such centers from the Foundation for Research on the Nature of Man, Durham, NC. The list included thirteen parapsychology research centers in the United States in 1978. Forty-five parapsychologists were interviewed at these centers. During the period of the participant observation study, some of those interviewed were working only part-time as parapsychologists and some terminated their employment (but maintained interest in the field). It is difficult to determine whether some individuals are "full-time" parapsychologists or not. College professors who maintain an interest in parapsychology might not be deemed as full-time parapsychologists. If only individuals working at what has been deemed a "center" and devoting all their attention to parapsychology are counted as full-time workers, then 16 of these individuals fall in this category. Besides the 45 individuals classified as parapsychologists working at the listed centers, 15 administrative, secretarial, or public-relations personnel working at the centers also were interviewed. During the participant observation study, other centers were located and key parapsychologists and former parapsychologists were also interviewed. Consequently, 10 American parapsychologists, 11 former parapsychologists, 7 European parapsychologists, and 14 individuals involved with the field but not members of the PA were also interviewed. A total of 102 interviews were conducted.

During this study, one center relocated and new centers were formed. A current listing (1983) of parapsychological research centers can be found in Appendix C. The word "parapsychologist" will be used to denote a member of the PA rather than the looser definitions often used by the media and the general public.

Participant observation study was conducted by visiting each center and staying at least a week at larger ones, by volunteering as a subject in experiments, by fraternizing with parapsychologists, and by attending parapsychological conferences sponsored by the PA and its regional affiliate, the Southeast Regional Parapsychological Association.

Information about the reaction of parapsychologists to deviant labeling is analyzed regarding its manifest and latent effects. Although parapsychologists have tended to increase their adherence to the ideology of science, their impact on the larger cultural process of science is negligible. This information is presented in chapter 6.

Information about the interaction between parapsychologists and the public also was acquired during the participant observation study. The desire of parapsychologists to adhere to all the norms of science has a latent effect on the field. Parapsychologists do not actively attempt to modify the distorted image of psi that has been accepted by various elements of the media and the general public. This distorted image of psi makes it seem less acceptable as a topic of inquiry than the image of it that parapsychologists have developed. This information is presented in chapter 7.

The purpose of this study is to explain the historical continuity of parapsychology, a realm of inquiry that can be considered a deviant science. This historical continuity can be explained as an aspect of the scientific ideology and the process of labeling parapsychology as deviant. The ideology of science aids scientists in differentiating anomalies that are allowed to affect the cultural process within science from anomalies that are rejected. By labeling as deviant those belief systems that have been derived from rejected anomalies, scientists engage in a rhetorical and political process. Scientists who have been labeled as deviant can create a stable relationship with orthodox science by increasing their adherence to scientific ideology and will tend to do so in response to being labeled as deviant.

2

Scientism and the Rejection of Extraordinary Anomalies

This chapter argues that certain features are necessary for a phenomenon to be accepted as a legitimate anomaly and for other phenomena to be rejected. Anomalous phenomena that are accepted for inclusion within the scientific process must have either the appearance of high to moderate replicability under laboratory conditions, or an explanation that does not violate any of the meta-physical assumptions of science. Rejected anomalies tend to be sporadic, experiential (not easily subject to measurement), and to occur infrequently. Rejected anomalies are deemed to be "extraordinary" or to have "extraordinary" explanations. Rejected anomalies, if they are to generate long-term research programs, must have experiential facets, that is, they must have aspects that can be experienced by the average person, in order to gain support from lay groups.

Because the resources of science are limited, criteria must be devised to govern their allocation. Some realms of inquiry have been very fruitful in producing "knowledge" while others have generated meager results. Since some fields deal with phenomena whose onto-logical status is very slight, virtually all scientific resources (funding, access to the scientific system of communication, access to the academic system of support, and so on) have been denied. This allows resources to be channeled into what is considered by the scien-tific community to be more worthwhile endeavors. The criteria that have evolved regarding the ontological status of anomalies constitute an aspect of scientism.

Scientism is an ideology that exists not only within the scientific community but also within the entire society. Consequently, it influences the social treatment of individuals who report anomalous experiences. A stigma is associated with the claim of having experiences that are deemed "unreal," which leads to fewer reports of their occurrence. This gives the impression that such experiences occur less frequently than they actually do. Therefore, the features (infrequent and sporadic) that led to the labeling of the phenomena as deviant are increased and the stigma attached to reporting the phenomena may also be increased. "What we learn from the study of social intelligence about anomalous events is . . . that the anomalous, if noticed, is kept secret. And it remains secret precisely because there are so many barriers to its emergence" (Westrum, 1982:96). In this way, a cycle can occur in which the experience of an anomalous phenomenon is labeled as deviant. This is an aspect of what has been called the "decline process" in figure 2-1, since the frequency of reports of the experience declines.

The labeling of scientists who undertake such investigations as deviant also contributes to the decline process. The stigmatized scientist may find that his or her sources of funding have vanished, that access to scientific systems of communication has been blocked, and that the chances for promotion in rank have diminished. Frequently, the scientist stops investigating the rejected anomaly, leading other researchers to believe that the claims of those supporting the phenomenon are invalid. An indirect result is that the stigma associated with reporting and investigating the anomaly increases.

Just as the labeling of an experience as deviant leads to its underreporting, so can such labeling contribute to its repetition. The creation of a category of rejected anomalies often allows individuals to associate these phenomena with metaphysical orientations that are antiscientistic or religious. This nonscientistic orientation is generally concealed, rationalized, and inexplicit. These lay groups tend to be opposed not to the methods of science but merely to *some* of the assumptions that constitute an aspect of scientism. Interested groups or individuals collect reported cases of the alleged phenomenon and analyze their data. Some rejected anomalies are subject to experimental laboratory procedures. The exceptional nature of the anomalous experience is reduced by seeking to gain a scientific understanding of it. The lay groups seek to organize their findings into future scientific paradigms.

Theoretical Model
Demonstrating Treatment of Rejected Anomalies and Means for
Long-Term Research Involving Rejected Anomalies

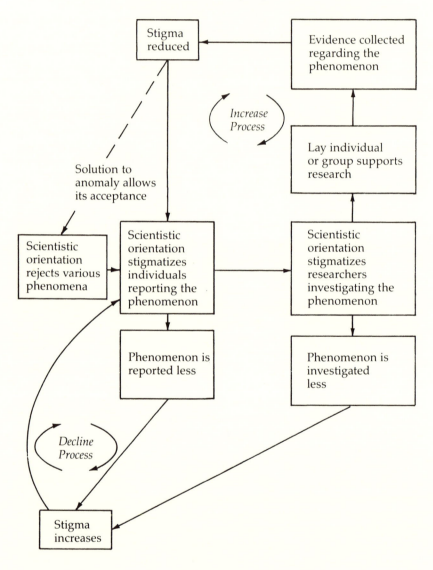

Figure 2-1.

This activity reduces the stigma associated with the experience of the phenomenon. Scientific investigation of a rejected anomaly increases its ontological status because possibilities are created for the phenomenon's verification, the degree of actual experience of the phenomenon can be revealed, and the high degree of reputability of some of the experiencers can be used in the quest for legitimacy. This cycle has been labeled the "increase process" in figure 2-1, in that the activity allows the reporting of the phenomenon to increase, thus its incidence seems to increase.

The tendency of mainstream scientists to incorporate some acceptable results of deviant science into the scientific/cultural process gives deviant science a function beyond entertainment value or revolutionary potential. Science's ability to absorb discoveries that do not conflict with scientism causes deviant science to have a residual nature and reduces its capacity to create revolution.

Dolby (1979:41, 42) notes three distinct patterns by which the claims of a deviant science can become respectable: (1) the deviant ideas are developed independently by orthodox scientists, (2) an idea associated with deviant science is taken up by mainstream scientists and found to be valuable within the orthodox framework, and (3) the deviant movement becomes orthodox. Since patterns 1 and 2 of Dolby's list occur within mainstream science, their analysis lies beyond this study. The present study tries to explain why some forms of deviant science seek orthodoxy yet fail to attain it. Figure 2-1 may be appropriate only for forms of deviant science that are associated with anomalistic experience. The changes which occurred in the scientific acceptance of such fields as osteopathy and Freudian psychoanalysis are not effectively modeled by figure 2-1.

The model in figure 2-1 fails to reflect fully the complexity of the social situation surrounding rejected anomalies. It merely attempts to illustrate the interaction between scientific ideology, rejected anomalies, scientific community, and lay groups or individuals. The actual interaction between a society and the frequency of reporting any particular rejected anomaly seems to vary over time and involves many more factors. An analysis of all these factors lies beyond the scope of this study. In Western societies, the reporting of some anomalies (such as werewolves, fairies, mermaids, dragons) seems to have declined drastically, whereas the reporting of other experiences (such as poltergeists and ghosts) has not (Roll, 1977).

Truzzi (1977) presents a method of differentiating claims within a

Table 2-1. Defining Normal Sciences and Protosciences by How
Claims Are Evaluated

In Terms of Institutionalized Science and Its Attitudes	In Terms of Scientific Method	
	Acceptable	*Unacceptable*
Acceptable	1	2
Unacceptable	3	4

1 = Normal science.
2, 3, 4 = Protosciences.
2, 4 = Pseudosciences.

Source: Adapted from Marcello Truzzi, "Editorial: On Psuedo-sciences and Proto-sciences," *The Zetetic*, 1 (Spring–Summer 1977), 5.

four-cell matrix (see table 2-1). A claim is considered acceptable or unacceptable in terms of the attitudes of established scientists. These individuals also evaluate the methods employed by proponents of the claim. Truzzi (1977:5) explains his matrix as follows:

In terms of this matrix, 1 refers to ordinary or normal science, and 2, 3 and 4 all refer to what I have called *protosciences,* insofar as all seek acceptance into ordinary science, 1, and allege to seek validation through use of the scientific method. Both 2 and 3 are called pseudosciences, but 2 is truly pseudo (false), while 3 is not; and 4 is a full-fledged pseudoscience which one would usually find labeled "quackery," since it is unacceptable both methodologically and institutionally (by, that is, the scientific community of "gate keepers"). Obviously those in category 4 usually claim they are in category 3. Unfortunately those in 2, who should be in 4, are accepted by those in institutionalized science along with 1—and are not usually perceived, therefore, as being pseudosciences.

Truzzi (1977) notes that, in general, the reason for rejection by the scientific community of a claim is its lack of "fit" with established theory. Rejected anomalies have an "extraordinary" quality that makes them unsuitable. Since rejection is a means by which scientism manifests itself, one objective of this present analysis is to shed light on the forms or qualities of anomalies that lead to acceptance or rejection.

The two criteria associated with Truzzi's matrix are the two main aspects of scientism, an ideology that:

1. supports science as a valuable *body of knowledge* which should be altered only with a certain degree of hesitancy;

2. supports science as a *method* that can be used to progress toward some absolute truth.

Actually these two aspects of scientism are mutually supportive. The scientistic perspective requires a certain commitment to the existing body of scientific knowledge, since it has accumulated through use of methodologies found to be valid in the past. Truzzi (1977:4) notes, "We recognize that the borders of scientific knowledge are fluid and that science continues to evolve. But scientific evolution grows in a fashion that continues to subsume its earlier explanatory perspectives. New data and relationships (once validated) must be absorbed into current science in a systematic fashion. Thus, science is by its very character *conservative* and *skeptical* toward extraordinary claims."

The community of "gate keepers" evaluates protosciences according to their attitudes as institutionalized scientists. Since the rejection of a protoscience depends on the attitudes of elite scientists, a poll of these individuals sheds light on this process. Such a poll is presented in chapter 5 with regard to parapsychology.

One claim of the "relativistic" orientation within the sociology of science is that a scientist's belief in the "reality" of a phenomenon affects his or her evaluation of research into the phenomenon. Collins (1974, 1975, 1976, 1981) noted this tendency among those interested in parapsychological phenomena, emotions in plants, high fluxes of gravity waves, and the transversely excited atmospheric pressure CO_2 (TEA) laser. The notion of what constitutes a valid replication of any experiment is constructed through social interaction. Travis (1981) extended the "relativistic" claim to include scientists who had conducted learning experiments with worms. The level of replication attributed to the investigation of any specific anomaly (such as worms' ability to learn) is associated with evaluations, in terms of scientific method, of other researchers' competency. Collins (1976, 1981) presents a matrix that explains the relation between attitude and evaluation of an experimental result with regard to any particular observer (see table 2-2). Believers in a phenomenon regard as valid those experiments supporting belief. Skeptics regard as valid those experi-

Table 2-2. Scientists' Tendency to Evaluate Research
so as To Support Their Prior Systems of Belief

FIND RESULTS CONSONANT WITH THIS BELIEF	BELIEF IN PHENOMENON BEING INVESTIGATED	
	Yes	*No*
Yes	1. Competent	2. Not competent
No	3. Not competent	4. Competent

SOURCE: Adapted from H. M. Collins, "The Place of the Core-Set in Modern Science: Social Contingency with Methodological Propriety in Science," *History of Science,* 19 (1981), 6–19.

ments supporting nonbelief. Individuals tend to reject research that does not support their beliefs. Collins (1976:24, 25) explains this matrix: "I would suggest that in fields where the existence of some phenomenon is universally accepted (or not) the right (or left) side of this classification, boxes 2 and 4 (1 and 3) disappear, and competence is then defined by the results found in the experiment. . . . In a controversial field, actors may be seen as arguing for either the right or left hand side of the table, and claims for replicability (or otherwise) are part of the rhetoric of these negotiations." Hence, replicability is part of the "rhetoric of scientific presentation." It is "a means of accomplishing objectivity rather than demonstrating it" (Collins, 1976:28).

When this idea is applied to Truzzi's (1977) method of defining normal science and protoscience (table 2-1), we note that an observer, who believed that a specific protoscience was invalid in regard to established scientific knowledge, would tend to find its methodology unacceptable. Cells 1 and 4 should have many cases while cells 2 and 3 would have few with reference to table 2-1 and to the way scientists tend to act. This hypothesis was tested by surveying elite scientists and was supported by the results that are presented in chapter 5.

Truzzi (1977) notes that anomalies are basically of two types. Anomalous *facts* (variables) concern a phenomenon that radically violates our expectations (for example, a unicorn). No shift in any

Table 2-3. The Differentiation of Anomalous Claims

VARIABLE (*facts*)	RELATIONSHIP (*processes*)	
	Ordinary	*Extraordinary (anomalous)*
Ordinary	A	C
Extraordinary (anomalous)	B	D

A = Ordinary science.
B = Cryptoscientific claims.
C = Parascientific claims.
D = Crypto-parascientific claims.

SOURCE: Adapted from Marcello Truzzi, "Editorial: On Psuedo-sciences and Proto-sciences," *The Zetetic*, 1 (Spring–Summer 1977), 7.

established paradigm would be necessary to accommodate acceptance of this observation. Acceptance of anomalous *processes* (relationships), on the other hand, would require serious changes in our current lawlike statements within science. For example, acupuncture hypothesizes that there is a relationship between ordinary pins placed in the body and the relief of ordinary pain. Accepting a relationship between these two would require serious reconceptualization of paradigms within neurophysiology. Truzzi (1977) notes that some anomalies fall in both categories of fact *and* process. For example, finding a mermaid might change our view of evolution and perhaps even of genetics. These distinctions allow Truzzi to define cryptoscience, parascience, and crypto-parascience through use of the matrix in table 2-3. Truzzi (1977:7) explains the matrix:

In this matrix A would constitute propositions found in ordinary science: ordinary (accepted) variables in ordinary relationships. An example of B would be an extraordinary variable (e.g., a unicorn, a sunken continent, a strange radiation) in ordinary relationship to other things. These would constitute what I would call *cryptoscientific* claims. An abominable snowman or Yeti would be a cryptozoological claim; a sunken continent (Atlantis) might represent a cryptogeographical claim. Ordinary variables in extraordinary relationship, as in C, I would label *parascientific* claims. Thus, telepathy would constitute a parapsychological claim (two people thinking the same thing is not itself extraordinary, but the claim that a thought can be transmitted to another person and cause a second, parallel thought is extraordinary). Acupuncture would involve paraphysiological claims. Those claims that involve extraordinary variables and relationships, as found in D, would combine both cryptoscientific and parascientific claims. Since no obvious term exists for these claims, I will simply call them *crypto-parascientific* claims. Since claims of the type D tend to have little support from the rest of science (since both the variables and the relationships are extraordinary), they tend to become more isolated and are often labeled quackery more readily than either cryptoscientific or parascientific claims. Quite commonly, these crypto-parascientific claims have support outside science (e.g., from religion) to keep them going. Often these claims border on science, or are seen as outside of science and as supernatural claims.   •

Truzzi (1977) notes that his matrix reveals significant differences about the strategies required of proponents in order that the anomaly might gain scientific acceptance. Cryptoscientific claims are (at least in theory) relatively easy to validate but difficult to disprove. For example, the capture of a live unicorn could be used to prove its existence but the failure to capture one does not disprove the existence of this animal. Parascientific claims are relatively easy to disprove yet difficult to prove. For example, a researcher might conduct a statistical test to disprove the validity of an astrological claim. If the experiment was successful in supporting the claim, the researcher would have to contend with alternative explanations, the need for replications, and so on.

This method of analysis seems to sort out anomalous claims and to reveal the strategy that proponents should use in their efforts to attain legitimacy. Difficulties arise when attempting to classify some example cases. What is extraordinary for one individual may not seem so to another. Moreover, extraordinary variables and facts are often linked (to various degrees) with extraordinary relationships even though this linking may not be logically necessary. For example, unidentified flying objects are often believed to be extraterrestrial in origin. In this case, an extraordinary fact is linked to an extraordinary relationship in many people's minds even though this linking is not logically required. Truzzi (1978:18, 19) notes, "The degree to which each of us may be surprised by a strange event is rather relative to our own experience and background. . . . It is far easier to make reasonable assessments of extraordinariness in relation to existing bodies of scientific knowledge and theory."

He also notes that such evaluations depend not only on the phenomenon itself, but also on the "extraordinariness" of the explanation of that phenomenon. It would seem that any extraordinary fact requires a somewhat extraordinary explanation (though not necessarily one that would cause a paradigm shift). For example, the claim that a Sasquatch lives in Oregon demands an explanation as to why scientists have not uncovered better evidence supporting the claim. Other animals have left far more traces of their existence. An officer of the International Society of Cryptozoology wrote me that he was uncertain that the discovery of a Sasquatch skeleton would convince his critics. They would merely deny its authenticity (as they do the sightings, casts of footprints, and film). Facts and relationships are often interwoven together and the evaluation of both is culturally specific.

It should also be noted that evaluations by attitude and evaluations in terms of scientific method are not dichotomous. The evaluation is not whether the protoscience is "acceptable" or "unacceptable." Each observer formulates a personal scale of acceptability using his or her own criteria and creating a ranking of various protosciences. Scientists share scientism as a source of criteria. Rosenthal (1982) notes that cryptoscientists experience rejection of their research because (1) they study things that may not exist (cryptoness) and (2) they study things that they "should not study" (tabooness). The evaluation of cryptoscientific claims varies on both of these scales. In a small survey, Rosenthal (1982) found that studies of death, heterosexual behavior, and suicide tended to be ranked low on tabooness and cryptoness. The study of "abduction by spacecraft" and of "ghosts" had just the opposite rankings on both these scales. "Language in apes" was ranked high in cryptoness and low in tabooness. The study of "religion" was deemed high in tabooness and low in cryptoness. We might speculate that the concept of "cryptoness" is derived from scientistic attitudes while "tabooness" is a more general, social component.

A "measure for crackpots" scale devised by Gruenberger (1964) was designed to differentiate pseudoscience from science. This multifactor scale attempted to separate individuals whom Gruenberger (1964) evaluated as "crackpots" (dowsers and "ESPers") from scientists he deemed as valid (physicists). The scale used factors such as "public verifiability," "predictability," "humility," "paranoia," and "statistic compulsion." Many of the elements on this scale illustrate the covert aspects of scientism. Gruenberger (1964) failed to note that scientists tend to evaluate individuals whom they consider to be "crackpots" as having the negative personality components that constitute aspects of his scale. The scale could also be used to demonstrate that psychologists and sociologists are more like "crackpots" than are physicists. This scientistic notion leads to evaluations both between and within realms of inquiry. For example, "Psychology, as a science, is considered second-rate by some representatives of the 'hard sciences.' And in psychology itself, some members of the Psychonomic Society regard the rest of psychology in a manner comparable to the way that most astronomers treat astrology" (Krippner, 1982:129). The historical events that have led to and that support this orientation will be discussed later in this chapter.

Although the scientistic orientation creates a continuum of evaluations regarding scientific claims, the ranking of these claims varies over time. Many scientists believe that experimental replication determines these shifting evaluations. Sociologists of science note that the use of experimental "replicability" as a criterion is part of the rhetoric of scientific struggle. In their study of paranormal metal-bending research, Collins and Pinch (1982:184) note, "It would seem that evidence is so bound up with the society or social group which gives rise to it that theories held by members of radically different scientifico-social groups cannot be adequately tested against each other by experiment."

A discussion of various example cases, some of which involve cryptoscientific claims and others parascientific claims, may shed light on this issue. The example cases have been selected with the idea of illustrating the factors that bring about changes in the acceptance of anomalous claims. All cases involve a process of argumentation that occurred almost totally within the scientific domain.

Example Case 1—Meteorites

The history of the investigation of meteorites illustrates the scientific acceptance of a parascientific claim. It also illustrates the "decline" and "increase" processes hypothesized in figure 2-1. The information on this case and the discussion of social intelligence about anomalies are derived from Westrum (1977a, b).

Meteorites can be classified originally as rejected anomalies. In the early 1770s, various papers were submitted to the French Academie Royale des Sciences concerning meteors and stones that were alleged to have fallen from the sky. At the time, no connection was made between meteors and the alleged "thunderstones," since "stones simply did not fall from the sky." The extraterrestrial origin of these stones was a parascientific claim since it associated "ordinary" stones with an "extraordinary" process. Chemical analyses submitted by Fougerous, Cadet, and Lavoisier concluded that the "thunderstones" had not fallen from the sky because their chemical analyses revealed nothing that was not in the earth. When highly reputable individuals such as the mayor and town attorney of La Grande de la Juillance sent in a formal document testifying their witnessing of the falling rocks, the physicist Bertholon, editor of *Journal des Sciences Utiles,* poured scorn on what was regarded as a scientific absurdity. John Pringle, a fellow of the Royal Society of London and later its president, stated in 1759 that there was no well-vouched instance of any meteor that had fallen. This observation is significant in that an article by Henry Barham concerning a meteor striking the earth in Jamaica about 1700 had appeared in the *Philosophical Transactions* of the same Royal Society of which Pringle was a fellow. This incident illustrates an aspect of the process of labeling certain experiential phenomena as deviant. Scientists often assume that their lack of knowledge of reports about a rejected anomaly indicates its nonexistence. Their knowledge depends on the information available and their willingness to seek and believe it. Their assumptions, as in the case of Pringle, often lead to a neglectful or disparaging attitude toward past observations of phenomena occurring infrequently and sporadically.

Scientists often fail to take into account the effect of the process of deviant labeling. This assumption is, in effect, "If phenomenon x were real, I would have heard about it by now." If a phenomenon occurs infrequently, sporadically, experientially, and without any mechanistic explanation, the process of deviant labeling will thwart reports of the phenomenon from coming to the attention of scientists. Their disparaging attitudes contribute, in turn, to the process of deviance labeling, and further low reporting (Westrum, 1977b).

The eventual solution to the puzzling reports regarding "thunderstones" illustrates a pathway toward overcoming the stigma associated with rejected anomalies. This has been called the "increase process" because the legitimacy and reporting of the anomaly are often increased through scientific investigation by those willing to ignore the stigma associated with the experience.

E.F.F. Chladni, a man familiar with factors that constitute evidence in courts of law, ignored the scornful abuse that had been hurled at those who had witnessed rocks falling from the sky. He apparently believed the witnesses' testimony that he had collected, and, by diligently comparing many reports, he solved the problem in 1794: shooting stars, meteors, and falling stones (meteorites) were all aspects of the same phenomenon. Later, methods of analysis were devised that supported Chladni's theory. His theory eventually removed the stigma associated with the observation of "thunder-stones," because of its newly perceived "ordinary" quality. Although this discussion oversimplifies what was actually a complex combination of events, it illustrates the nature of the solution required for a rejected anomaly to become accepted within the scientific process. The solution to the puzzle presented by meteorites did not require a paradigm shift.

Example Case 2—N-Rays

Some cryptoscientific claims have achieved almost an "ordinary" status until an incident occurs that stigmatizes the individuals investigating them. The history of N-rays illustrates the "decline" effect presented in figure 2-1 and the importance of the appearance of long-term experimental replicability in gaining acceptance for a claim. In this realm of inquiry, which existed entirely within the scientific community, high rates of "claimed replicability" were undermined by the stigma of a debunking incident.

N-ray research began in 1903, when the distinguished physicist M. Rese Blondlet, Professor of Science at the University of Nancy (France), observed an unusual phenomenon during the course of his X-ray research. N-rays, named after Nancy (the city of their discovery), supposedly increased the brightness of any luminous object through which they passed. The phenomenon was experiential in that the researcher generally evaluated the change in brightness visually. A high degree of consistency and apparent logic was evident in the investigation of N-rays. Newly developed photographic techniques seemed to verify their reality. Various laboratories replicated Blondlet's experiments. Nevertheless, in 1904, a skeptical physicist from Johns Hopkins University, Robert W. Wood, visited the Nancy laboratory, secretly removed a vital piece from the scientific apparatus, and watched with amusement as the N-rays were still "produced." This debunking brought N-ray technology to an end. The "decline process" had been set in motion. Although the Nancy group put up resistance, the concept of N-rays would never again enter into scientific journals. The extraordinarily great number of people in different laboratories who participated in this research remains unexplained except as a case of collective delusion. M. Rese Blondlet, Jean Becquerel, Gilbert Ballet, Andre Broca, Zimmern, and Bordier were not pseudoscientists or charlatans, and their other achievements as professors, consultants, and lecturers support this claim (Rostand, 1960; Klotz, 1980).

A comparison of the histories of X-ray and N-ray research illustrates the relationship between scientism, replicability, and the process of labeling a group as deviant. The discovery of X-rays by Roentgen in 1895 seemed more extraordinary than the "discovery" of N-rays in 1903. "Extraordinary" explanations were presented explaining the X-ray phenomenon, such as internal vibrations of electrons, ether vortices, irregular ether pulses, or particles resembling cathode rays (Stern and Lewis, 1971). The consistent ability to produce X-rays experimentally, however, led to their acceptance. In contrast, N-ray reseachers dealt mainly with an experiential phenomenon (personal observation made by the researcher) and were too thoroughly stigmatized by one debunking event to convince others to join in the research even though the "N-ray experience" had apparently occurred quite consistently for some. Some researchers even retracted their articles on N-rays before they could be published, in order to avoid the stigma following the debunking (Klotz, 1980).

The example case of N-rays and their relationship to X-rays warns the relativistic sociologist of science not to take *too* radical a position regarding Kuhn's original idea. Although the final evaluation of N-rays and X-rays resulted from a process of argumentation within science (a political and rhetorical process), one cannot help believing that inherent differences between the ontological qualities of these two rays contributed to this outcome. As Hardin (1982:126) notes, "No matter how explicitly you announce it, 'reality' *doesn't* mean 'that state of affairs which a given social group agrees is the case.' It *does* mean, simply, that which is the case." Hardin (1982:127) goes on to argue that certain philosophical assumptions underlie the totally "relativistic" position; these assumptions include:

(1) the tacit epistemological claim that we are incapable of knowing the truth about certain things, or

(2) the tacit metaphysical claim that in some cases there is no fact of the matter, or

(3) the tacit metaphysical claim that what is the case is constituted by what some person or group asserts to be the case.

Although I acknowledge the validity of Hardin's arguments, the relativistic position that I adopt allows an analysis of scientific *border* areas, where we, *at present*, do not know the truth of the matter and where rhetorical arguments have increased importance within the scientific process. A relativistic analysis can contribute to our understanding the tacit ideologies that exist within science.

A comparison between the acceptance of N-rays and psi reveals an aspect of the scientific ideology. N-rays originally gained a degree of acceptance owing to their similarity to X-rays. Explanations of N-rays had a "mechanistic" quality. Explanations for psi, on the other hand, have been not only "extraordinary" but also "nonmechanistic." This places psi firmly within the category of a parascientific claim and makes it more difficult to verify owing to higher scientistic requirements of replicability, theory, and so forth.

The example case of N-rays illustrates how a "decline" in reported experience (and in acceptance) can occur through the labeling of an anomaly's investigators as deviant. The events surrounding the social construction of replicability in this field fit the patterns noted by Collins (1975, 1976) and Travis (1981). Both the ontological status of N-rays and their very character were negotiated through a rhetorical process between skeptics and believers. After the debunking incident, N-ray proponents attempted to find special "characteristics" within the experimental process that were required in order to elicit the phenomenon. An "experimenter effect" (the notion that only some experimenters might be able to produce the result since the experimenter influenced the effect) was hypothesized to occur. This claim is not unlike that made by many parapsychologists, who find that not all researchers can elicit psi.

In the end, N-ray proponents lost the rhetorical struggle for legitimacy and had no means to gain support from nonscientific groups. The "N-ray experience" was not of the nature that individuals within the general population could have it or use it to support a religious or nonscientific ideology. The N-ray researchers were also unable to devise a mechanistic explanation that could explain the inability of other researchers to replicate their experiments; consequently, the research program eventually ended.

Example Case 3—Continental Drift Theory

The concept of "mechanism" is critical in explaining the acceptance of meteorites and the rejection of N-rays. A "mechanistic" explanation for "thunderstones" contributed to their eventual acceptance as meteorites. The failure of the proponents of N-rays to devise a "mechanistic" explanation for the failure of other scientists to replicate their experiments led to the decline of this realm of inquiry. A consideration of the history of continental drift can shed light on the concept of "mechanism" and its relation to the acceptance of anomalistic explanations.

In 1915, A. Wegener proposed the theory of continental drift, suggesting that at one time the continents were united and that they later broke and "drifted" apart (Wegener, 1924/1966). The proposal was received with hostility and gained only a few supporters. The standard historical account views the original rejection as due to the fact that "no one had devised an adequate mechanism to move continents . . . through a static ocean floor" (Gould, 1977:163). By the end of the 1950s some scientists came to believe that the continents had moved, and during the 1960s a "mechanism" was hypothesized (plate tectonics) which allowed the theory of continental drift to become established and even dominant. Frankel (1979) has portrayed the eventual acceptance of plate tectonics theory (which has obvious parallels to continental drift theory) as a rational episode in the history of science. A brief discussion of the history of continental drift theory will illustrate how the idea of plate tectonics evolved and will shed light on the notion of "mechanism."

Wegener's (1924/1966) original hypothesis sought to explain three types of observations—(1) geological evidence: the similarity of the coastlines and rock formations on the continents of South America and of Africa hinted that these continents had been connected; (2) "anomalistic" paleoclimatic evidence: geologists viewing paleo-climatic evidence might expect to find similar deposits at similar latitudes but did not (Wegener suggested that this might be explained by the theory that the continents had moved): and (3) fossil evidence: paleontologists found that fossil fauna and flora on the continents were very similar, suggesting that the continents may have been connected in the past (Laudan, 1980).

For the geologists of Wegener's era, the evidence was unclear. Mere coincidence might explain the patterns that Wegener used as supporting arguments. Alternative theories seemed just as satisfactory in explaining many of Wegener's "anomalies." Further, as Laudan (1980:288) notes, "The problem with drift was not simply that there was no *known* mechanism or cause, but that any *conceivable* mechanism would conflict with physical theory. . . . Evidence drawn from a wide range of fields, including astronomy, cosmology, and experimental physics, but especially seismology, suggested that the mantle of the earth, through which the continents were supposed to move on Wegener's theory, was solid." When we reject an anomalistic claim on the basis of its not having a suitable explanation, we indicate that it lacks a "mechanistic" explanation *that does not conflict with present physical theory.*

During the 1950s, paleomagnetic and oceanographic evidence changed the situation. New evidence that drift had occurred was gathered, and by the end of the 1950s a small group of scientists became convinced that continental movement was an event which needed to be explained (Runcorn, 1962). During the 1960s, it was suggested that huge rigid "plates," perhaps one hundred kilometers thick, moved slowly apart, creating the "drift" of the continents. By the early 1970s, the acceptance of so-called plate tectonics can be attributed to the verification of two predictions that were both based on the theory. The degree to which these hypotheses were verified seemed impressive to geologists. In one case, the theoretical plate movement agreed with actually measured movement to three significant figures.

Yet, the nature of the powerful force that causes the plates' motion remains unexplained. Laudan (1980:293) notes, "A *kinematics* of plate tectonics is essentially complete. Those historians and geologists who say that plate movement was accepted because a mechanism was found are thinking in terms of this kinematics. But the *causes* of plate movement are still a mystery. There is no lack of hypotheses, but no geophysicist would disagree with the claim that they are all tentative and fraught with difficulties. Those historians and geologists who say that plate tectonics was accepted in the absence of a mechanism are thinking of a *dynamics*."

Obviously, the acceptance of an anomalous claim is dependent on more than merely the development of a "mechanistic" explanation. The history of the theory of continental drift reveals that the idea was reconsidered *before* a mechanistic explanation was devised and that the explanation which was later accepted leaves many questions regarding actual "mechanisms." The idea of a "mechanistic" explanation seems to involve a description of how interrelated parts operate together in a machinelike fashion. The determination as to whether a particular theory successfully describes the working of these parts depends on the rhetorical and political processes of argumentation within science. The history of the theory of continental drift suggests that scientists *do* value and seek explanations which explain the interaction of components of a system in a machinelike fashion, and that "apparent" verification of hypotheses derived from "mechanistic" theories leads to success in the process of argumentation. This contributes to the reclassification of "extraordinary" claims into "accepted" ones. This history also hints that when scientists come to accept an anomalistic process, they are *then* motivated to devise a mechanistic explanation which explains that process. Resources are requested for the development of experimental tests which can support or refute the explanation.

A mechanistic explanation need not be tested empirically for it to aid in the acceptance of a claim; frequently the mere existence of a probable or possible mechanistic explanation causes scientists to deem a claim as "acceptable" rather than "extraordinary." Fire walking, which involves humans walking on a bed of hot coals without blistering their feet, seems impossible. Some skeptics have suggested that fraud is involved in preventing burns from occurring (Houdini, 1920/1981). The development of mechanistic theories explaining the phenomenon reduces its "extraordinary" quality. For example, one theory suggests that a barrier of superheated vapor protects the walker's feet (Walker, 1977). Another is that the fire walker's vascular system constricts to reduce blood circulation at the same time a substance called bradykinin (which is believed to play a part in the inflammation process) is being suppressed (Doherty, 1982). Although neither theory has been fully tested, the mere existence of these ideas allows scientists to increase their level of belief in the authenticity of the fire-walking phenomenon.

Feats of superhuman strength during emergencies also seem extraordinary, although an explanation for them exists within the scientific framework. Massive release of epinephrine within the person demonstrating the feat may explain the phenomenon. These examples support Truzzi's (1978) contention that the nature of the explanation of an event is very important in scientifically evaluating the event's ontological status. A suitable explanation (one that makes a claim "acceptable") need not *completely* describe a process, as long as it does not conflict with present physical theory.

Example Case 4—Behavioral Bioassay Phenomena

Investigation of behavioral bioassay phenomena furnishes a modern example of the process by which labeling a research field as deviant can terminate progress within that field. Unlike N-ray research, and like psi, behavioral bioassay phenomena can be studied in a statistical manner.

Two psychology graduate students at the University of Texas, R. Thompson and J. V. McConnell, attempted to condition (or "teach") a simple freshwater flatworm, the planarian, to contract when an electric light was turned on. They achieved results that indicated this was possible (Thompson and McConnell, 1955). This eventually led to an experiment in which "trained" worms were cut in half across the middle and allowed to regenerate. It was found that the tail section retained as much "learning" as the heads (McConnell, Jacobson, Kimble, 1959). A third set of experiments achieved results that were startling enough to attract interest within the scientific community and even the popular press. Worms that had been "taught" were cut up and fed to "unlearned" worms, and "learned" behavior was observed (McConnell, 1962). In 1965, the "behavioral bioassay phenomena" or "memory transfer effect" was demonstrated experimentally by four separate research groups in vertebrates (Travis, 1981). Yet, many attempts to replicate these experiments failed. In 1966, twenty-three scientists published a jointly signed letter in *Science* reporting their failure to replicate the memory transfer phenomenon (Byrne et al., 1966). Dyal (1971) counted 133 positive experiments, 115 negative, and 15 equivocal. The research effort continued. By 1973, thirty-four independent laboratories had reported positive results (Braud, 1973). Replications had been published in the respected journals *Science* and *Nature,* and a master's thesis had been presented relating to the field (Hoffman, 1971). A research group headed by G. Ungar claimed to have isolated and synthesized one of the transfer agents, "scotophobin," a peptide that was said to transfer fear of the dark. The compound was later said to produce dark-avoidance behavior in rats, mice, goldfish, and cockroaches (Travis, 1980).

Yet, the phenomenon seemed to violate a number of assumptions concerning memory, which was presumed to involve networks of nerve cells. Behavioral bioassay phenomena did not fit into prevailing theory and no mechanism existed explaining how the effect worked. Some researchers hoped that RNA (which had been discovered during this time) would explain the transfer process.

Eventually, the number of scientists investigating behavioral bioassay phenomena began to decline. *Science* began rejecting articles written about the effect. Braud (1979) suggests that this occurred because: (1) the field was too "extraordinary," (2) the replication rate was too low, (3) the hope that RNA was associated with the transfer was totally wrong, (4) the research was not theoretically oriented, and (5) a stigma was attached to those who successfully demonstrated the effect. Active research virtually ceased following the death in 1977 of G. Ungar, the major proponent of the field. Other researchers lost interest. At the covert level, some scientists implied that those who successfully replicated behavioral bioassay experiments were either incompetent or frauds. Travis (1980:167) notes, "The failure *can now be seen* as the failure of a logical progression of experimentation related to the concept of a *molecular* code for memory (analogous to the genetic code), and most reviews adopt this construction of events."

In his review of the transfer of memory phenomenon, Bennett (1982) notes that one problem was the inadequacy of "behavioral data to support a learning interpretation of the transfer effect. . . . The lack of many good replication studies, inadequate control in many of the studies, and improper statistical analysis of the data have prevented many of the experiments from showing definitively that learned information has been transferred" (p. 407). Furthermore, "the biological mechanisms required to produce the effect are unknown" (p. 407). This example case illustrates the need for a "mechanistic" explanation and the tendency for "inadequate" studies to be associated with "rejected" claims. Although Bennett (1982) suggests that some experimental results provide evidence for interanimal transfer of learned information, he also feels that the memory transfer hypothesis runs counter to our understanding of neural functions since it would require that a new macromolecule be synthesized for each response an organism learns to make. Braud (1983:1) suggests that "if this behavioral bioassay work would have occurred ten years later, it probably would have been accepted since the peptide carriers fit very nicely with the recently discovered endorphin and enkephalin peptides. The field wasn't ready before then."

Travis (1980) also cites McConnell's actions and attitudes as contributing to the field's demise. Perhaps in reaction to the hostility that greeted the transfer of learning experiments, McConnell's group adopted a self-deprecating and humorous attitude. They began circulating *The Worm Runners Digest* (McConnell, 1969). The tone was often humorous; scientific reports of experiments with planarians (and later memory transfer experiments with other animals) were mixed in with such articles as "Aversive Conditioning in the Dead Rat," as well as cartoons and poems. After some scientists complained about finding it difficult to differentiate serious articles from satire (until they had nearly finished reading the article), the group began distinguishing science from humor more clearly. *The Journal of Biological Psychology* contained straight scientific articles. *The Worm Runners Digest* started at the back cover and was "upside down."

Travis (1980) points out that this format (even in its revised form) "spoiled the act" because it violated "taken-for-granted distinctions in a subversive manner." The social rituals and etiquette of science require a certain decorum and demeanor. As was noted in chapter 1, the production of scientific knowledge involves a ritualistic process not unlike a court of law. The ritual itself helps to establish the scientific community. Those who violate norms of decorum are engaging in a form of deviant behavior. Travis (1980) notes that one of the important tacit norms for doing science is "the importance of being earnest."

Besides seeming "not to be earnest," Travis (1980) notes McConnell indulged in forms of "spoiling the act" by being too open or honest. He sometimes talked about his research in a casual or humorous way, which shattered the illusion of science as a serious affair. He allowed others "behind-the-scene" views of problems that existed in behavioral bioassay research. For example, McConnell wanted to determine if "learning" could occur through the mating of worms (a subject high in "tabooness"): "We got a species [of planarians] from Buckhorn Springs. Big worms. But as soon as we started training them, they stopped mating. If we stopped the training, they mated. It makes you wonder about the value of an education" (McConnell interviewed by Travis, 1980:178). Travis further notes: "McConnell *can be seen* to have followed a subversive strategy . . . by allowing backstage contingencies to show through. . . . It is a violation of the 'rules' of the institution of science itself, rather than an attempted subversion of a particular theory—a process which is expected to take place *within* the rules" (p. 178).

McConnell's lines of research have a "taboo" quality. The idea of memory transfer occurring through cannibalism or sex seems peculiar, "funny," and strange. The "funny" quality tends to "spoil the act" and makes the researcher seem less than totally earnest.

Parapsychologists sometimes violate this same norm (the need to be seen as earnest) when they present anecdotal reports on spontaneous PK or poltergeist cases. They do this by being too "open" about what they observe. For example, Hasted (1981) reported that a turkey liver ostensibly teleported (disappeared at one point and reappeared at another) from inside a turkey (sealed in a plastic bag) and was found outside the turkey on his kitchen table. In reviewing Hasted's (1981) book, H. Collins (1982:109, 110) notes: "Hasted has broken the norms of scientific publishing. . . . In mixing up personal anecdote with the more sober general reporting of the metal bending chapters, Hasted has spoilt his case. . . . The conservative scientific public may be willing to try to digest a little bit of the unusual, but to serve up a great multicolored gobbet is asking too much." The very nature of what occurs within field investigations of psychic phenomena "spoils the case" for parapsychology. The capricious (and silly) nature of some poltergeist phenomena (Gauld and Cornell, 1979) sometimes renders reports of them as ridiculous. Some parapsychologists (in their attempt to become legitimate) ignore all spontaneous psychic experience, but such an attitude can hardly be considered scientific (merely scientistic). Parapsychology is similar to the "transfer of learning" paradigm in that (1) it has problems with the "appearance" of replication, (2) it has not devised an acceptable explanation for

these problems, and (3) there are aspects within reports of spontaneous psychic experiences that "spoil the case." A difference seems
to lie in parapsychology's ability to maintain loose connections with
the crypto-parascientific claims that gain it public support. This allows
a longevity that behavioral bioassay phenomena could not attain.

Example Case 5—Ball Lightning

The group of phenomena labeled as ball lightning illustrates the
way that scientific assumptions have influenced the classification of
anomalous experience. Some anomalies are granted higher ontological status than others regardless of the quality of the evidence
surrounding their observation. Most scientists would grant higher
status to ball lightning than they would to UFOs or psi merely because
ball lightning seems to have a greater probability of being explained
within the realm of present science. This observation is illustrated by
the fact that UFOs and other forms of unexplained "nocturnal lights"
are sometimes explained as being "merely" ball lightning. Ironically,
none of these anomalous experiences has been completely explained.

Ball lightning denotes a luminous sphere (assumed to be electrical
in nature) having a lifetime of a second to several minutes and which
often is observed (although not exclusively) in the vicinity of thunder-
storms. Ball lightning can vary in size from as small as a pea to as
large as a house (Corless, 1982). No single theory satisfactorily
explains the more than one thousand observational reports that
constitute the main source of evidence for this anomaly. It may be that
more than one form of phenomenon is being observed and that more
than one theoretical explanation is required. The very existence of ball
lightning is still questioned by many scientists. Barry (1980:3) notes,
"The skepticism surrounding ball lightning is apparently a result of
its infrequent occurrence and its observation and report by generally
untrained observers: The reports and descriptions of the phenomenon have varied so greatly from occasion to occasion that the scientist who looks for consistency is frequently infected by doubt and
skepticism." Barry (1980) points out that bead lightning, which
appears as a string of small globular luminous masses that are apparently connected, seems to be accepted by the scientific community.
He notes, "Bead lightning, oddly enough, does not evoke the emotion

and disagreement that ball lightning does. The major difference between ball lightning and bead lightning observations is the personal involvement of the observer. Bead lightning is most often observed at a relatively large distance from the observer and is associated with normal cloud-to-ground and cloud-to-cloud activity. By contrast, ball lightning is most often observed nearby and may not appear to be related in any normal fashion to a direct lightning stroke" (p. 4).

Even though photographs of ball lightning have been deemed to have a higher probability of being valid than those of bead lightning, ball lightning has been granted lower ontological status (Barry, 1980). The emotional factor inherent in ball lightning's observation gives it greater "cryptoness."

This "cryptoness" is increased by the possibility that some ball lightning may be an optical illusion caused by a residual image retained by the eye after a normal lightning stroke. St. Elmo's fire may also be mistaken, in some cases, for ball lightning. The problem is compounded by the wide variety of ball lightning observations. Ball lightning has been observed to be violet, red, yellow, black, transparent, or even to change colors. Although usually spherical, it has also assumed the shape of rods, dumbbells, spiked balls, and balls with tails. Sometimes the phenomenon may even demonstrate a degree of intelligence, for example, exploring a room as if it perceives the objects about it (Corless, 1982).

The line of demarcation between ball lightning and "nocturnal lights" is not at all clearly defined (Corless, 1982). Corless (1977) divides nocturnal lights into various groups by virtue of the circumstances of their appearance: will o' the wisps (associated with swamps), ghost lights (associated with a particular locality), psychic lights (associated with psi or a religious interpretation), and moving and flashing lights (often called UFOs). Anomalous light effects (ball lightning?) also have been associated with earthquakes and meteors. This analysis reveals that the circumstances of a report frequently determine its interpretation. A ball lightning effect that occurred during an electrical storm would be termed "ball lightning" and might be reported to a meteorologist. Other cases with the exact same appearance but occurring in other circumstances would be called UFOs, psychic lights, or will-o'-the-wisps depending on the context and the observer's assumptions and interpretation. Consequently, some effects would be classified as cryptoscientific claims (ball lightning) and others as parascientific or crypto-parascientific claims (lights associated with psi, life after death, etc.). Ball lightning is merely the category of experiences that have been observed under situations which point to an explanation involving electricity, rather than a "nonmechanistic" explanation. This leads to a greater ontological status for it, even though attempts to simulate the phenomenon in the laboratory have not been completely successful.

Example cases taken from my interviews illustrate this point. One respondent, as a young child and while alone, observed a ball of light that was approximately one foot in diameter. As it approached, a window magically opened and the light entered the room. It then proceeded through the house and exited through the front door, which also magically opened and closed. The child's parents refused to believe this story but were unable to explain how the young child was able to open the window (which had remained open and was apparently "impossible" for the child to open). The respondent has not previously reported his observation (which he solemnly affirms to be true) to any authority, because it seems to defy classification and because of its unusual nature.

A second example case, taken from my interviews, concerns a family who claimed haunting experiences. One respondent described "bright balls of light which were suspended in the air." Other respondents reportedly observed a "bright globe of light." These experiences could be classified as ball lightning except for the context in which they occurred. Since the same respondents also reported hearing strange unexplained noises (footsteps, moans, etc.), seeing apparitions, and having unusual paralyses, the observations of luminous spheres should be classified as "psychic." Similar to the situation in which Hasted (1981) described the ostensible teleportation of a turkey liver, the respondents "spoiled the act" by claiming haunting experiences. If no haunting experiences had been claimed and if a thunderstorm had occurred during the time of the reported "bright globe of light" observation, the experience might be granted higher ontological status.

These example cases support Collins's (1976) contention that the social milieu within which scientific exploration takes place can determine how one result is accepted over another in the day-to-day work of science. The categorization of anomalies allows for only certain types to be collected. Barry's (1980) discussion of ball lightning makes no mention of UFOs, ghost lights, or psychic lights.

A brief discussion of Charman's (1979) review of the scientific literature on ball lightning illustrates the differences and similarities between this realm of inquiry and that of psychical research. Charman (1979:285) notes that "no theorist has yet found it possible to formulate a plausible mechanism that would account for all the available reports. At best, individual theories have attempted to give an explanation for a limited group of events." This statement could apply to psychical researchers, yet their realm of inquiry is far less legitimate.

The "three important characteristics," which Charman (1979:263) notes are reportedly associated with ball lightning, do not necessarily exclude psychic lights or UFOs from the domain of investigation: "First, they [ball lightning] are either mobile or, if stationary, can remain in mid-air without the need for any material support; they thus differ from discharges like St. Elmo's fire which remain anchored to the discharging object. Second, they have lifetimes which typically extend over many seconds, much longer than conventional lightning discharges. Last, their luminosity remains roughly constant throughout their life." These characteristics merely establish ball lightning as a valid anomaly, distinguishable from St. Elmo's fire and conventional lightning. It would seem that the eyewitness descriptions brought to the attention of (and accepted by) ball lightning researchers are selected by the researchers' need to devise a mechanistic explanation for this phenomenon. Experiences that seem to defy such an explanation are ignored.

Summary of Observations Regarding the Example Cases

These example cases reveal some of the factors that bring about changes in the evaluation of cryptoscientific and parascientific claims. The ability or inability to associate a claim with a suitable mechanistic explanation can be viewed as important in assigning status to that claim. Meteorites and continental drift theory gained status with the development of mechanistic explanations that did not conflict with physical theory. Proponents of claims which are deemed as highly unlikely are often stigmatized as incompetent. The investigators of N-rays and behavioral bioassay phenomena were unable to overcome this stigma. Without any means of public support, the investigation of these anomalies declined. Anomalies are sometimes grouped with regard to the explanation attributed to them rather than by observed qualities. The idea of a suitable "mechanistic" explanation (or lack of one) seems to be at the heart of the scientific rejection of anomalies that occur infrequently or sporadically, such as psychic lights or UFOs. To gain an understanding of the ideology regarding scientific explanation, a brief discussion of the historical evolution of scientism is necessary.

The Development of Science and Its Ideological Aspect

MacKenzie and MacKenzie (1980) reveal various assumptions made at the start of the scientific revolution during the seventeenth century which were important in the later development of science as an ideology. Although the Protestant Reformation helped set the stage for the eventual emergence of a cultural norm of rationality, these assumptions justified rationalism for Protestant and Roman Catholic countries.

One assumption was that no aspect of the physical world could be completely understood without the application of mathematics. This assumption, formulated by Galileo, Descartes, and others, carved out a domain of investigation for the natural sciences. Although the assumption had roots in the mathematical mysticism of Pythagoras, which had been revived during the Renaissance, early scientists were able to reformulate the concept to provide a foundation of modern science.

Philosophy is written in this grand book—I mean the universe—which stands continually open to our gaze, but it cannot be understood unless one first learns to comprehend the language and interpret the characters in which it is written. It is written in the language of mathematics, and its characters and triangles, circles, and other geometrical figures, without which it is humanly impossible to understand a single word of it; without these, one is wandering about in a dark labyrinth. (Galilei, 1623/1960:183–184, and quoted by MacKenzie and MacKenzie, 1980:136)

Galileo's concept of the world as a text is medieval in origin. His belief in mathematical language is more modern. The reification of mathematics led Galileo to distinguish between primary and secondary qualities. He claimed that some qualities were genuinely inherent in objects while others were not. Secondary qualities (according to Galileo) such as color, odor, or heat are "no more than mere names . . . they have their habitation only in the sensorium. Thus, if the living creature were removed, all these qualities would be removed and annihilated" (Galilei, 1623/1960:311, and quoted by MacKenzie and MacKenzie, 1980:137). Primary qualities such as hardness, size, and motion exist in objects even without observation.

In 1690, Locke presented a similar theory in *An Essay Concerning Human Understanding*. Solidity, shape, and numerosity are inherently within objects; color, odor, and pitch are not but are an aspect of the "power" of physical objects that allows us to perceive them. It is difficult for the observer to distinguish which qualities are primary and which are secondary. The suggestion is that primary qualities produce the illusion that secondary qualities are real when, in fact, secondary qualities exist only in the mind.

Galileo's formulations, based on his mathematical and metaphysical assumptions, presaged the development of modern empirical science in the West. Perceptions of primary qualities (size, shape, motion, etc.) could be used in empirical investigation if care were taken in measuring them, since these qualities were inherent within the objects themselves and were not subject to perceptual distortion. Secondary qualities could not be used as sources of data since they did not actually exist in the physical world. The distinction, adopted and refined by Descartes, Boyle, Newton, Locke, and others, came to play a vital part in the metaphysical foundation of science. Although Berkeley, in 1710, demonstrated the philosophical dilemmas in distinguishing between primary and secondary qualities, the distinction generally was assumed to have been verified by the ongoing success of science.

Because the physical sciences deal with more "primary" qualities (ones that are more subject to measurement), they have an elevated position within science. Human experience is a product of less valued, "secondary" qualities or faculties. The concept of mind exists as a residual category containing those "subjective" qualities not suitable for mathematical (and, hence objective, scientific) analysis. One historian of science observed:

It does seem like strange perversity in these Newtonian scientists to further their own conquests of external nature by loading on mind everything refractory to exact mathematical handling and thus rendering the latter still more difficult to study mathematically than it had been before. Did it never cross their minds that sooner or later people would appear who craved verifiable knowledge about mind in the same way they craved it about physical events, and who might reasonably curse their elder scientific brethren for buying easier success in their own enterprise by throwing extra handicaps in the way of their successors in social science? Apparently not; mind was to them a convenient receptacle for the refuse, the chips and whittlings of science rather than a possible object of scientific knowledge. (Burtt, 1932:318–319)

The concept of "mind" had been defined in a manner that made scientific explanation for it exceedingly difficult. Physiological theories might hope to account completely for mental processes by explaining the electrical and chemical events in the brain but theories based on "secondary" qualities would always be considered incomplete.

Even after science evolved from a hobby practiced by gifted amateurs to a massive social effort employing many of the brightest minds of all Western societies, these original metaphysical assumptions insured that the physical sciences would, by definition, be more scientific than the social sciences and that experiential phenomena, those based on "secondary" qualities, would be difficult for science to explore.

As science evolved it acquired a certain absolute and righteous quality (see Becker, 1932). Galileo referred to nature as acting through "immutable laws which she never transgressed." Although Newton might concede that the watchful eye of a deity might be required to repair cosmic breakdowns of the universal gears, he refused to allow the need for "hypothesis" in science. Science was composed of laws that were clearly deducible and verifiable from physical phenomena. These laws stated the mathematical behavior of nature. Qualities discovered as true within the experimental realm were considered universal, since nature was uniform (Burtt, 1932).

Eventually, it became unnecessary to mention God in explaining cosmic phenomena. More than a century after Newton published his *Principia* in 1684, Laplace was able to account for all planetary orbits without the requirement of a deity's intervention. The universe had finally gained a clockwork quality, governed by immutable, physical laws. When Napoleon asked Laplace about the place of God in his system, he replied, "I have no need of that hypothesis" (Durant and Durant, 1965:548). The universe was assumed to consist of a lawful and mathematically ordered system of matter in motion. The ongoing success of science seemed to support this assumption.

This brief description of the historical roots of the ideology of science reveals the criteria valued in defining the domain of science. Although various formulations of modern physics have evolved beyond the mechanistic model of reality, the scientistic orientation, derived from science's metaphysical foundations, still constitutes the source of criteria for differentiating science from nonscience. Experiential phenomena, those grounded in "secondary" qualities, are of only limited value to science. When such phenomena occur infrequently and sporadically, they seem to deny the lawful and mathematically ordered quality that reality is assumed to hold. When theories denying the scientistic orientation are developed to explain such phenomena, these theories are deemed "extraordinary."

Max Weber's belief in the disenchantment of the world as a historical process evolved from the success of the scientistic orientation. One of the values of science is that "there are no mysterious incalculable forces that come into play, but rather that one can, in principle, master all things by calculation" (Weber, 1962:573). Weber stated that individuals in past ages had been living in an "enchanted garden" populated by numerous incalculable forces. With advances in science, belief in these forces would decrease. The average person in modern times, although unable to understand completely the technology that science has made possible, assumes that scientific theory explains nature without the use of magic. Various tacit norms, such as Broad's (1978) "basic limiting principles," discussed in chapter 1, are derived from this assumption. Any attempt to grant validity to magical forces violates these norms.

It should not be surprising that the scientific ideology, so important in developing a mechanistic image of nature, should stimulate opposition among various groups. A discussion of one form that this opposition has taken, the "parapsychological tradition," will reveal the ideological foundation necessary for deviant science to exist as an ongoing endeavor.

The Parapsychological Tradition

The parapsychological tradition is, to some extent, a reaction against the mechanical model of nature supported by scientism. It includes Mesmerism, Spiritualism, the psychical research movement, and modern parapsychology. It can be viewed as a tradition of opposition to the rationalistic and materialistic (both implicit or explicit) ideology of the scientific revolution.

> The parapsychological tradition has embodied a direct and continuing reaction against the exclusion of uniquely mental or otherwise physically irreducible qualities from the "real" world, expressly including, in one way or another, the physical world. It is a tradition of trying to prove or demonstrate that there are forces, entities, phenomena in the universe other than those which orthodox scientists would allow—forces such as irreducible capabilities of the human mind, or of spiritual fields extending throughout the cosmos, such as could never be contained in any purely materialistic theory. (MacKenzie and MacKenzie, 1980:148)

The scientistic orientation renders the paranormal as a priori impossible and intellectually unacceptable. Although the parapsychological tradition is not consistent in describing the fields or forces it seeks to explain, it is consistent in visualizing them in a way that conflicts with the conception of the world as an ordered causal sequence. Paranormal phenomena are not just a collection of events that "happen to conflict with scientific conceptions of the world." This category of events would be termed anomalies. Rather, paranormal phenomena gain their label because they challenge the scientistic orientation and cannot be defined without referring to it. "Parapsychology is thus still definable as the study of phenomena that cannot be assimilated to a mathematico-physical conception of the world—roughly, of phenomena that cannot be given a reductive explanation but that interfere in some way with those that otherwise can" (MacKenzie and MacKenzie, 1980:161).

This tendency reflects what might be termed the "negative" definition of parapsychology. For example, Beloff (1974:1), a prominent parapsychologist and former president of the PA, has defined the field as "the scientific study of the 'paranormal,' that is, of phenomena which in one or more respects conflict with accepted scientific opinion as to what is physically possible." A field devoted to all phenomena which violate scientistic assumptions is doomed to remain a parascience. By collecting parascientific anomalies, it seems to challenge the common foundation of all scientific theories. It seems to increase the quantity of information that remains unexplained rather than decrease it. The array of rejected anomalies collected by parapsychology attracts the support of those expressing antiscientific and nonscientific ideologies and, consequently, incurs the continual opposition of the scientific establishment.

Some modern parapsychologists would disagree with this analysis. They feel that the so-called paranormal does not violate any of the tenets of modern physics. They choose not to use the term "paranormal," since they feel that the phenomena they investigate occur within the realm of nature and are, consequently, entirely normal. It can be argued that parapsychology is not necessarily incompatible with science and that quantum theory may support some of the "notions" which parapsychologists support (Collins and Pinch, 1982). In response to this idea, MacKenzie and MacKenzie (1980:161) argue: "Even if modern researchers are not driven by the motive of disproving mechanism, materialism, etc., the objects of their study are still phenomena barred from the universe by the assumptions and implications of the natural sciences. It is only this feature that ties together the wide variety of topics investigated by parapsychologists and distinguishes them from those of psychology, physics, etc."

Mainstream science attempts to absorb any finding that does not violate assumptions regarding the natural world. This tendency gives the parapsychological tradition a "residual" nature. It is a field that is socially defined as a collection of alleged anomalous events which science cannot absorb. It is a realm of inquiry containing the parts which remain after useful observations have been taken away.

Various historical examples support this observation. Whenever an investigation of a phenomenon within the parapsychological tradition generates an explanation that does not violate the mathematico-physical conception of the world, the fruits of this endeavor are removed from the realm of parapsychology.

The history of hypnotism illustrates how one realm of inquiry became legitimate by dissociation from the parapsychological tradition. Franz Anton Mesmer's use of "Mesmerism" associated what is now termed hypnosis with what is presently termed psychic phenomena (psi) and with vague occult forces. Later, researchers stripped the occult forces from their study of hypnotism, but still found it was related to psi (for example, by John Elliotson and James Esdaile in the middle of the nineteenth century). Elliotson took up the cause of "magnetism," and was opposed by almost the entire medical profession. Medical doctors were attempting to free themselves from past connections with astrology and magic and their reaction to

Elliotson's research reflected this effort. Elliotson was eventually discharged from his position at University College Hospital in 1846 because of his interest in "magnetism" (Gibson, 1980). Esdaile (1808–1859), a Scottish surgeon, performed over two hundred major operations with the use of "Mesmerism" and without the use of anesthesia. Still, hypnotists were labeled frauds and their work was reviled and denigrated in every way.

James Braid (1795–1860), a physician in Manchester, England, renamed Mesmerism "hypnotism" (from the Greek, *hypnos*, since he believed it was a form of sleep). His original hypothesis was purely neurological and "mechanical." He speculated that hypnosis was brought about by exhaustion of the nervous system. Although this theory was almost entirely erroneous, Braid's belief that suggestion caused the peculiar hypnotic "sleep" allowed the field to begin dissociating itself from its parapsychological roots. Braid's attempts to popularize hypnosis as a means of anesthesia were set back by the introduction of chloroform.

Jean Martin Charcot (1825–1893) of the Paris Hôpital de la Salpêtriere contributed to the field of hypnosis by supporting it. His mechanistic conclusion on the nature of the phenomenon was also erroneous. He considered it an abnormal condition possible only in people with an unusual nervous constitution, apparently because he did very little research into the matter. At the same time, his great reputation confirmed the field's respectability and helped set the field apart from the parapsychological tradition.

The use of hypnosis declined with the rise of psychoanalysis. In a way "replicability" was a problem, because Freud (1856–1939) felt that he was unable to obtain deep hypnosis in a sufficient number of his patients and, consequently, did not use the technique within psychoanalysis. When some medical practitioners lost faith in traditional psychoanalysis, they saw the value of hypnosis as an abbreviated form of therapy for the treatment of war neuroses during and after World War II. The development and acceptance of methods that combined hypnosis with traditional psychoanalysis also aided in the acceptance of hypnosis as a therapeutic tool. It was not until 1958 that the Council on Mental Health of the American Medical Association gave an official status to hypnotism as a therapeutic adjunct under responsible medical and dental direction.

This history illustrates the factors that can lead to the gaining of legitimacy for a protoscience. Although the SPR considered hypnosis as a topic for experimentation within the parapsychological tradition during the 1890s, modern parapsychologists recognize the field as distinct from their own. Hypnosis has been successfully associated with mechanistic orientations and practical applications. The field continues to dissociate itself from the parapsychological tradition, just as medicine attempted to reject more suspicious realms of inquiry in the past. Modern medical journals that are concerned with hypnosis make no mention of psi.

Various other examples can be furnished of phenomena that have been removed from the realms of parapsychological inquiry through the development of physico-chemical explanations. Pratt's (1953) study of the homing behavior of pigeons and migratory birds was published in the *Journal of Parapsychology* because he had hypothesized that psi was a factor in their navigation. The phenomenon ceased being of interest to parapsychologists when it seemed likely that birds use astronomical information even though the *exact* mechanism remained unclear. Bird navigation depends on stars, the sun, geomagnetic cues, olfactory cues, and variables in the atmosphere, factors that may or may not be sufficient to explain this ability. The means by which birds integrate these variables into their navigational system is unknown (Schmidt-Koenig, 1979).

Kirlian photography furnishes another example of a field that originally held interest for parapsychologists. A physico-chemical explanation for the phenomenon (Pehek, Kyler, and Faust, 1976) has made the field more suitable for physiological psychology even though this explanation has not solved all the puzzles surrounding the effect. Explanations that successfully use physico-chemical mechanisms or sensory-motor interaction with the world tend to remove a phenomenon from the field of parapsychology.

The case of Kirlian photography illustrates the interaction between the social milieu and the scientific establishment in the treatment of rejected claims. Because the Kirlian effect has been associated with human "auras" in Western society, scientists have shown little interest in fully investigating it. Soviet researchers, for whom it was never a crypto-parascientific claim, still investigate the phenomenon.

These examples illustrate an important aspect regarding the residual nature of parascience. The deviant researcher continually attempts to separate events that have a physico-chemical explanation from those that he or she believes do not. Although the former explanations may be valuable to the mainstream scientist, only events that seem to have no such explanation are useful to the deviant parascientist. This situation extends even into some forms of cryptoscience. For example, investigators of UFOs, Big Foot, or the Loch Ness monster attempt to distinguish valid sightings from those that have ordinary explanations. When a UFO is determined to be a weather balloon or Sasquatch footprints to be the result of a prankster, this evidence is separated from unsolved cases. Both of these forms of rejected anomalous phenomena have a tradition of investigation that is sociologically similar to that of parapsychology. All are privately supported for the most part. All deal with an experience that is stigmatized. In all these fields, the investigation of the experience tends to reduce the stigma when the investigator fails to find an ordinary solution. They have a residual nature in that only "unsolved" cases constitute evidence for the "extraordinary" theory.

Popular writers often lump together the systems of belief that are oriented around these phenomena. Berlitz (1975) linked the Bermuda Triangle with UFOs, visits by ancient cosmonauts, "pyramid energy," "psychic energy," the lost continent of Atlantis, and the American mystic Edgar Cayce. Each of these systems of belief contains aspects that are similar. Proponents of each believe in phenomena that occur sporadically, infrequently, and in a manner that cannot be objectively verified. Some individuals are apparently attracted to the very "extraordinary" solutions that combinations of these belief systems suggest. Such combining of anomalous phenomena makes the explanation so exceptionally "extraordinary" that eventual acceptance into the scientific/cultural process is even more difficult. The activity of combining claims tends to make cryptoscientific claims and parascientific claims into crypto-parascientific claims. While this decreases the possibility of scientific acceptance, it increases the support of antiscientistic and religious segments of the society and, consequently, aids in the long-term survival of deviant science.

Owing to the rejection of science, realms of inquiry that investigate these rejected anomalies usually depend on public funding. This has required investigators to interact with the public and the media, consolidating the scientist's deviant role. Continual interaction with the media is repugnant to established scientists and further supports their rejection of the deviant researcher. As Hagstrom (1965:272) notes, "Appeals to unqualified audiences induce anxiety among scientists and lead them to take retaliatory action." The offending scientist is considered to have failed to allow qualified audiences to effectively critique his or her work and, consequently, is considered to have violated the norm of skepticism. The appeal to nonscientists is also threatening in that it blurs the autonomy of science, a cornerstone of the scientistic orientation. Scientific reaction to such appeals to unqualified audiences can be quite hostile and effective. It has been alleged, for example, that leading scientists abused their positions of power and authority in dealing with Immanuel Velikovsky's book *Worlds in Collision*. The publisher of his books was successfully pressured to cease disseminating his ideas, and at least one of Velikovsky's defenders was dismissed from his job (Hagstrom, 1965:272).

Deviant scientists affect the theoretical explanation associated with anomalous experience through their attempts to remove the anomaly from the crypto-parascientific classification. Scientific proponents of UFOs refuse to place blind faith in the extraterrestrial nature of these anomalies, but merely consider them as "experiences." This tends to make the study of UFOs a cryptoscience. Parapsychological investigators of haunting cases point out that such experiences can be explained as a form of "super-ESP" (Gauld and Cornell, 1979). These experiences do not necessarily prove life after death, nor do they grant any ontological validity to the "ghost" itself. This tends to make psychical research a parascience, since the researchers still accept the existence of psi as an explanation.

Parascientists form a bridge between religious groups that accept crypto-parascientific claims and scientific groups that support parascientific claims. Cerullo (1982) argues that the research of the SPR founded in 1882 was a response to one aspect of a spiritual crisis that was occurring in Protestant countries in Europe. Science was challenging religion as the controlling intellectual force. Psychical research became a means of searching for an image of the self that was both scientifically credible and religiously significant. Cerullo (1982) terms this image the "secular soul," a mysterious inner part of the individual that is part of the spiritual order but nevertheless also part of our earthly bodies. The secular soul that some psychical researchers sought was a form of crypto-parascientific claim, since it involved more than a process. It also was something that the researchers hoped might be demonstrated as a fact. Cerullo (1982) suggests that the secular soul might have become more accepted scientifically had Sigmund Freud's concept of the "unconscious" not proven more satisfying to Western intellectuals. The historical link between religious ideology and parascience still serves modern parapsychology in that it supplies a channel for financial support.

The support of lay groups for cryptoscientists and parascientists is justified by the tendency of the research to reduce the stigma associated with the anomalous experience. This is done through the following activities:

(a) The scientist can gather evidence that increases the ontological status of the phenomena being investigated. UFO specialists, Big Foot enthusiasts, and parapsychologists have made films of their respective rejected anomalies. Parapsychologists have attained statistically significant results in their experimental research in order to demonstrate psi. A large number of anecdotal reports by highly reputable individuals constitute a form of evidence that reduces the stigma of an experience. The collection of anecdotal evidence demonstrates that various rejected anomalies are "socially real" in that some people act as if they are real, that is, they have changed their behavior and attitude following the experience.

(b) The scientist can determine the social and psychological characteristics of those who have had the experience of the rejected anomaly. By demonstrating that experiencers do not differ substantially from the general population, the stigma of the experience is reduced. Some researchers have found that UFO observers or those who have had psychic experiences seem as psychologically healthy as nonexperiencers (see McCready and Greeley [1976:129] with regard to psychic experience).

(c) The scientist can attempt to use scientific methods (for example, controlled comparison using standardized procedures for collecting data) as much as possible. When patterns emerge from this effort, proponents can claim this as evidence supporting the empirical facticity of the phenomena in question. This can reduce the stigma surrounding experience of the phenomena since the experience is made to seem an aspect of the natural world.

(d) Not all activities of protoscientists reduce the stigma surrounding anomalous experience. Often experiences that have been alleged to be anomalous have been debunked by researchers. The researcher decides that fraud or misperception is the most logical explanation for the experience, and the stigma surrounding similar experiences is increased.

The existence of a supportive individual or group is critical in the development of long-term research into a rejected anomaly. These groups have the following characteristics:

1. Groups need the media to aid in recruitment and funding. Consequently, the phenomenon must generate media interest. This can be accomplished if the phenomenon has the particular "funny" or "man-bites-dog" quality that attracts public interest. The "funny" quality, which "spoils the act" for the deviant researcher in his or her attempt to gain legitimacy within science, insures the public attention required by deviant science. Crypto-parascientific claims often fulfill this role.

2. Groups need a phenomenon that is experienced fairly frequently by individuals within the general public. This supplies a sufficiently large pool of believers (and potential group members).

The nature of the anomalous experience affects its capacity to attract public support. Some phenomena are basically experimental (related to what Galileo would term primary perception) in that they are "experienced" only by people wishing to "measure" them. Groups that investigate *experimental* phenomena (for example, behavioral bioassay) generally cannot withstand deviance labeling since no segment of the general public feels motivated to finance their research. The topic does not have sufficient emotional appeal. Some groups investigating *experiential* phenomena (related to what Galileo would term secondary perception) cannot locate elements within the public to support their deviant research for the same reason (for example, N-rays). Since the experience is not recognized to occur spontaneously within the general public, it generates little interest. Some *experiential* phenomena do not occur frequently enough to generate an interested research group. For example, the New Jersey vegetable monster, "a large beleafed anthropoid" (W. T. Rockwell, 1980), has been observed only once and attracts only humorous interest. Other groups investigating experiential phenomena (UFOs, Yeti, Loch Ness monster) successfully gain supportive groups and media interest since the investigated experiences seem to occur almost on a regular basis. The diversity of the phenomena studied under the rubric of parapsychology is especially suitable for maintaining the field's longevity as a deviant science. These alleged phenomena include both experimental and experiential anomalies and generate cryptoscientific, parascientific, and crypto-parascientific claims. These claims attract scientific, antiscientific, and religious interest.

The history of modern parapsychology illustrates the researcher's need to interact with the public, especially with elements in the public supporting crypto-parascientific claims. J. B. Rhine, often called the father of modern parapsychology, first attempted to make an impact on the scientific establishment by publishing *Extrasensory Perception* in 1934. He later presented his case before the public in his more popular book, *New Frontiers of the Mind*, in 1937. Rhine's success in establishing the parapsychological paradigm has often been attributed to his brilliant salesmanship. He was able to attract benefactors who left grants and bequests, yet who had no deep understanding of experimental parapsychology. Their actual motivation would seem to be the continuation of the search for what Cerullo (1982) termed the "secular soul." They hoped Rhine's research would support belief in life after death. Rhine was as interested in this question as the original founders of the SPR but wished to confine his scientific endeavor to questions that he felt could be resolved experimentally. The benefactors whom Rhine attracted were necessary for parapsychology. Upon his retirement from Duke, he was able to establish the nonprofit Foundation for Research on the Nature of Man (FRNM) in Durham, NC. FRNM was necessary for the development of parapsychology since its form of research did not continue at Duke University after Rhine's retirement. Mauskopf and McVaugh (1981) supply a more complete description of Rhine's early efforts in establishing the parapsychological paradigm.

The growth of parapsychology has continually been aided by private individuals who disagreed with the previously discussed metaphysical assumptions of science. Chester Carlson, one of the inventors of xerography, contributed substantially to both FRNM and, later, the American Society for Psychical Research (*FRNM Bulletin*, 1968). Parapsychologists have told me that he felt he was aided in the protection of his patent by forces from the "other side." An endowment for a research professorship at the University of Virginia stipulates that "the incumbent will devote at least fifty percent of his time to research into the question of the survival of the human personality after death" (*FRNM Bulletin*, 1969). This has allowed Ian Stevenson to study cases that are suggestive of reincarnation. Similarly, an Arizona prospector, Kidd, willed an estate of almost $300,000 to an unspecified institution that would attempt to find scientific proof of the existence of the human soul (Fuller, 1969). After a lengthy court battle, the American Society for Psychical Research (ASPR) was awarded the money, enabling the ASPR to study out-of-body experiences. Likewise, the Psychical Research Foundation (PRF) is supported partially by private benefactors through grants with the expressed purpose of the "exploration of the possible continuation after death of personality and consciousness" (*Theta*, 1980). This has led the PRF to investigate hauntings, poltergeists, and out-of-body experiences. The support for parapsychology from lay groups removes the need for continual experimental success as was demanded from N-ray and behavioral bioassay researchers. Indeed, numerous failures to replicate psi experiments occur; for example, Soal tested 160 individuals between 1934 and 1939 and found no direct evidence of psi (Rogo, 1975). Even the various cases of fraud that have occurred within parapsychology have not thwarted the movement. It would seem that as long as parapsychology can constitute a threat to the scientistic orientation or support religious belief, benefactors can be located.

Other protosciences have also evolved into institutionalized forms. The Center for UFO Studies, formed in 1973 in part through the efforts of Dr. J. Allen Hynek, had 1,639 American associates and 157 foreign associates at the end of 1982 (Timmerman, 1982). The International Society of Cryptozoology organized efforts concerning cryptozoological claims in 1982 and had almost five hundred members in May of 1983 (Greenwell, 1983). The evidence collected on these rejected anomalies is generated by researchers supported by lay individuals or groups. The research activity can reduce the stigma associated with anomalous experience through failing to find a "normal" explanation for the phenomena. This is not to say that *all* rejected anomalies are treated the same or that *all* lead to institutionalized forms which fulfill the role of deviant science. The example cases demonstrate otherwise. Parapsychology is unique among these realms of inquiry owing to its capacity to collect such a diversity of anomalous claims within one field. This increases the field's potential for longevity since it can attract benefactors with a variety of orientations.

A similar situation may be developing with the study of acupuncture. Although originally scorned by the scientific community, the investigation of acupuncture has gained some interest because of its susceptibility to experimental methodologies and its practical applications (Bowers, 1979). At the same time (as with other protosciences), political factors take on greater importance when systems of belief are labeled as deviant. Various elements within the medical community (surgeons, anesthesiologists, drug manufacturers) are unlikely to support acupuncture research, since acupuncture could replace some uses of general anesthesia. The American Medical Association vaguely opposes acupuncture (Duke, 1972). Although no totally suitable scientific explanation explains how acupuncture cures illness and disease, numerous individuals have reported satisfaction with their acupuncture treatments. It could be predicted that even if acupuncture generates the appearance of a low to nonexistent level of replicability under experimental investigation, it can still survive as a deviant science. Its ability to produce the experiences of healing and relief from pain in some individuals will generate sufficient support from lay groups so that the research effort can continue no matter what experimental results reveal.

This analysis portrays the processes of deviant labeling within science as not totally dependent on the ontological reality of the phenomenon that has been rejected. The point is that "facts" do not "determine" whether an anomaly is real. Facts, as in "factory" or "fabricate" (all from the Latin, *facta*), are things that are made. The rhetorical and political ability of elements in a society that seek power within, and over, science is of critical importance in this construction. Metaphysical assumptions, political processes, ideological interests, and group pressures contribute to the rhetorical and political construction of facts (R. Brown, 1977).

In conclusion, it should be noted that various realms of inquiry are labeled as deviant through a rhetorical and political process justified by the scientific ideology. Some deviant fields survive because of their ability to stimulate public support. Some of the attributes that lead to their rejection by the scientific community seem to generate sufficient public interest to insure long-term survival. The ability to attract media attention, to be associated with an anomalous experience shared by a sufficient number of "normal" people, and to devise a nonmechanistic or antiscientistic belief system contributes to the longevity of deviant sciences.

3

The Rhetorical Aspect of Parapsychology's Struggle with Its Critics

Scientific knowledge depends upon the changing judgments of scientific audiences on the meaning of statements that are directed to them (Overington, 1979). These judgments emerge through a process of persuasive argumentation. Continuously reasonable within the time frame within which they are made, these judgments are derived through the rhetorical and political process that produces rationality within science. Only in retrospect can the rejected anomalies that are today considered valid (for example, meteorites, continental drift, hypnosis) be differentiated from those whose ontological status is still uncertain (for example, psi and UFOs). The rhetorical nature of the conflict surrounding parapsychology does not make the field unique. Although beyond the scope of this study, it seems probable that all of science has an important rhetorical component (see Brown, 1977; Gusfield, 1976; Overington, 1977; Perelman, 1969).

Perelman (1969) conceives of four essential aspects of persuasion: speaker, argument, situation, and audience. For the purpose of this discussion, "argument" will be considered rhetorical in nature. The other aspects (speaker, situation, and audience) will be considered political and explored in chapter 4. As Perelman (1969) notes, each aspect is interdependent in that a speaker selects his arguments for a particular situation and audience. Even though this is the case, the aspects of speaker, situation, and audience are political in that a social process occurs determining who is allowed to speak, the conditions under which the message is conveyed, and the audience who receives the message.

Rhetoric can be defined as the effective use of language intended to persuade. Those who most effectively use the art can most successfully claim theoretical validity for their belief systems. If suitable political conditions exist, those who use rhetoric best are able to persuade the highest percentage of their audience. The fact that a major element of the struggle between parapsychology and its critics is rhetorical does not reflect negatively on either side of the conflict, but illuminates one aspect of this scientific issue. Moreover, I do not wish to imply that rhetoric is opposed to science or to rationality. Instead, "rational arguments" are themselves a special form of persuasive discourse, ones particularly (and normatively) favored by scientific speakers and audiences in scientific situations. Indeed, a first requirement of any scientific speaker is to convince his audience that his discourse *is* rational and objective and should be accepted as scientific.

A sociological analysis of the conflict's rhetorical nature may seem on the surface to be pro-parapsychology. This is not necessarily the case. The difficulty arises from the unmasking, demystifying quality of sociological analysis. Science, like much of human activity, does not function in the fashion often assumed. Certain processes occur that place some belief systems in a deviant role. Sociological analysis does not necessarily decry the process it reveals, although the general tendency is to view it this way. J. B. Rhine (1979) stated that he felt sociologists of science would "gently chide" science to grant parapsychology a more legitimate status, since they could reveal the prejudicial nature of mainstream science's reaction. It is not certain that this will occur, but the tendency of sociology to relativize science may produce greater tolerance for scientific systems of belief that have been labeled as deviant. In the present instance, of course, this relativity, as a product of the methodological perspective, is itself relative. Explanations in terms of sociological assumptions are being sought. Consequently, no absolutist claims for either the assumptions or the findings can be made. They are valid or invalid only within the limits of a sociological domain of discourse.

What is being employed for this study, then, is a relativistic, sociological perspective in which rhetoric is an important aspect of the construction of scientific knowledge. This does indeed grant a *possible* future legitimate status for parapsychology, but it does not *in itself* grant such status. Theoretical validity itself is a political and rhetorical construct that, in this case, is yet to be determined. Moreover, from a functionalist perspective, one might predict that certain social needs of the scientific community are served by the deviant role of para-psychology. Recognition of the rhetorical tools used to maintain parapsychology in this deviant role may not necessarily abolish its maintenance.

Collins and Pinch (1979) have previously described the strategies and tactics of parapsychologists and their critics within what they term the "constitutive" forum (formal journals and publications) and the "contingent" forum (popular and semipopular publications and informal communications). They argue that, in the case of parapsy-chology, the constitutive and contingent forums within science have interacted, thereby violating the norm that they should be separate.

The analysis in this chapter borrows heavily from that of Collins and Pinch (1979). Rather than demonstrating the crossing of consti-tutive and contingent forums, however, various tactics will be described as rhetorical strategies in order to demonstrate the power of verbal skill and argument within this conflict. It can be demonstrated that no key experiment can resolve the issue, and that the rhetorical strategies of parapsychologists and their critics tend to occur on different levels of discourse.

Collins and Pinch (1979) list the following strategies:

Constitutive Forum

Parapsychologists
Use of the symbolic and technical hardware of science.
Critics
  a. Blank refusal to believe.
  b. Using the symbolic hardware of philosophy.
  c. Association of psi claims with unscientific (especially occult) beliefs.
  d. Accusations of the triviality of psi evidence.
  e. Attacks on the methodological precepts of the parapsycholo-gists.
  f. Unfavorable comparison with canonical versions of scientific method.
  g. Accusations or presumptions of fraud.

Contingent Forum

Parapsychologists
    a. Attempts to metamorphose themselves in the public's eye into
       academic scientists.
    b. "Laundering the funds" by playing down the sometimes
       embarrassing sources of private funding while seeking to
       enlarge respectable (government) funding for psi research.

Critics
    a. Ad hominem attacks.
    b. Magnifying anecdotal evidence.
    c. Denying orthodox publication outlets.
    d. Diluting orthodox publication through special editorials, re-
       buttal efforts, etc.

The present analysis will reorganize these strategies as rhetorical
arguments. Each argument, when used by a speaker in the proper
situation before a suitable audience, has a persuasive effect. It will be
argued that because these strategies are carried on at different levels
of discourse, the resolution of the conflict may depend on elements
outside the scientific process, that is, the needs and desires of future
elite groups. Parapsychologists attempt to base their strategies on
empirical claims whereas their critics successfully use a priori philosophical arguments that are rooted in the scientific orientation itself.

Each of these strategies has produced counterstrategies, and
counter-counterstrategies. Following a discussion of the major rhetorical strategies of each side, an outline of a typical pattern of argument
will be developed. This outline reveals the importance of the process
of deviance labeling in defining the modes of rhetorical conflict.

Major Rhetorical Strategies of the Parapsychologist

1. Use of the Empirical Methodology of Science

The major strategy of parapsychology is to declare that by
adhering to the strictest canons of scientific methodology, it is possible
to (a) demonstrate the existence or nonexistence of psi, and (b) gain

knowledge concerning psi (if it exists). Because of this adherence to scientific methodology, parapsychologists claim that mainstream scientific recognition and legitimacy are rightfully theirs. The difficulty (and potential for conflict) lies in the fact that an overall review of parapsychological literature (which numbers in the thousands of articles) indicates that psi does indeed exist and even reveals various patterns that seem to be related to its occurrence (Palmer, 1978; Wolman, 1977).

Numerous experiments could be cited as evidence that the existence of psi has been proven. For the purpose of illustration, Beloff (1980) has listed seven experiments that can be considered as highly evidential in support of the existence of psi.

(1) The Brugmans' experiment with the subject Van Dam at the University of Groningen, 1920 (Murphy, 1961; Schouten and Kelly et al., 1968; Zorab, 1976).

(2) The Blom and Pratt experiment with the subject Stepanek in Prague, 1963 (Blom and Pratt, 1969; Keil, 1977; Pratt, 1964, 1973; Pratt and Blom, 1964; Pratt et al., 1968).

(3) The Musso and Granero experiment with the subject J. B. Muratti in Rosario, Argentina, 1967 (Musso and Granero, 1973).

(4) The Roll and Klein experiment with the subject Harribance at the Psychical Research Foundation Laboratory, August 1969 (Roll and Klein, 1972; Stump, Roll, and Roll, 1970).

(5) The Kanthamani and Kelly experiments with the subject B. D. (Bill Delmore) at the Foundation for Research on the Nature of Man (FRNM), February 1972–April 1973 (Kanthamani and Kelly, 1974; Kelly and Kanthamani, 1972; Kelly, Kanthamani, Child, and Young, 1975).

(6) Helmut Schmidt's experiments on PK in selected subjects using a binary random number generator at FRNM, 1973 (Schmidt, 1973).

(7) Terry and Honorton's "Ganzfeld" experiment with student volunteers at the Maimonides Laboratory, Brooklyn, New York, 1975 (Harley and Sargent, 1979; Honorton, 1977; Terry and Honorton, 1976).

Beloff (1980:94) concludes that although the skeptical option remains "open and valid," it is his personal opinion "that these seven different investigations represent an overwhelming case for accepting the reality of psi phenomena."

Any one of these experiments, if accepted at face value, could constitute "proof" that psi exists. Parapsychologists point to a history of past successful experimental programs and they maintain a community of individuals who act as, and claim to be, scientists. This history and continuity of research effort constitutes a powerful rhetorical resource. Their rhetorical strategy is successful to the degree that it appears the canons of scientific methodology are upheld. Readers of results from experimental research generally have not been present during the experiment (Gusfield, 1976). Rhetoric is involved in the social construction of the meaning that is attributed to the experiment.

The editor of the *Zetetic Scholar* allowed commentaries by both critics and parapsychologists following Beloff's (1980) article. Some parapsychologists wished to include additional individual experiments (for example, experiments conducted by William Braud), or to point to the entire body of parapsychological literature as evidence, or to place emphasis on statistically reliable relationships between psi scores and other variables as better evidence for the reality of psi (Palmer, 1980; Morris, 1980; Stanford, 1980). Counterstrategies, used to negate this method of argumentation, will be discussed in the section of this chapter devoted to "major rhetorical strategies of the critics."

2. Metamorphosis of Parapsychologists into Legitimate Scientists

A second major rhetorical strategy used by the parapsychologists is termed by Collins and Pinch (1979) as "metamorphosis." Parapsychologists attempt to metamorphose themselves, in the public's eyes, into academic scientists. They seek to ignore their spiritualistic heritage and the fact that the field is almost completely funded through private benefactors. Parapsychologists point proudly to the affiliation of the PA with the AAAS and to the high percentage of PA members who hold PhDs. Various distinguished scientists in the past have expressed support for psychical research, and the capacity to attract modern support is a counterstrategy to the process of labeling the field as deviant. In like manner, critics of parapsychology have successfully marshaled distinguished scientists to speak out against claims of the paranormal. The strategy of metamorphosis illustrates the point where rhetorical and political strategies meet. If the field of parapsychology is allowed to metamorphose itself, it can no longer be labeled as deviant.

3. Ability to Gain Support from Qualified Experts

The ability to gain support from qualified experts is a valuable rhetorical strategy for both parapsychologists and their critics. This strategy is closely related to political aspects of the process of argumentation, since the more qualified the expert, the more successful the strategy.

Parapsychology benefited from its ability to convince statisticians that the statistical methodology used by J. B. Rhine was valid. It also benefits from the support of qualified conjurers who have supervised experimentation and have given validation to the research methodology. Various respected physicists have given their opinion that the existence of psi does not violate the theories associated with quantum mechanics, and some theories even hint that the "paranormal" may be "normal."

Critics have used the counterstrategy of relying on the support of scientists, philosophers, and magicians who are hostile to parapsychology. The renown of the "debunkers" who have been assembled to form the Committee for the Scientific Investigation into Claims of the Paranormal has also made this counterstrategy valuable to the critics.

A community of "experts" exists in the Soviet Union, Japan, Western Europe, China, and Australia. These "experts" are scientists who have been convinced of the validity of parapsychological research through their own endeavors. Reference to the research conducted in the Soviet Union is sometimes cited in an effort to gain support for American parapsychological research. It is highly possible that Soviet researchers may be attempting to use psi for military purposes. CIA and DIA reports and scientific research articles from the Soviet Union and China indicate that this may be true. For a discussion of Soviet and Warsaw Pact research in parapsychology, see Pratt (1977), Wortz et al. (1976), Defense Intelligence Agency (1978), and Ebon (1983). Referring to these "experts" constitutes a weapon in the rhetorical arsenal of American parapsychologists in their attempt to gain support.

Major Rhetorical Strategies of the Critics

In order to prevent parapsychology from gaining complete legitimacy, numerous rhetorical strategies for resistance to the field have evolved. They derive their strength from the scientific orientation and from the process of labeling parapsychology as deviant.

1. The Strategy of Blank Refusal to Believe

Scientific prejudice is not that unusual when applied to deviant belief systems. For example: "Why do we not accept ESP as a psychological fact? Rhine has offered enough evidence to have convinced us on almost any other issue. . . . I cannot see what other basis my colleagues have for rejecting it; . . . my own rejections of [Rhine's] views is—in the literal sense—prejudice" (Hebb, 1951:45). Generally, an individual does not use this strategy since it is deemed unscientific. A rational dialogue is difficult against such a position. As a counter-strategy, parapsychologists can easily point out its unscientific nature. If some opinion is not intuitively obvious, however, some form of active belief is often required. Refusal to believe in psi is certainly not unusual and it constitutes a form of skepticism that is valued within the scientific community. The refusal to believe the evidence for psi constitutes an intuitive platform that can be the (often unstated) basis of more sophisticated rhetorical strategies.

2. The Strategy of Philosophical Argument

This strategy makes no attempt to be scientific, in an empirical or experimental sense, but is philosophical in nature. As such, it can be considered a sophisticated derivation of the first strategy, a kind of a priori argument that the paranormal is impossible. Often criticisms are derived from Hume's argument concerning miracles, Occam's razor, or the belief that nothing is true that conflicts with what is now known. If this were the case, there could be no scientific progress. Yet arguments derived from this philosophical position help create the conservative orientation within science, and aid in giving it a form of stability and respectability.

Hansel's (1960:177) statement regarding telepathy takes the form of the a priori argument: "But, when I say that telepathy is impossible, I mean that processes do not occur in nature as we know it which permit its occurrence. . . . When examining the experiments, it is not unreasonable to assume that telepathy cannot occur in view of the *a priori* arguments against it; and in fact a vast amount of the experimental work has failed to give a satisfactory demonstration of its occurrence."

Hanlon (1974:185) demonstrates the use of Occam's razor in his critique of the Stanford Research Institute team who investigated various psychics: "By Occam's Razor it is only necessary to show that plausible normal explanations have not been excluded [in order to prefer such explanations] . . . and their experiments fail the Occam's Razor test." A major rhetorical strategy involves derivations of Hume's argument as described by Price (1955:360): "Now it happens that I myself believed in ESP about 15 years ago, after reading *Extrasensory Perception After Sixty Years*, [a book by Rhine] but I changed my mind when I became acquainted with the argument presented by David Hume in his chapter, 'Of Miracles' in *An Enquiry Concerning Human Understanding*." Hume's argument is that since a miracle is a violation of the laws of nature (which have been established by experience), no testimony is sufficient to establish a miracle, unless it would be even more miraculous if the testimony were a lie.

Philosophically sophisticated arguments form the basis for numerous other rhetorical strategies for opposing parapsychology. One more moderate variation states that "exceptional claims require exceptional proofs." In its extreme form, this could mean that it is not possible to produce a proof for certain claims because of their extraordinary nature. Parapsychologists have attempted to counter these arguments by pointing out that exceptional scientific claims in the past have, in many cases, been found to be valid, and that to exclude such claims for any philosophical reason is unscientific. Indeed, they argue that if extraordinary claims cannot be proven, then there would be no scientific progress.

What is at issue in this argument is the quality of the claim that psi exists. The labeling of this claim as extraordinary and the philosophical implications of that label thwart parapsychology's progress toward legitimacy. Acceptance of the critics' philosophical arguments is a reflection of the process of labeling parapsychology as deviant and of agreeing with the scientistic orientation.

3. The Strategy of "Unpacking" Any Successful Experiment

This strategy, although derived from the philosophical strategies, has in the past made various valuable contributions to parapsychological methodology. The logical unfolding of the argument is as follows:

    a. The long-term demonstration of psi is highly improbable if proper scientific methods are followed.

    b. Parapsychologists claim to have demonstrated psi after long-term experimental programs.

    c. Hence, it is highly improbable that parapsychologists are following proper scientific methods.

The goal of the critic using this strategy is to "unpack" and examine in detail any experiment, and to demonstrate how methodological flaws could have entered into the experimental process, thereby producing an invalid result. Any experiment contains many shared assumptions inherent within the paradigm in which it is conducted. The critic refuses to make various of those assumptions and by doing so attempts to discredit the research finding. When conducted logically, this strategy is a part of the legitimate scientific process and, as such, appears to occur within a scientific framework rather than a philosophical framework, although these frameworks cannot be totally distinguished.

An example of the unpacking of an experiment will reveal the nature of the process. One of twenty pictures is used as a target in an ESP experiment. An agent attempts to send the image mentally. The subject successfully chooses the target. The critic reads a description of the experiment. He questions, Was the agent or anyone else who knew which picture was the target allowed to touch the target? If so, this may have left some sensory cue that allowed the subject to identify the target. The critic would be concerned about undetectable, unconsciously registered clues. The critic might be assured that no such touching was allowed. The critic then thinks of some other methodological flaw that *could* have occurred. How was the target selected? Who checked the process of randomization? His or her "unpacking" of methodological assumptions tends to render the experiment into an anecdotal form. Some chain of sensory contact must occur for an experiment to have been "successful," the critic reasons. ESP, by definition, requires no direct sensory contact, but indirect contacts would bias the results. This unpacking strategy makes the "perfect" ESP experiment an impossibility. Sooner or later, the critic will ask for information that is no longer available, or for a degree of experimental control and exactitude that is desirable in principle but impossible in practice.

One rhetorical ploy is to demand total perfection. It is always possible for critics to think of more rigid methodological procedures after an experiment has been conducted. For example, referees have required that mechanical recording devices be used in place of hand recording of data in experiments with only limited data to be recorded. Referees also have suggested that skeptical magicians must be present even during experiments in which sleight of hand was not logically a possible explanation. At the same time that it aided critics of psi, the unpacking strategy also assisted early psychic researchers in increasing the methodological sophistication of their procedures. Indeed, the level of methodological sophistication of many modern psi researchers is generally greater than that of their critics and some parapsychologists complain that few of their critics are of value to them. They argue that critics are using the "unpacking" strategy irrationally, that the safeguards and standards of precision which critics desire make experimentation impossible; therefore, it is not a strategy used in good faith. In this sense, the strategy is irrational, self-contradictory, and unscientific.

When used in an extreme form, the "unpacking" strategy does produce farfetched criticisms. Some critics have even hinted that results can be explained by poor eyesight or advanced age in researchers. At times, skeptics have insinuated that a parapsychological researcher is absurdly incompetent. The a priori arguments of the critics mean it is highly logical to assume that, within all experiments which successfully "prove" the existence of psi, there must be an "error some place" (Honorton, 1975).

4. The Strategy of Demanding Higher Replication Rates

The demand for a replicable experiment is selectively applied to deviant science as a rhetorical strategy to deny legitimacy. Most para-psychologists claim that a degree of replication does exist and that this indicates that psi is probably real.

Replication is not an all or none phenomenon. It admits of degrees. Psychological phenomena are not replicable to the same degree as physical phenomena are. Admittedly parapsychological phenomena are even less replicable than most psychological phenomena. This is not to say, however, that psi phenomena are not replicable. Honorton (1978) compiled a list of all the experiments known to have been carried out employing Schmidt's type of random event generator. Of the 54 experiments carried out in seven different laboratories, 35 reached a 5% level of significance. Studies employing meditation, hypnosis and ganzfeld stimulation as well as ESP and DMT [Defense Mechanism Test] studies gave comparable results with a replication rate above fifty percent. (Rao, 1980:108)

The demand for a *higher* rate of replication (rather than a perfectly replicable experiment) is a more powerful and subtle rhetorical strategy. In fact, it is similar to the demand for "progress" from any science. Numerous parapsychologists believe that experimental progress *has* been made, that this in itself verifies the existence of psi, and that modern experiments are more replicable than past ones owing to advances in methodology.

The demand for higher rates of replication appears to spring from a basic difficulty in "believing" in psi. Many parapsychologists have expressed similar opinions. Often they refuse to accept other researchers' conclusions until a higher rate of replication is achieved.

The nature of the philosophical argument over replicability is illustrated in an exchange of letters between a parapsychologist and a skeptic. The parapsychologist wrote, "The response in science cannot be that you demand they do it all again because you don't believe them—such a charge could always be made. Instead, since you are stating a position, that position must be falsifiable" (from the files of Theodore Rockwell). Ironically, the critic's position is also "scientific." The norm of skepticism is a cornerstone of science.

The demand for a replicable experiment is actually an aspect of the demand for a solution to the puzzle that psi presents. A totally replicable experiment would require recognition of all the factors associated with the occurrence of psi. Frequently, such a solution is required of any deviant science before it is granted legitimacy. But anomalies, by definition, are phenomena that lack such solutions. When anomalies are granted high ontological status, they generate research programs using scientific resources to seek answers to the questions they present. The demand for a replicable experiment from a deviant science is thus a strategy to deny scientific resources for investigating the rejected anomaly. Deviant scientists work toward developing a replicable experiment, but their inability to devise such a research tool would not be considered grounds for denial of legitimacy if the anomaly they investigated was not deemed "extraordinary" by the scientistic orientation.

5. Demanding a Better Theoretical Orientation

This strategy is also selectively directed toward systems of belief that have been labeled as deviant. Fields such as sociology or psychology do not have a single theoretical orientation, yet are still considered legitimate. Similarly, numerous theories have evolved within parapsychology. These theories have had the capacity to generate hypotheses that might be considered more "testable" than many sociological theories. All scientists wish that their fields had better theoretical orientations.

One aspect of this strategy is to claim that lack of a single theoretical orientation makes psychic research trivial or uninteresting. Hoagland (1969) states that "unexplained cases are simply unexplained. They can never constitute evidence for any hypothesis." Stevens (1967:1) believes that "the signal-to-noise ratio for ESP is simply too low to be interesting." Critics claim that statistical demonstrations of the paranormal do not mean anything.

To numerous proponents of psi, the phenomena have a great deal of meaning. They feel that some of the scientistic assumptions are invalid. This meaning exists as a rallying point for antiscientistic groups and individuals. The use of this meaning labels the field of parapsychology as deviant, yet insures the public support necessary to create an ongoing research endeavor.

The demand for a valid theoretical orientation is also a demand for a solution to the puzzle that psi presents. Such a solution is not required of other, "ordinary" anomalies that have been granted higher ontological status. Scientific resources are expended in the search for solutions to these anomalies even though they may not be associated with a theoretical orientation. Anomalies, by definition, lack a solution. The demand for a valid theoretical orientation explaining psi is a derivation of the philosophical rejection of the phenomena as "extraordinary."

6. The Strategy of Associating Parapsychology with Nonscientific
Activities or Belief Systems

Critics of parapsychology often attempt to lump together parapsychologists with proponents of UFOs and various systems of occult
belief. Rawcliffe (1959) considers ESP research as a cult of the supernatural in technical dress. The psychoanalyst H. Hitschman is quoted
by Dommeyer (1966) as describing interest in psi as a narcissistic
tendency related to infantile cravings. Zusne and Jones (1982:43) list
the information that John G. Fuller is a "flying-saucer enthusiast" as
a reason for dismissal of his writings regarding psychic phenomena.
Price (1955:362) stated, "In short, parapsychology, although well
camouflaged with some of the paraphernalia of science, still bears in
abundance the markings of magic."

Parapsychologists themselves are particularly concerned with this
rhetorical strategy and try to counter it by dissociating themselves
from other belief systems that have been labeled as deviant. Parapsychology does indeed spring from the faddish Spiritualist movement occurring in the 1890s, a fact that parapsychologists attempt to
negate through the strategy of metamorphosis. Evans (1969:640)
attempts to counter the metamorphosis strategy as he states, "Most
striking, of course, is the way in which, to all but the totally
committed, psychical research and its subject matter seems so hopelessly, woefully out of date."

The accusation of nonscientific activity often includes labeling
parapsychologists as incompetent. They are pictured as having their
judgment so clouded by their occult belief systems that they are incapable of conducting valid scientific research. Such accusations also
border on the ad hominen arguments that will be discussed later in
this chapter.

7. The Strategy of Accusation of Fraud

This is the last resort of critics, which can prove successful when
all other strategies fail. The logical pattern for this argument is as
follows:

  a. Since psi phenomena are improbable, their experimental
     production probably involved either methodological flaws or
     fraud.

b. Critics are unable to find methodological flaws in every case.

c. If no methodological flaw occurred, fraud probably occurred.

Skeptics use a derivation of Hume's argument to support this logical pattern. Miracles should not be accepted as long as the possibility exists that their supporting evidence has been produced fraudulently. Psi is miraculous because it is incompatible with our most basic assumptions about the universe. The fact that fraud has occurred, at times, within psi research strengthens this argument. On the other hand, accusations of fraud by critics are generally unproved. Some critics have retracted their accusations of fraud. Famous examples include Price's (1972) retraction of claims of fraud against Soal and Rhine, and Wheeler's (1979b) "correction" of his slanderous claim of fraud on Rhine's part.

Price's (1955:363) discussion of Soal's research illustrates the sweeping scope of the accusation of fraud strategy: "Since I know of no evidence of this nature showing that Soal did or did not cheat, all that I am trying to do in the next two sections is to demonstrate that Soal *could* have cheated if he wanted to, and that therefore we should demand better evidence than his before we believe in the supernatural." After corresponding with Rhine, Price retracted his claim of fraud; yet, ironically, evidence was later discovered that Soal probably *did* manipulate his data (Markwick, 1979). Forcing critics to resort to this strategy is, in a way, a victory for parapsychology, since this was a goal set by Henry Sidgwick in a presidential address to the SPR: "We must drive the objector into the position of being forced either to admit the phenomena as inexplicable, at least by him, or to accuse the investigators either of lying or cheating or of a blindness or forgetfulness incompatible with any intellectual condition except absolute idiocy" (Sidgwick, 1882:12). In the early days of parapsychological research, claims of fraud as an explanation may have been a more powerful rhetorical strategy. At present, the field has expanded to such an extent that using fraud as an explanation for all experimental effects would require a huge conspiracy of psi researchers. Although accusations of fraud have occurred in other sciences, it is unusual that it is used as a rhetorical strategy against a whole field of science. Price (1955:363) develops a rationale for this:

. . . we must recognize that we usually make a certain gross statistical error. When we consider the possibility of fraud, almost invariably we think of

particular individuals and ask ourselves whether it is possible that this particular man, this Professor X, could be dishonest. The probability seems small.
But the procedure is incorrect. The correct procedure is to consider that we
very likely would not have heard of Professor X at all except for his psychic
findings. Accordingly, the probability of interest to us is the probability of
there having been anywhere in the world, among its more than 2 billion
inhabitants, a few people with the desire and the ability artfully to produce
false evidence for the supernatural.

This rhetorical strategy allows the critic to dismiss any experimental results if it is possible for the critic to design a scenario in
which fraud could have occurred. C.E.M. Hansel (1966) makes extensive use of this strategy in his book *ESP: A Scientific Evaluation*.
Some parapsychologists have reacted to this strategy with multi-
experimenter research designs, machine recording of subject
response, and video-taping of experiments in progress. But the
hypothesis of fraud cannot be refuted when it is pushed to the
extreme. Fraud could always occur through conspiracy, sleight of
hand, tampering with data, and so on. Likely methods of fraud are
limited only by the critics' imagination.

Sometimes these scenarios seem farfetched, though not impossible. Joseph Hanlon (1974) suggests that Uri Geller used a hidden
radio transmitter and receiver embedded in his tooth to deceive his
Stanford Research Institute investigators into believing they were
observing ESP. Hanlon failed to point out that this idea (which he
believes discredits the paranormal quality of the results) was
suggested to him by the investigators themselves.

Critics have demanded that a skeptical magician be incorporated
into the research design and execution in order to prevent fraud. This
would not eliminate the fraud hypothesis, since the magician's
competence would then be open for debate, or the magician could be
assumed to be part of a conspiracy. Price (1955) suggested that a truly
valid parapsychological experiment would require twelve hostile,
respected scientists who would monitor the parapsychologist, preventing methodological flaws and fraud.

In order to gain a better understanding of the interaction between
parapsychologists and their critics, I decided to conduct a parapsychological experiment (McClenon, 1981c). Since I had, on various
occasions, discussed these interactions with the assistant editor of a

science journal, I contacted him again, hoping he might recommend a skeptical and respected scientist who would monitor my experiment. The assistant editor was quite hesitant to help me. After many phone calls and weeks of effort on my part, he finally suggested two scientists. I assumed that these individuals were of the caliber to referee a parapsychological article that might be submitted to his journal. The first scientist I contacted stated that since the possibility of psi was so slight, parapsychological research was pointless. He declined to participate. The second scientist also declined because he "did not have the time" (although the experiment had been designed to be monitored with little time and effort). The point is that the social stigma surrounding parapsychological research seems to preclude the possibility of satisfying some critics' demands.

Sociological discussion of the strategy of claiming possible fraud seems to place the critics of parapsychology in a bad light. Collins and Pinch (1979) even go so far as to apologize to the critics following their discussion of the fraud hypothesis since their analysis seems to render the strategy absurd. Following their analysis, they state, "The point of the above discussion of the fraud hypothesis is not to ridicule the critics of parapsychology—we must apologize for any unintentional sarcasm—but to show its universal applicability and therefore to beg the question of its infrequency of use in the rest of science" (Collins and Pinch, 1979:24).

Parapsychologists attempt to turn the fraud factor to their advantage through elaborate precautions against possible fraud and by revealing whenever it is discovered within their own ranks (Collins and Pinch, 1979). The most recent case of fraud involved W. J. Levy, then director of the Institute of Parapsychology, the research arm of the Foundation for Research on the Nature of Man. After discovery of the fraud by Levy's coworkers, Rhine (1974) published a statement in the *Journal of Parapsychology* announcing that all of Levy's experimental reports were to be considered unacceptable, and that any of Levy's work that had been replicated must be evaluated entirely on the strength of the replicated work alone.

Another conflict within parapsychology involved the method of handling failures to replicate Levy's work. Some researchers desired (and achieved) an even more open disclosure of failures to replicate Levy's experiments than was desired by Rhine. The manner by which parapsychology handled Levy's fraud might be pointed out as tending to legitimate the field rather than the opposite (Collins and Pinch, 1979; McConnell, 1975).

8. Ad Hominem Arguments

Often critics point out personal factors that are irrelevant to the claims being made. Various critics of the research concerning Geller at the Stanford Research Institute (SRI) noted that many of the investigators are Scientologists (Hyman, 1977; Gardner, 1975; Hanlon, 1974). Hanlon (1974:182) was most specific: "Puthoff has gone through encounter groups and other West Coast fads, and is now a Scientologist (as is Ingo Swann [a psychic subject used at SRI]). In an area where observation is difficult anyway, have the SRI investigators taken enough precautions to ensure that their natural desire to see Geller succeed does not cause them to unconsciously make errors or misinterpret the data to Geller's benefit?" Various skeptical respondents whom I interviewed were even more direct. The accusation was that a Scientology conspiracy was occurring at SRI with regard to psi research. The claim was that a large number of researchers, all Scientologists, had conspired to produce fraudulent experimental results which were consistent with church doctrine. The fact that non-Scientologists were involved with the research was not pointed out. One respondent interviewed by Collins and Pinch (1982:44) stated: "I do not think that Targ and Puthoff are very competent personally and I think the scientology thing is a very important condition to be aware of. . . . There is definitely some sort of scientology conspiracy. . . . There is a very strong ideological religious bias in their work. Scientology and that sort of stuff is something that appeals to second-rate scientists quite a lot."

Ad hominem arguments are also used by proponents of psi to explain what they consider to be "irrational" behavior on the part of their critics. It is claimed that some critics harbor hostility to psi because of their religious beliefs, others because they have no religious beliefs.

The critics also regard belief, and scientific specialty, as factors explaining what they consider to be incompetent research. Targ and Puthoff have been criticized for being laser physicists, and hence, not competent to do parapsychological research. Parapsychologists are criticized because they tend to be "believers" in psi. This contradiction is noted by Collins and Pinch (1979:256): "These criticisms begin to be reminiscent of 'Catch-22.' The experimenters' background in psi makes them suspect as observers, while their background in physics renders their psi-experimental expertise suspect. The personal history of a scientist's involvement in the field is rarely considered a relevant factor in orthodox science, at least not explicitly, but when orthodoxy is challenged, this type of factor is apparently considered important."

9. The Strategy of Labeling Scientific Endeavor as Socially Undesirable

Paul Kurtz, the founder of the Committee for the Scientific Investigation of Claims of the Paranormal, has often maintained that the actions of his committee are taken with the interests of the greater society in mind. The public must be protected against an increasing antiscientific, antirational movement involving the occult. Although Kurtz (1979) has stated that he is not actually against scientific parapsychologists, his activities seem designed to block the funding of parapsychologists. One parapsychologist exclaimed to me, "They [the critics] would make it seem as if to do parapsychological research is a heinous act." Sometimes this effort on the part of critics takes the form of a kind of holy war against the tide of rising irrationality that they consider acceptance of the paranormal to represent. For example, Dr. E. U. Condon (1969:7,8), nuclear physicist, past president of the AAAS, and former director of the Bureau of Standards, has stated, "There used to be spiritualism, there continues to be extrasensory perception, psychokinesis, and a host of others. . . . Where corruption of children's minds is at stake, I do not believe in freedom of the press or freedom of speech. In my view, publishers who publish or teachers who teach any of the pseudo-sciences as established truth should, on being found guilty, be publicly horsewhipped, and forever banned from further activity in these usually honorable professions."

Some parapsychologists use a counterstrategy to this argument by portraying the future (when ESP is accepted) as more open and honest (Hastings, 1973). Such a future world might be more suitable for the nuclear age. They also compare themselves to Galileo during his struggles with the Roman Catholic hierarchy. They maintain a belief in the ultimate value of empirical truth.

10. Magnification of Anecdotal Evidence and Accusations Thereof

Both sides use this strategy. Critics have observed informal conditions in parapsychological pilot studies and later inferred that such conditions are standard in all psi research (Diaconis, 1978). Some parapsychologists have presented anecdotal cases as evidence for psi. Both sides attempt to portray their arguments as valid and their opponents' evidence as anecdotal. The political power of the critics of parapsychology has allowed them to use this strategy to a greater extent before scientific audiences than the proponents of psi have been allowed. Consequently, the scientific community tends to be informed of anecdotes regarding possible fraud and poor statistical and methodological procedures that have been used in parapsychological research (Diaconis, 1978). Parapsychologists claim that these anecdotes are not representative of the field and that magnification of such claims is a form of intellectual dishonesty or poor scholarship.

Patterns of Argument

As was noted by Perelman (1969), one key to persuasion is the adjustment of argument to the situation and audience. When parapsychologists interact with their critics, typical patterns of argument result.

Figure 3-1 illustrates the typical patterns of argument and demonstrates the major realms of discourse used by parapsychologists and their critics. It reveals the two major points of rhetorical conflict involving the philosophical meaning of psi and the conduct of parapsychological research.

Parapsychologists tend to believe that it is possible to demonstrate psi in an experimental manner. They argue that critical strategies based on philosophy are invalid and that critics must point out the errors or fraud in a particular piece of research for their arguments to have validity.

Some critics argue that the probability that psi exists is so low that it has not been proven empirically. This situation occurs because "exceptional claims require exceptional proofs." No proof has been deemed satisfactory for such an exceptional claim as psi. Various strategies are available to the critic to reveal the unsatisfactory nature

Typical Patterns of Argument in the Rhetorical Conflict Between Parapsychologists and Their Critics

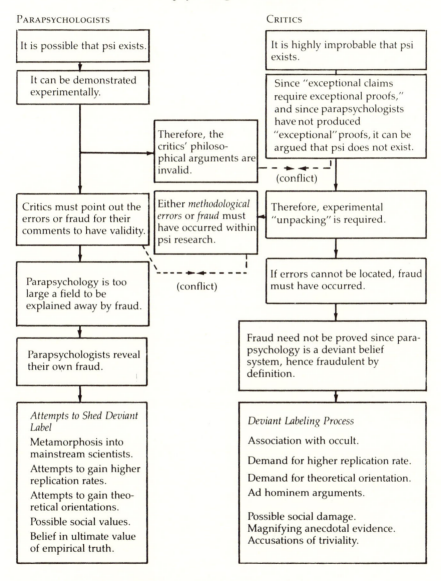

PARAPSYCHOLOGISTS

It is possible that psi exists.

It can be demonstrated experimentally.

Therefore, the critics' philosophical arguments are invalid.

Critics must point out the errors or fraud for their comments to have validity.

Either *methodological errors* or *fraud* must have occurred within psi research.

Parapsychology is too large a field to be explained away by fraud.

Parapsychologists reveal their own fraud.

Attempts to Shed Deviant Label

Metamorphosis into mainstream scientists.
Attempts to gain higher replication rates.
Attempts to gain theoretical orientations.
Possible social values.
Belief in ultimate value of empirical truth.

CRITICS

It is highly improbable that psi exists.

Since "exceptional claims require exceptional proofs," and since parapsychologists have not produced "exceptional" proofs, it can be argued that psi does not exist.

(conflict)

Therefore, experimental "unpacking" is required.

If errors cannot be located, fraud must have occurred.

Fraud need not be proved since parapsychology is a deviant belief system, hence fraudulent by definition.

Deviant Labeling Process

Association with occult.
Demand for higher replication rate.
Demand for theoretical orientation.
Ad hominem arguments.

Possible social damage.
Magnifying anecdotal evidence.
Accusations of triviality.

(conflict)

Figure 3-1

of any proof of psi. Experiments that successfully demonstrate psi are "unpacked" (analyzed step by step) in the search for methodological flaws. Fraud is always an alternative hypothesis for results claimed to demonstrate the existence of psi. Fraud need not be proved since the field of parapsychology has been labeled as deviant. The process of labeling it such involves many strategies (association with the occult, demand for higher replication rates, demand for better theories, ad hominem arguments, magnifying anecdotal evidence, accusations of triviality, and the possible social damage that might result from belief).

Parapsychologists use counterstrategies that reflect the process of deviant labeling. They reveal their own fraud when they discover it; they seek to become accepted as legitimate scientists (metamorphosis); they work toward achieving higher replication rates within their experimentation; and so on (see figure 3-1).

The irony of this rhetorical struggle is that dialogues between parapsychologists and their critics are usually rare. In only a few recorded instances has a critic of parapsychology visited a psi research center. This situation can be explained not only by the unequal political power of the two groups but also the different levels of discourse at which the argumentation is occurring. The creation of Marcello Truzzi's *Zetetic Scholar* in 1977 has allowed for more discussion of philosophical and methodological issues. Critics were officially part of the program at the annual PA meetings in 1982, which may mark the beginning of greater interaction.

An additional irony exists in the fact that parapsychologists frequently use the rhetorical strategies of their critics against one another. This is a result of their reaction to being labeled as deviant. They adhere more strongly to the scientistic orientation as a counterstrategy to criticism. The high degree of skepticism and adherence to scientistic orientations within this realm of inquiry will be discussed more fully in chapter 6. Obviously, this situation makes consensus on psi virtually impossible, since parapsychologists themselves frequently play the role of "critic."

Sociologically, these in-house feuds are predictable. The parapsychological community itself induces, sustains, and permits deviant behavior by some of its members. Deviant behavior helps to maintain group equilibrium, which is useful to the field (though obviously such infighting has dysfunctional aspects). Some forms of inquiry are labeled as deviant by the parapsychologists demarcating acceptable from unacceptable forms of research. Parapsychologists, as scientists, use scientistic assumptions to make this demarcation, which contributes to the field's "metamorphosis" away from its occult roots.

The typical patterns of argument demonstrate the difficulty of resolving any major issue. Two example cases, one illustrating a philosophical issue and the other a methodological issue, illustrate this dilemma.

In one exchange of letters, a parapsychologist and a critic argued the findings of parapsychological research. The critic refused to accept their legitimacy. Arguments focused on the improbability of psi and the critic's unwillingness to believe other people. Discussion involved a certain amount of questions about "belief." The critic, accused of being biased, responded:

Let me add that I do not consider myself an "unbiased critic" in any usual sense of the term, any more than I consider you an unbiased defender. Naturally, my opinion of contemporary parapsychology colored my article, just as your opinions color every paper of yours I have seen. Let's not either of us get into the absurd position of calling people biased who hold contrary views, and regarding ourselves as "unbiased." Have you ever met a true-believer in anything who didn't consider all his critics "biased"? I am willing at any time to grant the possiblility of PK. Where we differ is on the degree of probability we each assign to it . . . we each bring to bear on our estimate a lifetime of "biases" that are the product of our knowledge, experience and metaphysical dispositions. [From the files of Theodore Rockwell]

After a somewhat acrimonious exchange of letters, one writer concludes:

As you can see, our exchange of questions and answers has accomplished nothing except taking up both of our times. Our opinions are exactly the same as before, each would be highly critical of the other's responses, and nothing will be gained by exploring them in greater depth. [From the files of Theodore Rockwell]

Like many philosophical conflicts the issue is often not clarified by argument when each speaker maintains separate metaphysical dispositions. Philosophical resolution of parapsychological and critical orientations seems improbable.

Conflicts regarding methodological errors follow a different pattern. The critic is attempting to "unpack" the experiment to discover where possible methodological flaws or fraud could have occurred. The critic attempts to create a scenario in which the psychic subject being investigated was able to create a fraudulent effect. The researcher attempts to convince him or her that the scenario is not plausible.

A typical pattern of exchange might be as follows:

Critic: Did you take into account the possibility that "situation X" could have occurred? That might explain your experimental result through fraud on the part of the subject.

Parapsychologist: Yes, "situation X" can be precluded as a possible explanation for the results because of "precaution A."

Critic: What about "scenario Y"?

Parapsychologist: "Scenario Y" could not have occurred because we took precautions against that ("precautions A, B, and C").

Critic: I would suggest that "situation X" combined with "scenario Y" could have occurred because you did not take into account the possibility of "situation Z."

Parapsychologist: "Situation Z" can be ruled out by "precautions A, B, and C."

The question about whether "situation Z" can actually be dismissed becomes part of a philosophical argument on the improbability of the final paranormal claim. In another exchange with a critic, a parapsychologist notes, "There arises in one's mind, as one reads some of your material, the question, 'could such arguments and attacks, particularly those concerning poor procedure, fraud and cheating, be raised against other areas of science equally well?' Well, of course they could" [from the files of Theodore Rockwell].

Because of the critics' political ability to label research in parapsychology as deviant, parapsychology's rhetorical strategies take the form of a reflection of, and a reaction to, the philosophical arguments of the critics. The inability of parapsychologists to overcome effectively the philosophical opposition illustrates the social nature of scientific conflict. Resolution of the conflict requires one side to cease rhetorical activity, since the issues are occurring at different levels. If parapsychological research ceased, the issue would be closed. If criticism ended, parapsychology could become a "normal" science.

It is possible to imagine each side's meeting the other's arguments on the same level (parapsychologists using philosphical argument or critics doing empirical research). However, it seems doubtful that this would bring about a quick resolution of the question. No amount of experimentation by critics would convince the parapsychologist that psi is impossible, since the parapsychologist finds it highly probable through his or her own research. For parapsychologists to engage in philosophical argumentation removes the issue from the domain of science, since the scientistic orientation declares that science is essentially empirical.

Basically, the philosophical opposition to psi springs from the logical argument that "exceptional claims require exceptional proofs." A new rhetorical argument might be added if parapsychologists claim that psi is not particularly exceptional. Frequent exposure to other people's psi experiences would add psi to the list of sane experiences available to the average individual. Development of rhetorical strategies using the media which demonstrate the frequency and unexceptional nature of psi could weaken the philosophical arguments of critics. This analysis would conclude that media usage might be critical in the eventual resolution of the conflict between parapsychologists and their critics. The degree to which psi is considered "exceptional" is the fundamental issue.

4

The Political Struggle of Parapsychology for Legitimacy

The political struggle of parapsychology for legitimacy revolves around controlling the means for presentation of argument. Each rhetorical strategy devised by both parapsychologists and their critics has proven successful when presented to suitably receptive individuals. Each strategy appeals to a certain percentage of interested audiences. The political struggle occurs when some elements supportive of a claim attempt to thwart the presentation of their opponents' counterstrategies.

The political nature of scientific progress is hidden, because part of the ideology of science is that political support is unimportant in the acceptance of any particular theory. The assumption is that since science is a "value-free" process, theories that are "true" will eventually be accepted. This leads to the assumption that if a theory has been rejected, then it is probably untrue. For this reason, political activity that restricts a rhetorical strategy of an opponent can be especially effective in weakening that opponent's position. It can lead to the assumption, by some, that his or her theories are untrue. From a sociological perspective, however, the acceptance of a theoretical system depends on the political and rhetorical processes of science. The political process includes:

a. the creation or licensing of persons who are deemed qualified to speak before scientific audiences (for example, the granting of funds to a scientist for research);

b. a situation in which the speaker can present his or her rhetorical strategy (for example, scientific journals and conferences);

c. a scientific audience that can evaluate the presentation, thereby indicating what status it has as knowledge (scientists pass judgment on the journal article or conference presentation).

Scientific knowledge emerges from this process because it is created by scientific audiences through their reaction to persuasive argumentation (Overington, 1977).

The tendency of elite groups within science to prevent deviant scientists from entering into the process of argumentation before larger scientific audiences prevents the resolution of issues regarding psi. This explains, in part, the enduring nature of the conflict. The continuity of the field of parapsychology is also partially explained by its ability to present arguments through the media that reach the general public. This creates a situation where the field is able to produce "public knowledge" but not "scientific knowledge."

The attempts on the part of parapsychologists to shed their label as deviants can be illustrated by using the theoretical model devised in chapter 1 (see figure 4-1). Scientism, the ideology of science, generates criteria that allow the rejection of various anomalies and justifies the labeling of scientists who investigate these anomalies as deviant. The attempts of these scientists to shed their deviant label is generally thwarted by the political process of science. Deviant scientists attempt to shed their label (dotted line in figure 4-1) through rhetorical and political strategies. The greater political power of their critics creates latent effects from this attempt. These latent effects tend to support the scientistic orientation and will be discussed in chapter 6. A discussion of four example cases will reveal the political aspects of this struggle.

Example Case 1—Scientists Interested in J. B. Rhine's Research

My analysis of the controversy that took place over Rhine's (1934) *Extrasensory Perception* is based on Mauskopf and McVaugh (1979). Initially, the debate took place between the parapsychologists and a few psychologists and centered on Rhine's statistical techniques. Rhine evaluated the statistical significance of an aggregate of trials through a standard algorithm. He divided the Mean Chance Expectation by the Probable Error and termed this the "Critical Ratio."

The Political Process in Deviant Science

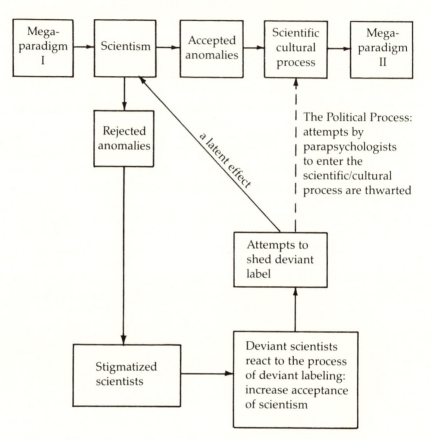

Figure 4-1.

These critical ratios could be converted into probability values by using a table of probability computed from the normal probability integral.

The debate arose owing to the incredibly high levels of statistical significance that Rhine claimed his research indicated. These data indicated that the probability that his research results were occurring by "chance" or "luck" was extremely slight.

This aroused the distrust of various critics. One wrote Rhine asking:

> . . . don't your "astronomical" odds ever give you the suspicion that something may be wrong? Must we trust alleged "scientific method" even when it tells us things we know can't be so? Consider the figure $x = 10^{-50}$ which is by no means the largest of your figures; have you ever tried imagining a proposition to which odds of that size could reasonably be ascribed? That the sun will rise tomorrow morning? Not at all; if we had all the records back to the Nebular precursor of the solar system, they wouldn't give us warrant for half these odds. (Willoughby, 1934)

The logical format of this rhetorical strategy seems derived from the a priori assumption that psi does not exist:
1. We know psi "can't be so."
2. A statistical evaluation indicates that psi is so (and even seems to place greater faith in psi than in the sun's future rising).
3. Therefore, the statistical evaluation must be invalid.

This debate took place through private dialogues which attracted little attention.

Chester E. Kellogg, a psychologist at McGill University, published his criticisms of Rhine's statistical methods in the semipopular *Scientific Monthly* in the fall of 1937. Curious mathematicians and statisticians also responded with their own studies of the statistical methods used by Rhine (Huntington, 1937; Sterne, 1937; Stuart and Greenwood, 1937). Although statistics was an undeveloped field in the 1930s, the complexities of this issue caught the interest of statisticians who saw it as a puzzle that could be investigated within their existing paradigms. Indeed, the issue was solved through the intervention of Burton Camp, then president of the Institute of Mathematical Statistics. Camp (1938) issued a ringing statement in support of the statistical procedures used by Rhine: "Dr. Rhine's investigations have two aspects; experimental and statistical. On the experimental side mathematicians of course have nothing to say. On the statistical side, however, recent mathematical work has established the fact that assuming that the experiments have been properly performed, the statistical analysis is essentially valid. If the Rhine investigation is to be fairly attacked it must be on other than mathematical grounds."

Issues, such as the argument concerning Rhine's statistics, are resolved through consensus achieved within the audience in question. The audience of mathematicians and statisticians who were aware of this statistical issue apparently agreed with Camp. H. T. Davis of Northwestern University attended the meeting of the Institute of Mathematical Statistics at which Camp made his statement. Davis (1938) concurred "that, on this mathematical question, there was not a single dissenting voice at a meeting attended by several hundred eminent mathematicians."

The resolution of this issue reveals an aspect of the rhetorical and political nature of science. Parapsychologists effectively used the rhetorical strategy of invoking support from qualified experts. The decision of these experts that Rhine's statistical techniques were valid removed this form of criticism from the rhetorical arsenal of the field's critics. This case illustrates how an audience's decision can affect the future process of argumentation. Criticism of ESP work by psychologists shifted away from statistical techniques in 1938.

Example Case 2—Parapsychology's Affiliation with the AAAS

The AAAS exists as the major scientific audience in America. Two major means (situations) exist for scientists to communicate with this audience. One is to present papers at meetings of the AAAS and a second is to publish articles in the official organ of the AAAS, *Science.*

A major effort in the political arena by parapsychologists began with their attempt to gain affiliation with the AAAS. The first step was forming the PA in 1957. As with all professional associations, an implicit purpose was to secure legitimacy for the field (Collins, 1979). The PA was formed with three overt purposes: to advance parapsychology as a science; to disseminate knowledge of the field; and to integrate the findings with those of other branches of science. To achieve these goals, it was important for the PA to gain affiliation with the AAAS, thereby enhancing the scientific status of parapsychological research (Dean, 1970). The history of the PA's struggle to gain affiliation with the AAAS and to present its rhetorical strategies to that scientific audience reveals the role of elite elements in the process of argumentation, and the ability of these elite elements to define that process.

The procedure for gaining affiliation with the AAAS is a sequential one that requires a majority vote from various elite groups. This sequence has changed over the years, and the approving groups have been as follows: through 1967—Committee on Affiliation, Board, Council; 1968–1970—Committee on Council Affairs, Board, Council; 1971–1973—moratorium on acceptance of applications for affiliation (during preparation of new bylaws); and 1974 to present—Committee on Council Affairs, Council.

This sequential procedure reveals the various elite groups within the AAAS that control the process of delineating science from non-science through the granting or denial of affiliation. The PA's degree of legitimacy might be measured by its ability to gain support from these various groups. Applications by the PA for affiliation were rejected in 1961, 1963, 1967, and 1968. The 1961 rejection by the AAAS Committee on Affiliation was on the ground that "at present, parapsychology is not firmly or generally accepted as a science" (AAAS minutes supplied by C. Borras). The decision by this committee could be considered an affirmation of the critics' counterstrategy to the parapsychologists' claim to be able to gain support from qualified groups (an aspect of metamorphosis). In 1962, in reviewing the committee's 1961 action, the Board stated that "no area of inquiry could arbitrarily be designated as lying outside the realm of science, but that the use of unscientific methods of inquiry by an applying society could properly be used as a basis for denying affiliation to that society" (AAAS Files, 1962). The Committee on Affiliation responded to that comment in 1963, stating it was "not satisfied that the applicant meets this criterion, and feels that the burden of proof rests with the applicant." The committee used a variation of the critic's strategy by questioning parapsychology's research methods. The decision reveals an aspect of the process of argumentation within elite groups. The Committee on Affiliation effectively prevented the PA from presenting its rhetorical strategy to any greater audience than the committee itself. It is the role of such elite groups to exercise this power, that is, to deny various proponents the right to act as speakers to scientific audiences.

The 1967 application was approved by the Committee on Affiliation, but the Board withheld approval "in view of the impending transfer of responsibility for affiliation from the Committee on Affiliation to the Committee on Council Affairs." The Affiliation Committee's statement of approval follows: "Inasmuch as the Parapsychological Association meets the stated criteria for affiliation with the AAAS, the Committee recommends that it be granted affiliation. This recommendation should not be interpreted as meaning that the Committee believes the scientific validity of the phenomena of ESP to have been established. However, the Committee believes that the continuing scientific investigation in this area by the Parapsychological Association should be encouraged" (minutes, Committee on Affiliation, November 22, 1967). The committee accepted parapsychology's strategy of claiming use of the empirical methodology of science.

During the December 29, 1967, meeting, the Board granted affiliation to four other applicants but voted to withhold any recommendation concerning the PA until the Committee on Council Affairs had had an opportunity to review and make recommendation to the Council on standards and procedures for granting and for withdrawing affiliation. Members were seeking a more absolute and definitive criterion than social labeling. The scientistic orientation claims that science can be distinguished from nonscience on logical grounds. A social definition of this demarcation should, therefore, be a reflection of some underlying epistemological reality, they felt. With an awareness of the criteria given importance by the scientistic orientation, Margaret Mead, an advocate of approval, advised officers in the PA that they should "stress the use of scientific *methods* as the relevant claim."

On November 18, 1968, the Committee on Council Affairs considered the Committee on Affiliation's approval, but voted (4 to 3) against recommending affiliation and passed a motion suggesting that the Board of Directors set up a committee to review and revise the criteria of affiliation. On December 27, 1968, the Board of Directors agreed to suggest to Walter Berl that a symposium be scheduled for the 1969 meeting "to discuss the criteria of what constitutes a science and a scientific approach to a problem." Metaphysics had found a very practical application.

The Council minutes of December 30, 1968, regarding the PA reveal that the Board of Directors had agreed to appoint a Committee on Criteria for Affiliation, "with the incoming President to serve as

Chairman and with the members drawn from the Board of Directors and the Committee on Council Affairs. Because of the variety of problems and points of view involved in efforts to define what is a science or what is a scientific society, the new committee will be encouraged to seek the advice and services of the chairmen of the AAAS sections."

This decision illustrates the process of argumentation that occurs among elite audiences. A consensus is sought for decisions that will determine future speakers and situations for argumentation within the greater scientific audience.

On November 19, 1969, the Committee on Council Affairs voted 5 to 2, with 1 abstention, to recommend to the Council that the PA be elected as an affiliate of the AAAS. On the same day, Dael Wolfle's report of the Committee on Criteria for Affiliation demonstrates the effect this decision had on the development of criteria: "Before the Committee on Criteria for Affiliation had met, the Committee on Council Affairs voted to recommend to the Council that the Parapsychological Association be elected as an affiliate. The immediate reason for reconsidering the criteria for affiliation was, therefore, removed as far as the Committee on Council Affairs is concerned. However, the Board is responsible for stating the criteria for affiliation, and the Board should, therefore, give the Committee on Criteria for Affiliation further instructions."

At the Board of Directors' meeting on December 28–29, 1969, the Board voted 5 to 2 to recommend to the Council that affiliation be granted to the PA. Action on criteria for affiliation was deferred and did not come up again at any later Board meeting. The decision to recommend that affiliation be granted seemed to negate the requirement that criteria for affiliation be modified. This decision allowed the AAAS Council to act as an audience for the rhetorical strategies of the opposing forces.

It would seem that the action of recommendation by the Committee on Council Affairs exists as a form of "common law" criteria for affiliation. This action removed any need for revision of existing criteria and illustrates a function of deviant science. Deviant science demarcates what is accepted as science from what is rejected. Such criteria are tacit and implied in that they are developed as a form of "common law."

The activity of E. Douglas Dean, a past president of the PA and PA secretary in 1969, demonstrates the effort expended in presenting parapsychology's best rhetorical strategies before the various elite audiences. Dean spent about three weeks each year working on these applications for affiliation with the AAAS.

> These applications are no easy matter. They cost about $150 each. To each of twelve scientists on the AAAS Committee is sent about 4½ pounds weight of materials. These are reprints of the best, most recent parapsychological research papers, copies of the P.A. Constitution and By-Laws, and articles in encyclopedias . . . in addition, about 20 typewritten pages were included in answer to reasons why the P.A. wanted affiliation, whether the P.A. satisfied six procedural matters, and seven points concerning the criteria of affiliation. (Dean, 1970:2, 3)

Dean also included the results of a poll of PA members showing that two-thirds of those replying were AAAS members and that nine were also AAAS fellows (the strategy of metamorphosis).

Dean had skillfully presented parapsychology's case. Although the Council members could not possibly determine the actual state of parapsychological research with its thousands of research results, those interested could read Dean's presentation of selected results. With the thoroughness of a skillful lobbyist, Dean attended the AAAS Annual Convention and made certain that a typing mistake which stated that four PA members were AAAS fellows (when in fact, nine were) would be corrected.

Dean's (1970) description of the AAAS Council vote on December 30, 1969, reveals four speakers addressing the audience. A man whose name Dean could not hear said, "In our agenda, it states that the 'aims of the P.A. are to advance parapsychology as a science, to disseminate knowledge of the field, and to integrate the findings with those of other branches of science.' These so-called phenomena of parapsychology do not exist and it is impossible to do scientific work in this area, so that we have a null science. I, therefore, will vote against this notion" (p. 4).

This speaker presented the strategy of "the blank refusal to believe." Afterward, a woman member said, "We are not familiar with what parapsychology is and so we are not qualified to make a vote on this association" (p. 4). This comment illustrates a facet often evident in the process of argumentation. The audience must make its decisions on the grounds of the rhetorical strategies that are available to it. Although the PA had mailed several items of literature describing parapsychology to all 530 delegates, this woman apparently felt uncomfortable with the limited information available to her. The limited information available to audiences in ambiguous situations sometimes makes the decision process seem irrational. Nevertheless, decisions must be made.

Following this woman's comment, H. Bentley Glass, president of the AAAS, addressed the Council: "The Committee on Council Affairs considered the P.A.'s work for a very long time. The Committee came to the conclusion that it is an association investigating controversial or nonexistent phenomena; however, it is open in membership to critics and agnostics; and they were satisfied that it uses scientific methods of inquiry; thus, that investigation can be regarded as scientific. Further information has come to us that the number of AAAS Fellows who are also members of the P.A. is not four as on the agenda, but nine" (p. 5).

Glass presented examples of the major rhetorical strategies of the parapsychologists (use of scientific methodology, metamorphosis). Following his statement, he asked, "Is there any further discussion?" Margaret Mead then spoke: "For the last ten years, we have been arguing about what constitutes science and scientific method and what societies use it. We even changed the By-Laws about it. The P.A. uses statistics and blinds, placebos, double blinds and other standard scientific devices. The whole history of scientific advance is full of scientists investigating phenomena that the establishment did not believe were there. I submit that we vote in favor of this Association's work" (p. 5). Her statement reiterated the rhetorical strategies used by parapsychologists. Following this statement, Glass raised the question of a vote. Approximately 160 to 180 members voted for granting affiliation with the AAAS to the PA. Approximately 30 to 35 were opposed.

The vote granting affiliation illustrates the political aspect of the process of argumentation. Although parapsychologists did not devise new rhetorical strategies (for example, a replicable experiment or a major theoretical orientation), they did develop the political skill required to present their arguments. Dean's lobbying for the parapsychologists' cause was instrumental in the PA's gaining affiliation. Margaret Mead's support should also be considered important.

Events following the election of the PA as an affiliate demonstrate the ability of elite elements to thwart parapsychological speakers in their attempts to address scientific audiences. "Upon its election as an affiliate, the P.A. enrolled in Section J (Psychology). Officers of the Section protested but had no authority to deny the enrollment. However, the Section did not accept P.A. contributions to its annual meeting programs. In 1973, the P.A. withdrew from Section J and enrolled in Section X—General" (enclosed with agenda for Board Meeting, April 20–21, 1979, AAAS Files).

Although enrollment in Section X has had advantages for parapsychology, the field has been treated as less than totally legitimate. Affiliation with the AAAS increases the PA's ability to use the strategy of metamorphosis. It also has allowed parapsychologists to address various symposiums sponsored by the AAAS, but as of yet, no parapsychologist has been allowed to publish a research article in *Science*. One former president of the PA noted, "The real 'Catch-22' in the relationship between parapsychology and the rest of science is this: the scientific community is not familiar with the better research in parapsychology because the editors of establishment journals are still, for the most part, reluctant to publish positive findings in this area" (from the files of Theodore Rockwell).

Researchers have been distressed that no matter how carefully prepared and executed their parapsychological experiments were, the editorial staff of *Science* has refused to publish them. Charles Tart wrote requesting the support of Margaret Mead in this matter. *Science* refused to publish his research demonstrating evidence of and factors related to psi. "Can you help me?" he asked. In a letter dated October 9, 1975, she discouraged his "pursuing this matter any further," that is, seeking political aid in urging *Science* to publish parapsychological articles. This illustrates the parapsychologist's failure to gain political support for his contention that he is qualified to address the AAAS audience.

One group of parapsychologists (Honorton, Ramsey, and Cabibbo, 1975) evidently tried to embarrass *Science* after their research article had been rejected. They published their article in the *Journal of the American Society for Psychical Research* and also included the comments from the referees whom *Science* had selected to judge the article. The referees' comments seemed to indicate either poor scholarship or a bias against parapsychology.

It would seem that the selection of referees by an editor will determine whether a parapsychological research article is favorably reviewed or not. The editor constitutes an audience who selects the speakers whose arguments he or she will consider. Parapsychologists are concerned that they have not been allowed to serve as referees for articles related to their field while their critics *are* selected.

Collins and Pinch (1979:257) note that surveys "indicated a bias against publishing the positive results of parapsychologists in contrast to the space given in these journals to the skeptics such as Bridgman, Brown, Price, and Hansel." Collins also noted a comment made to him by the editor of *Nature* regarding Collins's experiments with metal benders of the "Geller" type: "The editor has indicated that if an experimental report of this correspondence type had contained positive findings, it would not have been accepted" (Collins and Pinch, 1979:259).

Elite elements within science can choose to ignore the arguments of proponents of deviant sciences, if they wish. This strategy might be labeled as "stonewalling," or merely ignoring the arguments of a group that is politically weak.

One PA member, Theodore Rockwell, became a central lobbyist on behalf of the PA's effort to gain access to the AAAS audience through *Science*. His summary of his interaction with Philip Abelson (editor of *Science* magazine), William Carey (the AAAS executive officer), and various other AAAS officials reveals the ability of scientific elites to control the scientific means of communication, often through ignoring presentations of the proponents of psi (stonewalling).

Science Saga

12 Feb   75   TR [Theodore Rockwell] wrote to Abelson (Editor of *Science*), expressing admiration for his work and suggesting that psi phenomena might be getting overlooked. Suggested 30–45 min. discussion. NO REPLY.

18 Mar   75   TR sent copies of Feb 12th to Abelson's home and other office, with note suggesting perhaps it had not been received. Suggested meeting with staff member if Abelson too busy. NO REPLY.

April 75   TR placed several calls to Abelson, with request to call back. NO REPLY.

Thru 75–76   Several attempts to get *Science* to consider articles, research notes, news, letters or book reviews; all produced NO RESULTS. Some of the reasons given:

> *Nature* published an article once, "expecting a storm of outrage and criticism. But there was none, which I think discouraged the editor from publishing any more papers of the kind."
>
> The subject is "unbelievable."
>
> One or more reviewers always object.
>
> "We don't accept unsolicited book reviews."
>
> "The work is non-replicable." (But a later paper was rejected because "it does not report new results, being the replication of work of others.")

18 Dec 76   Council of Parapsychological Association (PA) directs its AAAS representatives to write Abelson re: situation, offered to assist in improving it. If no response, second letter. If none, then letter to AAAS Exec. Offr. and Publisher of *Science*. If no action, then to Pres., AAAS.

28 Mar 77   1st letter, PA to Abelson, NO REPLY.

 2 June 77   2nd letter, NO REPLY.

15 Jul   77   PA to Carey (AAAS Exec. Offr.), enclosing previous letters, and asking "that you assist us in determining *Science* publication policy, practice, and conformance of these to AAAS policy statement on *Science*."

25 Jul   77   Abelson to PA. "I cannot understand what happened to your two earlier letters." *Science* relies on reviewers. They generally do a good job. We can't favor borderline material.

27 Sep 77   PA to Carey. "Abelson's reply unresponsive to the issues." Described the problem. Enclosed several rejection letters from *Science*, with their reviewers' comments. Pointed out that names were deleted, to focus on letters themselves, which were "disgraceful." Again offered to work with AAAS, propose qualified reviewers, etc.

21 Oct   77   Abelson replied, "If you will supply the names, I will examine our files and make an effort to determine whether the reviewers

involved have a high reputation for objectivity and freedom from bias."

Oct	77	PA tried repeatedly to reach Carey by phone, to determine if Abelson's note was the entire AAAS response. NO REPLY.
3 Nov	77	TR met with Coates, Sec'y of AAAS Section to which PA belongs. He suggested we write AAAS Council or the *Science* Editorial Board, but try AAAS President first.
4 Nov	77	PA to Carey: Do you intend to address the issues we raised? NO REPLY.
17 Nov	77	PA to President Daddario and President-Elect David, reviewed the entire picture, emphasized that peer review was the issue, and offered to help. Quoted AAAS Policy Statement that AAAS "Selects the Editor" and reviews *Science* "at least once a year" to ensure that *Science* operates "as a primary activity of the AAAS."
13 Dec	77	David to PA: "the doors of *Science* should not be closed to papers on parapsychology. . . . We would not be justified in providing a special referral procedure . . . asked the editors to be especially watchful in the future in selecting qualified reviewers who are neither partial towards nor prejudiced against parapsychology."
22 Dec	77	PA to David: Thanks for your help. We don't want "special procedure"—want to be treated like other scientists. Want peer review: competence *in the field* is the issue, not prejudice toward or against. "We intend to proceed on the basis that our concern has been resolved."
6 Jan	78	Learned from *Science* staff that "a major article on para-psychology" was in preparation. No one in the field knew about it, and *Science* gave no further information.
14 Jul	78	*Science* ran sweeping condemnation of all psi research, by Perci Diaconis, a Stanford statistician. Many errors of fact and unsupported conclusions. No competent peer review (i.e., by researchers in the field). Stanford University News Service issues press release.
July–Aug	78	Numerous letters sent to *Science*, pointing out errors in Diaconis's article.

7 Aug 78   PA to *Science*. Protested Diaconis's article:

> Article had no input from scientists in the field. Did not meet usual standards for accuracy, objectivity, information.
>
> No peer review.
> Reviewed some previous examples of this type in *Science*. Copy to David, with request to investigate.

25 Aug 78   Copies of some letters to *Science* criticizing the Diaconis article sent to David by PA.

11 Sep 78   David to PA: "While this situation may not always seem comfortable, it is not an unusual situation. . . . I am confident you will continue to pursue your objectives."

(Rockwell, 1978a)

Rockwell did continue to pursue his objectives. In November 1978 he submitted a resolution for consideration by the Committee on Council Affairs. This resolution was entitled, "Responsibility of Scientists in Dealing with Controversial Findings." The Committee on Council Affairs (CCA) referred the resolution to the Committee on Scientific Freedom and Responsibility (CSFR) for review and advice, but took no action on the CSFR's recommendation that "the CCA request the Editorial Board of *Science* to review the allegation in the resolution of bias on the part of *Science*" (Borris, 1981).

Rockwell's attempt to act as a speaker before elite audiences within the AAAS reveals their capacity to ignore or reject his arguments. One tactic was suggested to him by a member of the CSFR in a conversation on September 18, 1978. She said that Rockwell had to "accept that such situations are primarily political, not technical." Rockwell was concerned that the parapsychologists "couldn't even get an open discussion of the subject." She suggested getting some allies outside the field such as:

—a well-known scientist to endorse an article or a resolution (preferably the former).
—the APA or other larger organization to join in.
—a Congressman to ask "Why don't we hear about this research?" . . . when the NSF budget is up for review.

(Rockwell, 1978b)

This suggestion supports attempts of parapsychologists to use the rhetorical strategy of support from qualified experts along with the increased use of political strategies. Success in using these strategies may be more important than the efforts of parapsychologists in conducting valid research as far as the field's "metamorphosis" is concerned.

During 1978 and 1979, various critics of parapsychology addressed audiences within the AAAS in the attempt to end the PA's affiliation. For example, on November 15, 1978, the Committee on Council Affairs was informed of a communication from a physics professor protesting the affiliation of the PA with the AAAS. The minutes of the committee read that "in the absence of evidence that the Parapsychological Association no longer meets the criteria governing admission of affiliates to AAAS, the Committee took no action." Without the presentation of a rhetorical strategy, the speaker was unable to sway this elite audience.

John Wheeler, a highly regarded physicist, had a greater effect on the scientific audiences he addressed. At the annual meeting of the AAAS on January 8, 1979, in Houston, Wheeler made a public appeal to "Drive the Pseudos Out of the Workshop of Science" (reprinted in the May 17, 1979, issue of the *New York Review of Books*). He also wrote William Carey requesting that consideration be given to revoking the affiliation.

Wheeler's comments (Gardner, 1979b) illustrate the rhetorical strategies available to the individual who is critical of parapsychology. Some of Wheeler's arguments included: "There's nothing that one can't research the hell out of. Research guided by bad judgement is a black hole for good money. . . . Where there is meat, there are flies" (p. 41). Wheeler expressed concern about the use that parapsychologists have made with their affiliation with the AAAS and hinted that the PA has misused it (antimetamorphosis). Wheeler hoped to begin an investigation into the quality of parapsychological research. Has parapsychology produced any "battle-tested findings?" (p. 40) he queried (the strategy of demand for higher replicability or better theory). Wheeler presented parapsychology as a means for unscrupulous individuals to fleece wealthy benefactors (the strategy of associating parapsychology with nonscientific groups and as having negative social consequences). Wheeler concluded his AAAS presentation with the statement, "Now is the time for everyone who believes in the Rule of Reason to speak up against pathological science and its purveyors" (p. 41). When asked to comment on the actual experimental work, Wheeler stated that J. B. Rhine, as an assistant to William McDougall, had been exposed as intentionally producing spurious results and that Rhine "had started parapsychology that way" (AAAS Files). This statement was apparently intended to provide a basis for dismissing the experimental work in parapsychology (the strategy of accusation of fraud).

Since Wheeler's accusation was untrue, it could have been considered slander. He later published a "correction" in *Science*, retracting his accusation of fraud against Rhine. On the advice of legal counsel, the AAAS disallowed the distribution of a cassette tape containing Wheeler's accusation.

The reaction within the AAAS illustrates how elite groups establish the "situations" in which the process of argumentation can take place. The minutes of the Board of Directors meeting on April 20–21, 1979 note: "Mr. Carey thought it would be imprudent to ask the Council to revoke any organization's affiliation in the absence of established criteria for disaffiliation. He proposed that the Board ask the Committee on Council Affairs to draw up such criteria for presentation to the Council at its 1980 meeting, without reference to any individual affiliate. The Board agreed" (AAAS Files).

The result was that the Council of the AAAS adopted on January 7, 1980, "Procedures for Termination of Affiliation: Related By-Law Amendments." These procedures make it fairly difficult for any affiliated organization to be terminated. It required, among other procedural matters, that two-thirds of the Section Committee members in which the organization in question is enrolled vote for disaffiliation. Then, two-thirds of the Council members must vote for termination of affiliation before disaffiliation could occur. These procedures specify the degree of consensus necessary to disaffiliate a deviant group.

It would appear that all scientific knowledge is constructed through rhetorical and political processes in that speakers present arguments in specific situations to qualified audiences in order to create that knowledge. The ambiguity and passion associated with deviant science merely reveals this process of argumentation more clearly. Elite scientific groups constitute special audiences who have the power to select the speakers to whom they will listen and to define and determine the situations under which the process of argumentation will take place. Elite scientific groups have the right (and indeed the duty) to defend the ideology of the greater group that they represent.

Example Case 3—The Students at the University of California at Santa Barbara

Students also constitute special audiences. The process of argumentation is often restricted in the classroom situation. Generally, the information being presented in a science course has already been accepted as "knowledge." This makes the process of hiring professors very important to emerging realms of inquiry. A parapsychologist who successfully teaches a course in the field contributes to its "metamorphosis" by demonstrating the possibility that parapsychologists have generated knowledge. Parapsychologists who address college classes often convince students of the possibility that scientific argumentation can take place within this realm of inquiry. A discussion of a sample case concerning a course taught at Santa Barbara illustrates how the process of argumentation can determine the situations in which speakers can address college audiences.

The conflict involving teaching parapsychology at Santa Barbara has been documented in a proposal submitted by David Phillips to the Executive Committee of the College of Letters and Science of the University of California. As a result of three yearly grants given to the Tutorial Program by the Parapsychology Foundation in New York, courses in parapsychology were taught each quarter from the fall of 1974 through the spring of 1977 by Robert Morris. Four major courses were taught: Tutorial 131, Introduction to Parapsychology; Tutorial 136, Internal States and Parapsychology; Tutorial 135, Research Methods in Parapsychology; and Tutorial 15, Religion and Parapsychology. After three years, an economic downturn forced the Parapsychology Foundation to discontinue Morris's grant. Morris left Santa Barbara and accepted a teaching position in psychology at the University of California at Irvine. David Phillips taught one course in parapsychology at Santa Barbara on a part-time basis, then attempted to gain university support for the course so that it could continue. An Ad Hoc Committee on Parapsychology studied his proposal in order to recommend whether the course should continue and, if so, how it should be funded and administered. The Committee's report contains a very brief history of parapsychology, the past content of parapsychology courses taught at Santa Barbara, and the Committee's recommendations. The report reveals a typical difficulty of individuals who must deal with this issue; the Committee found that no criteria for evaluations of new sciences exist nor were there established criteria for evaluation of courses at the University of California.

In chapter 2, it was argued that scientism, the ideology of science, establishes criteria for the rejection of various anomalies. Such criteria evolve from scientific megaparadigms that are normally tacit. The need to explicate them arises when users desire to invoke them as a rhetorical instrument for labeling and social control. But the actors participating in the elite audiences having power to make decisions are normally problem solvers within the scientific paradigm. They find it difficult to explain their assumptions since they are in the habit of using these assumptions as a resource of explanation rather than as a topic to be explained.

The Ad Hoc Committee on Parapsychology developed three criteria for course approval that they decided best served the purposes of the university:

1. The course is based on a substantial body of established knowledge or proven technique.
2. A qualified instructor is available.
3. Sufficient student interest exists.

These criteria coincide with the main aspects of the process of argumentation. A qualified "speaker" must have suitable "rhetorical arguments" to present to an "audience" of students in order for the Committee to allow the class "situation" to occur. The issue concerns the suitability of parapsychological "knowledge" and the technique for producing that knowledge.

Through choosing the rhetorical arguments of the critics of parapsychology as more valid than those of its proponents, the Committee justified its conclusions. These conclusions were derived from the committee's evaluation of parapsychological "knowledge" and were based on the "negative" definition of psi.

The Committee's report states:

In considering courses in parapsychology, it is important to attend to exactly how that field is defined. Parapsychology is defined as the study of psi phenomena, that is, the study of effects in which all known modes of communication of influence have been *ruled out*. In our judgment, no course in

parapsychology can at present satisfy the first criterion. There is no phenomenon for which this ruling can be said to be established. Only if the definition
of parapsychology were to be loosened to include effects obtained in
controlled laboratory experiments where known factors *appear* to be ruled out,
can we speak of a body of parapsychological knowledge. This is hardly
substantial, consisting at best of a few statements about factors which are
related to the occurrence of apparent psi phenomena. (Phillips, 1979)

The Committee defined psi such that it could not be considered
related to a substantial body of established knowledge. It was
presumed that "science" describes "reality" and parapsychology
describes "appearance." If all "known" modes of communication
have been ruled out regarding a phenomenon, it would be impossible
for a body of knowledge, that is, things "known" about the phenomenon, to exist.

Phillips could argue that the course was based on a substantial
body of argument concerning the nature of psi, that the course
presented various aspects of that body of argument, and that proven
scientific techniques were available to resolve the arguments. Use of
these techniques has led to a certain amount of agreement within the
audience of parapsychological researchers.

The Committee was swayed by the philosophical contradictions
that their definition of the nature of psi had generated. They decided
"not [to] recommend the use of University funds for the teaching of
courses in this area at this time" but to allow the previously taught
courses to be condensed into a single course should extramural
sources of funding provide for all costs associated with the course.

The Committee's decision reflects the social definition of parapsychology. As a field that studies rejected anomalies, it seems to lack
the ability to generate scientific "knowledge." As long as the anomalies in question are denied examination within the process that
produces scientific knowledge (speakers, arguments, situations, audience), no "knowledge" can be generated. The parapsychological
community has attempted to set up its own process of argumentation,
but its "speakers" have not been granted authority to address the
greater scientific community.

Phillips spent a great deal of time and effort attempting to meet
the Committee's requirements so that a single course could continue.
He located outside funding for the course and a highly qualified
instructor, Joseph Rush, to teach it. Unfortunately for the field of
parapsychology, the Tutorial Program under which the course was to

be taught was abolished by an unrelated budget cut. Phillips could not convince the head of any other department to accept the course.

The history of this example case reveals the ability of an elite audience (the Ad Hoc Committee on Parapsychology) to define the situation in which a speaker (Joseph Rush) could address an audience (the students of the University of California). This case illustrates the entrance of extraneous factors (the ending of the Tutorial Program) in changing the situation and the effect of elite audiences in terminating the process of argumentation (the various department heads refused to allow the course to be taught). Although the student audience maintained a high enrollment and expressed a great deal of interest in all the courses, an elite audience restricted the process of argumentation before the student audience.

Various other courses in parapsychology have been taught at the university level. Gaining permission to teach such courses seems to depend on the political skill of the requesting instructor. One individual told me of the ease with which he got his first course approved. He found that he needed permission from a particular department head. The particular department chair's daughter had recently had a remarkable psychic experience and the chair's interest in the paranormal had already been awakened. Other parapsychologists describe department conflicts, denied promotions, strange political struggles, and harassment of students who are interested in parapsychology.

Parapsychology courses might become more prevalent in the future if colleges must compete more effectively for students. Curricula may be designed for the consumer of knowledge rather than the producer. Parapsychology courses attract student interest, require limited facilities, and tend to be profitable for the supporting institution. They often are successful within adult education programs. Exposing future scientists to the rhetorical positions of parapsychologists would help the field progress toward legitimacy.

Example Case 4—Members of the General Public Who Are Exposed to the Media

Like students, individuals who constitute audiences within the public cannot be said to generate scientific knowledge. Only scientific audiences engage in that activity. At the same time, students and scientists are also members of the general public and are exposed to speakers who address that audience. Elite scientific groups restrict the process of argumentation regarding psi within the scientific community. Ironically, this has led to the popular media serving as the major source for scientists of information about the paranormal (this is discussed in chapter 5). As one parapsychologist noted during my interview with him, "If we can't get a hearing in the scientific press, the popular press is our only hope." Owing to the fact that information on psi reaches scientists through the popular media, the media contribute to the process of argumentation within science in an indirect manner.

The media also allow the field of parapsychology to locate research subjects and sources of funding. Consequently, parapsychology's ability to use the media is critically important.

This example case will discuss an attempt by the Committee for the Scientific Investigation of Claims of the Paranormal (CSICOP) to influence the media coverage of alleged paranormal phenomena. The inability of this Committee to restrict the presentation of rhetorical strategies favored by proponents of psi demonstrates the needs and desire of elites controlling the media.

Paul Kurtz, a philosophy professor at the State University of New York at Buffalo, and some sympathetic supporters, persuaded no fewer than 186 leading scientists to sign a statement that astrology had no merit. The great quantity of media coverage that this incident generated encouraged an informal group of individuals, who were concerned about false claims of the paranormal, to organize formally. They founded CSICOP around such notable individuals as science fiction writer Isaac Asimov, psychologists Theodore X. Barber and B. F. Skinner, magicians Milbourne Christopher and James "the Amazing" Randi, *Time* senior editor Leon Jaroff, astronomer Carl Sagan, and *Scientific American* writer Martin Gardner. The attack on astrology by such a prominent group was eminently newsworthy. The Committee hoped to use this situation for its own aims.

The evaluation of elite elements within the media is of critical importance for CSICOP to accomplish its goals. *Science News* (August 20, 1977) noted that reaction to the Committee's plea for equal time for skeptics was mixed. They noted that the *Washington Star* chided the group for overseriousness and overkill: "It is classic gnat-killing by sledgehammer." The *New York Times* echoed most of the Committee's concerns: "Science is not the be-all of existence, but its enemies can all too easily be the end-all." The participation of *Time* editor Leon

Jaroff and *Scientific American* writer Martin Gardner has allowed those publications to present the rhetorical positions of parapsychology's critics (for example, Gardner, 1979a).

CSICOP gained extensive media coverage when it filed a complaint in November 1977 with the Federal Communications Commission (FCC) against an NBC-TV documentary entitled, "Exploring the Unknown." The program, produced by Alan Neuman and narrated by Burt Lancaster, was aired nationally on Sunday night prime time. CSICOP was concerned that various phenomena were presented as valid and/or paranormal when in fact their paranormal and valid quality was not certain. CSICOP felt that the program failed to present the critical orientation. *Time* magazine might be said to have factually but one-sidedly reported the affair concerning the suit, since not one member of the parapsychological community was quoted by *Time,* nor was Alan Neuman or anyone else connected with the program quoted.

The following July, the FCC dismissed as baseless the charges of CSICOP that the documentary was biased. Their four-page statement declared that the FCC Fairness Doctrine, designed to prevent one-sided presentations on controversial issues of public importance, had not been violated (J. White, 1979). The FCC considers programs involving the paranormal as generally falling under the category of "entertainment" rather than the category of "news." CSICOP could not convince this elite audience that it was important to require presentation of the critics' rhetorical strategies.

Parapsychologists have not been opposed to all efforts to correct media distortion. Some support the idea of a kind of psi consumer protection agency "to inform and advise on things psychic" (Bartlett, 1977). Many are concerned about misrepresentation of the work of parapsychologists by the media (see chapter 7). The issue regarding CSICOP and the FCC was outside the concern of the PA, since only one of its members participated in the TV show.

Unlike scientific or student audiences, the general public often demands entertainment from its speakers. This demand favors the presentation of the rhetorical strategies of parapsychology. On July 16, 1981, NBC rebroadcast a segment of NBC News Magazine in which Soviet parapsychological efforts were discussed. This "news" presented a rhetorical strategy of the parapsychologists, the strategy of claiming support from appropriate experts (in this case, the Soviet scientific bureaucracy). The critics of parapsychology could not gain the right to use their counterstrategies against these arguments, thus allowing proponents of psi to present their arguments without opposition before the general public.

CSICOP's attempt to influence media coverage of the paranormal has not been without effect. Some media representatives whom I talked with in 1982 showed an increased awareness of the critical argumentation on the paranormal and seemed to feel that the FCC does require a balanced presentation of this issue. It would seem that the presentation of *conflicting viewpoints* supplies a form of entertainment that is suitable for mass audiences.

Observation of the example cases discussed in this chapter reveals that scientific, academic, and media elites have different criteria for evaluating a speaker's claims and for serving the greater audience that they represent. Scientific elites tend to use criteria derived from the ideology of science, whereas media elites wish to respond to the public's desire for entertainment. Academic elites tend to serve their institution rather than the student audience. The example cases indicate that elite audiences determine the speakers and situations and, indirectly, the rhetorical strategies used to address greater audiences.

The inability of parapsychologists to present their rhetorical strategies to a greater scientific audience allows the process of labeling them as deviant to continue. The inability of groups critical of parapsychology to restrict the proponents of psi in their argumentation before the public allows the field to reach the lay individuals and groups that it requires for funding and personnel. Although proponents of psi may be restricted in the generation of scientific knowledge, they are free to enter into the generation of the "social knowledge" produced by public argumentation. Consequently, it might be predicted that in the future the public will become more receptive to the idea of psi, even if the scientific community remains skeptical. This can be expected as a result of elite audiences restricting various speakers in the process of argumentation within science but not within the media.

Of special importance in the generation of scientific knowledge are the attitudes of scientists who form the administrative elite of science. Understanding these elite scientists' attitudes is necessary if the process of labeling parapsychology as deviant is to be fully revealed. This analysis of example cases illustrates the role that elites play in structuring the process through which scientific knowledge comes into existence.

5

A Survey of Elite Scientists:
Their Attitudes Toward ESP,
Parapsychology,
and Anomalous Experience

Analysis of the rhetorical and political aspects of the conflict between parapsychology and its critics reveals the importance of elite groups in determining the speakers, situations, and audiences that take part in producing scientific knowledge. In order to gain a greater understanding of this process, a questionnaire was designed and administered to Council members and selected Section Committee representatives of the AAAS. The questionnaire requested opinion of ESP, parapsychology, and anomalous experience. It was designed to compare responses of the "elite" AAAS members to studies that have been conducted with other populations in the past. These members are "elite" in that they are in positions of leadership and, therefore, constitute an aspect of the "administrative" elite of the AAAS. Such individuals are especially important in forming policy on border and deviant realms of inquiry.

Major findings of this study are that:

1. Although recent studies hint that belief in ESP may be increasing among the general population and scientific community, the elite scientific group polled by this study demonstrated

A briefer version of this chapter was published in the *Journal of Parapsychology* 46, 2 (1982), 127–152.

the highest level of skepticism of any major group surveyed within the last twenty years.

2. Some sections within the AAAS demonstrate greater degrees of skepticism than others. Elite pharmacists and engineers have a greater tendency to be believers. Anthropologists and those in the History and Philosophy of Science section tend toward skepticism.

3. Belief in ESP is not strongly correlated with age within this elite scientific group. Even among the youngest quartile, only 39 percent can be considered "believers" in ESP.

4. Among this elite group, believers in ESP tend to cite personal experience as grounds for belief. Skeptics tend to cite a priori reasons as grounds for disbelief.

5. Familiarity with psi research (as reported by the respondent) is faintly correlated with skepticism over ESP.

6. The elite scientists who responded to this questionnaire report a far lower level of anomalous experience than has been reported by the American population (McCready and Greeley, 1976). The present study found that reporting such experiences is highly correlated to belief in ESP.

7. Answers from this elite group of scientists tend to explain the resistance of scientists to the work of parapsychologists in a completely different manner from the arguments chosen by members of the PA (Allison, 1973). Choice of arguments explaining this resistance tends to be correlated with belief in ESP.

8. The findings support the belief that an ideological resistance to parapsychology exists within the a priori philosophy of science and that this philosophy is associated with status within science. These findings tend to support the theoretical orientations devised in chapters 1 and 2.

Theoretical Orientation

Elite scientists play a critical role in the process of labeling certain systems of belief as deviant. An understanding of the attitudes of this elite may explain the process more fully.

The scientific elite is created by a series of processes in which professional recognition is distributed unequally. There can be no doubt about the unequal distribution of scientific rewards, prestige, and administrative control within science: "At all levels of scientific recognition, from the Nobel Prize down to the routine citing of research findings, the same marked separation of a small élite from the great majority of scientists is apparent" (Mulkay, 1976:449). Although scientific elitism is a complex multidimensional phenomenon (Amick, 1974), elite scientists tend to have certain attributes. They tend to be significantly older than non-elite scientists, to have come from a small number of elite centers (for example, Harvard, Columbia, Berkeley, Princeton, Oxford, Cambridge), and to have made at least a respectable and usually a major contribution to scientific knowledge (Mulkay, 1976).

Although the intellectual elite and the administrative elite within science are not synonymous, the processes of selection associated with these groups tend to make them overlap. Membership within the administrative elite is considered "a form of service to the profession of a presumably scientifically useful nature" (Amick, 1974:2) and allows considerable control over the systems of communication within science, over the allocation of funds, and over the selection of future elites.

There is speculation among sociologists concerning the size of the administrative elite within science. Wood (1964) considers these scientists as an "apolitical elite."

For federal issues, Christopher Wright has estimated that there are between 200 and 1,000 men and women who significantly and directly influence the availability of scientific knowledge and ideas and their technical application. James Killian is inclined to fix the number of the consistently influential at 200—the lowest point of Wright's estimate. In an initial empirical exploration, Howard Rosenthal screened names from the *American Men of Science* according to five measures of elite participation in advisory posts, professional associations, and mass media recognition to arrive at a core group of approximately 900 members. But Rosenthal's calculation of an "active elite"— participation in at least two elite capacities—resulted in a group numbering only 392. (Wood, 1964:48; also see Wright, 1964; Gilpin and Wright, 1964; Greenberg, 1969)

It would seem that the nature of the particular issue involved would determine the size of the scientific elite exercising authority over it. For the purpose of this study, the field of inquiry has been restricted to the AAAS and the population to be polled has been arbitrarily set at approximately five hundred.

Elite scientists act as a kind of buffer betwen science and society. In performing this role, they continually define the nature and meaning of science and, therefore, tend to demonstrate the highest commitment to an ethos that might be considered central to science (Mulkay, 1976:462). This ethos is derived from a priori assumptions underlying the development of science since the seventeenth century (MacKenzie and MacKenzie, 1980). One aspect of this ethos (zeitgeist, ideology, worldview, etc.) is the labeling of some realms of inquiry as deviant. Inasmuch as parapsychology is part of a tradition that covertly opposes this scientific worldview, it might be predicted that elite scientists would reject the field of parapsychology and its ideas more than does the average scientist or citizen. These scientists might also be expected to employ a priori explanations to a greater degree, as a means of justifying this rejection.

The Pretest Process

A lengthy questionnaire was designed for use in interviewing scientists and was used as a means for developing a final mail-out questionnaire. The interview questionnaire was administered in person to over thirty-five professors at the University of Maryland. No attempt at a random selection of interviewees was made. Physicists, chemists, biologists, psychologists, and anthropologists were interviewed. The patterns of response regarding opinion of ESP were similar to those found by Wagner and Monnet (1979) in their random sample of college professors. In addition, I observed the following features:

1. Some professors became anxious when they realized that the questionnaire involved parapsychology. Merely directing their attention to this field seemed to make them tense.

2. The subject matter was not one to which the average professor had given much thought. Many individuals seemed puzzled, disturbed, or uninterested.

3. Some skeptical scientists regarded the questions as biased in favor of belief. Some professors, especially physicists and chemists, stated that they held sociologists in low regard and that they normally did not answer questionnaires of any form. For them, sociology was only one step more legitimate than parapsychology. Some saw no possible value in any sociological study that involved parapsychology.

4. Individuals who firmly believed in, and those who were extremely skeptical of, paranormal claims seemed to enjoy being interviewed.

Numerous modifications were made in the questionnaire during the pretest phase in response to the comments made by professors. For example, a question on attitudes of colleagues toward ESP was dropped when it appeared that most scientists had never discussed the issue with their colleagues, and assumed that their colleagues agreed with their own opinion. Generally, scientists told me that they had barely enough time to keep abreast of developments in their own field much less keep informed about parapsychology. A typical attitude was one of little interest or opinion. A minority (especially among biological scientists) believed in ESP and wished to relate the personal experiences that had created their belief. Sometimes their descriptions seemed quite convincing. A second small group of scientists vehemently denied that any valid paranormal experience was possible.

A final questionnaire was devised that contained the following items (see Appendix A for a full listing of questions):

1. Questions used by Wagner and Monnet (1979) regarding sex, field, age, and attitudes toward ESP and parapsychology, which had been administered to a random sample of college professors (Items 1–6).

2. An open-ended request for additional comments concerning attitude toward parapsychology (Item 7).

3. Items measuring self-defined familiarity with parapsychological research and attitudes toward science (Items 8–10).

4. Questions regarding the frequency of anomalous experience, from McCready and Greeley's (1976) study in which they polled a random sample of the American population (Items 11–15).

5. An open-ended request for a description of any paranormal or psychic experience that the respondent might have had (Item 16).

6. Questions regarding the resistance of scientists to the work of parapsychologists, from Allison's (1973) study in which he polled members of the PA. An additional argument and an open-ended question were added to Allison's list as a result of the pretest process (Item 17).

Although Palmer (1979) has devised a better scale for measuring paranormal experience, the McCready and Greeley (1976) scale has the advantage of brevity and of having been administered to a random sample of the entire American population. Although this scale is not particularly valid in measuring psi experience, it can be said to test some aspects of anomalous experience. Item 11 (concerning déjà vu) was modified slightly to improve grammatical clarity.

The reasons for resistance listed in Item 17 might be considered unsophisticated. The choice of questions was largely dictated by the need for comparability with prior studies and thus reflects popular misconceptions about parapsychology. A more sophisticated study on conflicting beliefs in ESP can be found in McConnell (1977).

Mailing the Questionnaire

A population of individuals was selected from the membership of the Council and selected section committees within the AAAS.* The AAAS is governed by a council and is organized into nineteen sections. Each section contains representatives from its member organizations. The criteria for selection of sections were that (1) sections must have a degree of involvement with the subject matter associated with parapsychology or must at least have the potential for future involvement; and (2) a manageable population (fewer than five hundred individuals) was required. The selection of sections was necessarily arbitrary. Table 5-1 supplies a list of sections that were selected. Examples of sections which were not selected (but which may or may not have been appropriate) are the Agricultural Sciences Section and the Meteorology Section. All members of the Council and the section committees that were selected were mailed questionnaires. These 497 individuals constitute an "administrative elite" within science and are a population that has power to grant or deny status to parapsychology.

The questionnaire in Appendix A was mailed out on January 9, 1981. Each individual received a cover letter on University of Maryland letterhead stationery, a questionnaire, an addressed and stamped return envelope, and an addressed and stamped post card which would signify that the anonymous questionnaire had been returned. The individual's address was obtained from the *Handbook of the AAAS*. Scientists who were listed more than once among the

---

*This study was conducted under the auspices of the Department of Sociology of the University of Maryland. It was not supported, authorized, or endorsed by the AAAS.

Table 5-1. AAAS Sections Receiving Questionnaires

GROUP WITHIN AAAS	NUMBER OF SCIENTISTS
Council Members	86
Section B—Physics	22
Section C—Chemistry	23
Section G—Biological Sciences	66
Section H—Anthropology	14
Section J—Psychology	29
Section K—Social and Economic Sciences	29
Section L—History and Philosophy of Science	15
Section M—Engineering	37
Section N—Medical Sciences	47
Section S—Pharmaceutical Sciences	8
Section T—Information, Computing, and Communication	34
Section U—Statistics	15
Section X—General	72
Total	497

Council and section committees were included within the group in which their name first appeared. The respondent could check a block on the post card indicating that he or she wished to be mailed a preliminary report on the questionnaire results. Reminder post cards were sent out on January 20 and 29, 1981. A replacement question- naire, with a revised cover letter, was sent out on February 20, 1981, to those who had not mailed back a post card.

Method of Analysis

Generally, analysis was conducted by comparing column percent- ages across rows. Pearson product correlations were calculated (using the 1108 Univac computer at the University of Maryland) in order to supply a measure of strength of relationship between variables. This statistic was always calculated using "uncollapsed" data that were not grouped into the categories shown in each table.

Because the group of 497 scientists constitutes the test population, tests of statistical significance are inappropriate. Tests of statistical significance reveal the probability of a result's being due to sampling error. Random sampling was not an aspect of this study. Since the computer supplies information on statistical significance without extra effort, it has been furnished on some tables. Generally, the strength of a relationship in which the Pearson product correlation (r) is greater than .3 has been deemed "strong." Relationships with r's between .2 and .3 are considered "moderate," and r's between .1 and .2 might be termed "weak." An r of .1, calculated which an N size of 300, demonstrates statistical significance at the .05 level but should not be considered particularly meaningful.

If one classifies as "believers" those who feel that ESP is "an established fact" or a "likely possibility" and classifies as "skeptics" those who feel that ESP is "merely an unknown," "a remote possibility," or "an impossibility," then observing attitudes toward ESP is simplified. This is the same classification system used by Wagner and Monnet (1979).

This system of classification will be used throughout the present study and might be considered improper by some proponents of psi. They might be alarmed by use of the term "believer" since they feel an evaluation of evidence does not require "belief" in psi and that "belief" is a term unsuitable for use by scientists. From the outset, it should be recognized that the term "believer" is meant not in a negative sense but merely as a convenient definition for a collection of individuals who have responded to the ESP opinion question in a particular manner. A similar dilemma exists with the term "skeptic." A true skeptic (for example, Truzzi, 1980) suspends judgment concerning all questions and, consequently, could not deem any phenomenon as impossible. The reader is requested to ignore the philosophical problems that are involved. The use of the terms "skeptic" and "believer" allows a labeling of these groups and a means of quickly noting the difference (or lack of differences) between the individuals falling into these categories.

Results

This survey achieved a 71% rate of response based on the questionnaires that were mailed out. Five of the 497 questionnaires were returned either because the potential respondent had moved and left

Table 5-2. Relationship Between Opinion of ESP
and Questionnaire Return

Opinion of ESP	Return Data: Individual Is Responding To			Total
	Original Mail-Out (response received before Jan. 22)	*Reminder Post Cards* (response received Jan. 22–Feb. 23)	*Replacement Questionnaire* (response received after Feb. 23)	
Believer	63 (28%)	23 (33%)	13 (32%)	99
Skeptic	165 (72%)	47 (67%)	28 (68%)	240
Total	228 (100%)	70 (100%)	41 (100%)	339

$r(339) = -0.02$

no forwarding address or was deceased. Questionnaires were returned by 353 individuals thus yielding a response rate for possible responders of 72%. In reality, some of these "responders" supplied little or no information on themselves or their opinions. If "response" is defined as making a choice on Item 4 (the "opinion of extrasensory perception" question), then 339 individuals fell into this category. This indicates a 69% response rate for possible responders (68% of questionnaires mailed out). This should be considered a high rate of return for this type of mail survey. The results of the survey will be described under eight subtopics.

Evidence Testing the Validity of Wagner and Monnet's (1979) Survey of American College Professors

One valuable means of analysis involves comparing the results of this questionnaire with the results of similarly worded questionnaires. The possibility exists that these studies suffer from bias because of nonresponse. The methodology used in this present study sheds light on the probability that this form of bias intrudes into these types of questionnaires. If believers in ESP tend to respond to these types of questionnaires, a greater percentage of them should be in the group of original responders. A lesser percentage should be among those who required the stimulation of reminder post cards. Even fewer should have required a replacement questionnaire before their response was obtained. If such a difference occurred, it would throw doubt on Wagner and Monnet's (1979) contention that their results truly reflect their sampled population since their survey collected only the response of those stimulated by a "one shot" questionnaire.

The data in table 5-2 indicate that there are no tendencies for later responders to have less belief in ESP ($r[339] = -.02$). Of those who responded before January 22, 1981, 28% could be classified as believers. A larger percentage of believers (33%) responded between January 22 and February 23, and after February 23, 32% of those who responded were believers. This result suggests that bias owing to nonresponse is not a problem in either Wagner and Monnet's (1979) or this present study.

A Comparison of Attitudes toward ESP and Parapsychology among the Various Previous Studies and This Study

Warner and Clark (1938) and Warner (1952) polled members of the American Psychological Association to determine their attitudes toward ESP and parapsychology. Warner and Clark (1938) received 352 replies out of 603 questionnaires sent out (58%). Warner (1952) received 349 replies from 515 sent out (68%). In both cases, those considering ESP an established fact or a likely possibility constituted a small percentage of the sample (8% and 17%, respectively). ESP was considered a remote possibility or an impossibility by 50% and 49%, respectively.

The most extensive survey of attitudes toward parapsychology to date was conducted among the readers of the English journal *New Scientist* (Evans, 1973). From the 71,000 copies of the journal that were sold, 1,416 replies were received. A surprisingly high level of belief was expressed, with 67% responding that ESP was either an established fact or a likely possibility.

Various other studies reveal aspects concerning belief in ESP. Moss and Butler (undated) are reported by Wagner and Monnet (1979) to have surveyed their psychology colleagues (N = 37) and their students (N = 80). The professors were found to be significantly more skeptical. A reverse relationship between education and belief was found by a Gallup Poll (June 15, 1968) in which 51% of 1,553 adults stated belief in ESP. A greater percentage (two-thirds) of those with college backgrounds believed in ESP.

Wagner and Monnet's (1979) study (conducted in 1973) is the most methodologically comprehensive. A random sample of college professors was selected from 120 colleges and universities that also were selected at random from the 1968–1969 Cass and Birnbaum *Comparative Guide to American Colleges.* The only requirement for inclusion in the sample was that the institution must have at least 1,000 students and more than 100 faculty. The questionnaire was similar to those used by Warner and Clark (1938), Warner (1952), and Evans (1973). Wagner and Monnet's (1979) results indicated a favorable attitude toward ESP similar to that found by Evans (1973) and by Gallup (1979) in 1978. Wagner and Monnet (1979) found that 66% of their college professor sample were favorably disposed and only 23% considered ESP either a remote possibility or an impossibility.

The present study finds a remarkable difference in opinion when compared to previous, recent studies (see table 5-3). Only 29% are favorably disposed (consider ESP an established fact or a likely possibility) while 50% consider it a remote possibility or an impossibility. It seems certain that this population of elite scientists is far more skeptical about the existence of ESP than the average college professor or the average responder to the *New Scientist* poll.

A comparison of the percentage who consider the investigation of ESP a legitimate scientific undertaking reveals a similar trend (see table 5-4). Only 69% of the responding elite AAAS members consider this type of inquiry a legitimate scientific undertaking while 14% would deny its legitimacy. This percentage of individuals denying the legitimacy of the investigation of ESP is greater than has been found in any major study. Certainly an irony exists in the fact that such a large number of elite individuals within science oppose the scientific investigation of a question considered valid by a majority of college professors.

A comparison of the natural and social scientists within Wagner and Monnet's (1979) study with those who responded in this present study also reveals major differences in attitudes toward ESP (see table 5-5). Slight differences exist between natural and social scientists in

Table 5-3. A Comparison of Respondents' Attitudes Toward ESP in the Literature (by percentage)

RESPONDENTS THINK ESP IS:	WARNER AND CLARK (1938) N = 352	WARNER (1952) N = 349	*New Scientist* (Evans, 1973) N = 1,416	WAGNER AND MONNET (1979) N = 1,188	THIS SURVEY OF ELITE SCIENTISTS (1981) N = 339
An established fact	1	3	25	16.3	3.8
A likely possibility	7	14	42	49.3	25.4
Merely an unknown	40	34	12	10.9	21.2
A remote possibility	36	39	19	19.4	41.0
An impossibility	14	10	3	4.1	8.5

both the Wagner and Monnet (1979) sample and in this present sample. The present study's sample reveals greater skepticism within both the natural and social scientists. For example, 28% of the natural scientists and 20% of the social scientists within Wagner and Monnet's (1979) sample feel ESP is a remote possibility while 39% and

Table 5-4. Do You Consider the Investigation of ESP a Legitimate Scientific Undertaking? (by percentage)

	WARNER AND CLARK (1938) N = 352	WARNER (1952) N = 349	EVANS (1973) N = 1,416	WAGNER AND MONNET (1979) N = 1,188	THIS SURVEY OF ELITE SCINTISTS (1981) N = 339
Yes	89	89	85	84	69
No	10	9	—	8	14

Table 5-5. Relationship Between Academic Field of Scientist and
Attitude Toward ESP (by percentage)

Respondents Think ESP Is:	Natural Science College Professors (Wagner and Monnet, 1979) N = 294	Elite Natural Scientists[a] (this study, 1981) N = 119	Social Science College Professors (Wagner and Monnet, 1979) N = 239	Elite Social Scientists[a] (this study, 1981) N = 61
An established fact	10	3	10	7
A likely possibility	46	27	47	13
Merely an unknown	15	19	13	25
A remote possibility	28	39	20	49
An impossibility	3	12	11	7

[a]Physicists, chemists, and biologists were considered natural scientists. Psychologists, sociologists, economists, philosophers, and anthropologists were considered social scientists.

NOTE: Percentages have been rounded off to nearest figure, thus the addition of values is not always equal to 100%. This practice has been used in all percentages.

49%, respectively, of the present sample feel this way. Elite scientists differ in opinion not only from the typical college professor but also from the typical scientist teaching at a college.

The Relationship Between Section of the AAAS and Belief in ESP

Wagner and Monnet (1979) found a major difference in belief between psychologists and other social scientists. Of the psychologists in their sample, 34% were believers while 56% of all social scientists in their study fell in that category. Among the elite psychologists in this present study, only 5% were believers, whereas

32% of those within the social and economic group have that attitude (see table 5-6.) This finding, therefore, replicates that of Wagner and Monnet (1979).

On the other hand, Wagner and Monnet (1979) found that 100% of all the social scientists in their study who felt that "ESP is an impossibility" were psychologists. This finding of such extreme skepticism among psychologists was not replicated. Only two out of the twenty-one elite psychologists who responded felt that ESP was an impossibility.

The theoretical orientation described earlier in this present study would predict that Council members, being of higher status, might be more skeptical of ESP than other elite scientists. This prediction was supported to some extent (only 16% were believers). Other sections demonstrating a small percentage of believers were Anthropology (0%), History and Philosophy of Science (0%), and Psychology (5%). Sections demonstrating a high percentage of believers were the Pharmaceutical Sciences (60%), the General Section (42%), and Engineering (40%).

These data are particularly significant in that a movement was initiated (Wheeler, 1979a) that sought to disaffiliate the PA from the AAAS. These data indicate that such a movement would, at present, be unlikely to succeed. Present AAAS "Procedures for Termination of Affiliation: Related By-Law Amendments" require that two-thirds of the Section Committee members of the AAAS section in which the organization in question is enrolled and two-thirds of the Council members vote for termination of affiliation before disaffiliation can occur. Since the PA is affiliated with the General Section, termination of affiliation seems improbable.

Differences in Sources of Belief in ESP Between Previous Studies and This Study

This study contained a question that was used by three previous studies, on the sources of the respondent's opinion of ESP (Wagner and Monnet, 1979; Warner, 1952; Warner and Clark, 1938). Respondents could check which sources they used in developing an opinion of ESP. A comparison between the various previous studies indicates the differences between source of belief or rejection of ESP. The elite scientists cited newspapers as a source of opinion more frequently

Table 5-6. Attitude Toward ESP and Parapsychology by Members of AAAS Sections

Section	Number of Questionnaires Mailed	Number Responding[a]	Percentage Responding	Percentage "Believers"	Percentage Denying Legitimacy to ESP Investigation (N = 338)
Council Members	86	43	50	16	11
Section B Physics	22	11	50	18	25
Section C Chemistry	23	18	78	33	38
Section G Biological Sciences	66	53	80	34	11
Section H Anthropology	14	8	57	0	43
Section J Psychology	29	21	72	5	5
Section K Social and Economic Sciences	29	19	66	32	5

continued

Section L History and Philosophy of Science	15	9	60	0	0
Section M Engineering	37	30	81	40	20
Section N Medical Sciences	47	29	62	28	10
Section S Pharmaceutical Sciences	8	5	62	60	0
Section T Information, Computing and Communication	34	24	70	38	4
Section U Statistics	15	11	73	18	8
Section X General	72	55	76	42	15
Total	497	336	68%	29%	14%

[a]This number represents those who allowed the use of their section name and who responded to Item 4 of the questionnaire.

Table 5-7. A Comparison of Source of Opinion
Concerning ESP (by percentage)

Source of Opinion	Warner and Clark's (1938) Psychologists	Warner's (1952) Psychologists	Wagner and Monnet's (1979) Professors	This Study's (1981) Elite Scientists
Newspapers	29	24	54	67
Books by Rhine, etc	47	48	19	22
Journal reports	41	35	26	30
Hearsay	8	8	12	14
A priori	34	32	18	25
Personal experience	2	8	11	28
Television	—	—	—	15
Other	—	—	—	18

than any other group that has been polled. Of these scientists, 67%
cited this source of opinion (54% of Wagner and Monnet's sample of
college professors cited this source). The elite group also cited
a priori reasons and personal experience (25% and 28%, respectively)
more frequently than did the college professors (18% and 11%,
respectively).

Physicists and chemists led all fields in their citing of a priori
reasons as a source of opinion on ESP (30% and 42%, respectively,
chose this source). Those in the social and economic sciences cited
this source least frequently (only 5% chose a priori reasons as a
source). Yet no clear pattern emerges as to the relationship between
scientific field and belief in ESP or source of opinion regarding ESP.
Wagner and Monnet (1979) speculate that psychologists may be more
negative toward ESP, since they have read more journal articles and
books by Rhine, and have a greater familiarity with research design
and potential pitfalls in experimental research. This present study
finds that the elite psychologists cite journal articles as a source of
opinion more frequently than any other group of elite scientists.

Table 5-8. Relationship Between Belief in ESP and Belief
That the Investigation of ESP Is Legitimate

In Your Opinion ESP Is:	Do You Consider the Investigation of ESP a Legitimate Scientific Undertaking?		
	Yes	*Not Sure*	*No*
An established fact	12	1	0
	(5%)	(2%)	(0%)
A likely possibility	75	10	1
	(33%)	(17%)	(2%)
Merely an unknown	44	19	7
	(19%)	(32%)	(16%)
A remote possibility	92	26	18
	(40%)	(44%)	(40%)
An impossibility	7	3	19
	(3%)	(5%)	(42%)
Total	230	59	45
	(100%)	(100%)	(100%)

$r(334) = 0.37$
$P < .001$. The reader should be reminded of the caveat concerning tests of significance mentioned in chapter 5, "Method of Analysis" section.

This study replicates Wagner and Monnet's (1979) finding that modern scientists are apparently less familiar with books and journal articles about parapsychology than psychologists were in 1938 and 1952. This is demonstrated by the fact that these sources of opinion were cited less frequently by the elite scientists than by previously polled psychologists.

Factors Related to Attitude Toward ESP

As would be predicted by the theoretical model presented in chapter 1, belief in ESP is highly correlated to opinion on the legitimacy of its investigation: r (334) = .37. This supports the contention that parapsychologists are labeled as deviant because scientists do not believe in the anomaly that they investigate. Although it would be

Table 5-9. Relationship Between Birthyear of Elite Scientist
and Opinion of ESP

OPINION TOWARD ESP	BIRTHYEAR OF ELITE SCIENTIST			
	1918 or Before	*1919–1927*	*1928–1936*	*1937 or After*
Believer	22	20	32	24
	(25%)	(19%)	(39%)	(39%)
Skeptic	67	84	52	37
	(75%)	(81%)	(61%)	(61%)
Total	89	104	84	60
	(100%)	(100%)	(100%)	(100%)

$r(332) = -.16$
$P < .002$. See caveat, table 5.8.

theoretically possible to conduct a valid scientific investigation of ESP without the phenomenon being "real," belief in ESP and the legitimacy of its investigation is highly correlated within this elite scientific group.

Various factors were found to be unrelated to attitude toward ESP. No correlation was found between the "attitudes toward science" questions (Items 9 and 10) and attitude toward ESP or legitimacy of its investigation. Nor were sex and month of birth related to these attitudes.

Wagner and Monnet (1979) noted that "attempts to relate age, sex, or month of birth to attitudes toward ESP were unsuccessful." This present study finds no strong relationship between age and attitude toward ESP: r (332) $= -.16$. Younger elite scientists are slightly more predisposed to accept the probability of the phenomenon. However, anyone who hopes that the demise of the most elderly elite scientists will herald a scientific revolution in which ESP becomes an accepted anomaly will probably be disappointed. Of scientists born during 1918 or before, 25% are believers. Of those who were born during 1919 but before 1928 (31%), only 19% are believers. Of those born during 1928 but before 1937, 39% are believers. Of those born during 1937 or after, 39% are believers (see table 5-9).

Table 5-10. Source of Opinion
Regarding ESP and Belief in ESP

Source of Opinion	Percentage Believers of Those Citing Source	Percentage Skeptics of Those Citing Source	Percentage of Total Responders Who Cite Source	Times Cited (N)
Newspapers	30	70	70	236
Books by Rhine, etc.	25	75	22	76
Journals	23	77	30	107
TV	47	53	15	54
Hearsay	33	67	14	50
A priori	7	93	25	88
Personal experience	54	46	29	101

Believers tended to cite different sources of opinion on ESP from those of skeptics (see table 5-10). Believers constituted 30% of those who cited newspapers, 25% of those citing books by Rhine, etc., 23% of those citing journals, 47% of those citing TV, 33% of those citing hearsay, 7% of those citing a priori reasons, and 54% of those citing personal experiences. This would indicate that belief is related to personal experience and TV, while skepticism is most related to a priori reasoning.

The importance and role of personal experience would probably have been revealed more fully if that term had been clearly defined. Of all physicists who mentioned a source of opinion, 48% chose "personal experience." Many indicated in the open response sections of the questionnaire that it was their "personal experience" that ESP was very unlikely. A large percentage of this group (46%) reported never having either a déjà vu experience or any of the other anomalous experiences about which they were questioned. Only 16% of those in the Physics Section (and 13% of those who chose physics as their "field") were believers. Chemists also tended to be skeptical. An equal percentage of those in that field were believers (13%), yet only

Table 5-11. Relationship Between Familiarity with Psi
Research and Opinion of ESP

	How Familiar Are You with Psi Research?				
Opinion of ESP	Not at All	Slightly	Somewhat	Fairly well	Very
Believer	26	43	22	6	2
	(39%)	(27%)	(26%)	(25%)	(100%)
Skeptic	40	115	64	18	0
	(61%)	(73%)	(74%)	(75%)	(0%)
Total	66	158	86	24	2
	(100%)	(100%)	(100%)	(100%)	(100%)

$r(336) = 0.10$
$P < .03$. See caveat, table 5-8.

16% cited personal experience as a source of opinion and 41%
reported never having had any of the experiences about which information was requested. It would seem that chemists (and most of the
other scientists) regarded "personal experience" as "anomalous
personal experience," while physicists felt that their experimentation
constituted "personal experience."

Comments written by the respondents in the various open-ended
sections of the questionnaire reveal the impact that parapsychological
literature has had on this elite group. J. B. Rhine is mentioned 14
times. In 13 cases, he is mentioned by a skeptic (often in a negative
context). Harold Puthoff and Russell Targ are the only living parapsychologists mentioned by a respondent. They are referred to once
by a skeptic in a negative context. Only 9 of the 351 responding scientists cited a parapsychological journal as a source of information
regarding the field (5 were believers, 4 were skeptics). It would seem
that reports of modern parapsychological research are not reaching
this elite group and that past research has not had a particularly
favorable impact.

To the question "How familiar are you with parapsychological
research?" the most frequent response was "slightly," with 47% of all
respondents choosing this category (see table 5-11). Virtually no relationship exists between familiarity with psi research and opinion of

ESP: r (336) = .10. Those who consider themselves more familiar tend to be more skeptical (yet the two individuals who termed themselves as "very" familiar with psi research were certain of the reality of psi).

Analysis of the relationship between frequency of anomalous experience and opinion concerning ESP demonstrates the close relationship between these two factors (see table 5-12). Those who report belief in ESP also report a greater frequency of anomalous experience. The experience of clairvoyance is especially related to belief in ESP: (r = .28). Merely to report any one of the experiences on any occasion is highly correlated with belief (r = .33). This "cumulative experience" scale is also the best predictor of an individual's opinion on the legitimacy of ESP research of any item on the questionnaire (disregarding the ESP opinion question itself). Those who have had anomalous experiences are far more likely to grant legitimacy to ESP research, and the more experiences, the greater the probability of granting legitimacy: r (312) = .27.

These findings indicate that opinions on parapsychology and ESP are not formed by analysis of the findings of scientific experimentation. Many elite scientists who have not had an anomalous experience consider the paranormality of such experiences to be impossible. Others, who have personally had these forms of experience, feel that they constitute evidence supporting the possibility of the paranormal.

A Comparison of the Quantity of Anomalous Experience Within the Elite Scientific Population and Within the General American Population

It might be hypothesized that since differences in attitude toward ESP within the elite scientific population can be explained by differences in the level of anomalous experience, differences between the elite scientist and general population might follow the same pattern. This is indeed the case; the elite scientists who responded to the survey have a lower level of anomalous experience than the general American population (see table 5-13). Only the experience of déjà vu is reported by an equivalent percentage of these two populations. The most marked difference occurs in the reporting of the ESP experience. Of the elite scientists, 26% reported this experience, while 58% of the American population reported it.

Table 5-12. Relationship Between Belief in ESP and Anomalous Experience

Type of Experience	Percentage Who Reported One or More Experiences	Percentage of Believers Who Reported One or More Experiences	Percentage of Skeptics Who Reported One or More Experiences	Pearson Product Correlation Between Belief in ESP and Frequency of Experience[a]
Déjà vu	59	76	52	.23
ESP	26	47	17	.27
Clairvoyance	4	14	0.4	.28
Communication with the dead	10	17	7	.17
Out-of-body experience (with spiritual force)	20	33	14	.14
Any of the above experiences	65	90	56	.33

[a]All these values are significant at the .005 level, but see caveat, table 5-8.

Table 5-13. Percentage of Individuals Who Report Having Had
a Particular Experience Once or More

TYPE OF EXPERIENCE	GENERAL POPULATION— McCREADY AND GREELEY (1976)	ELITE SCIENTISTS IN THIS STUDY
Déjà vu	59	59
ESP	58	26
Clairvoyance	24	4
Communication with dead	27	10
Out-of-body experience (with spiritual force)	35	20

Factors Related to the Respondent's Evaluation of Reasons Explaining the Resistance of Scientists to Parapsychology

One section of the questionnaire requested the respondent to evaluate various arguments that could explain "the resistance of scientists to the work of parapsychologists." Table 5-14 lists the arguments that the respondents evaluated. The respondent was asked to rank each argument as to its importance in explaining scientific resistance. Each argument could be evaluated as "extremely important," "very important," "somewhat important," "slightly important," "not at all important," or "I do not know or cannot answer." As table 5-14 indicates, these rankings were found, in most cases, to be correlated with opinion of ESP.

A comparison of Allison's (1973) results regarding the PA members' evaluation of various arguments and the results of this study reveals major differences between the importance assigned to these arguments by the two major groups (see table 5-14). While the PA members evaluated the arguments "Parapsychology threatens the established mechanistic world view . . . " and "Scientists are simply unfamiliar with the present evidence . . . " as most important, the elite scientific group considers these arguments as least important. The argument considered least important by the parapsychologists ("There is insufficient evidence for psychic ability") is deemed most

Table 5-14. Percentage Who Consider Argument "Very Important" or "Extremely Important"

	Parapsychological Association Members (Allison, 1973)	Present Study Total	Present Study Believers	Present Study Skeptics	Present Study: Correlation between Rating of Argument & Opinion of ESP	N Elite Scientists
a. Parapsychology threatens the established mechanistic world view of scientists.	67	13	17	11	= + .11[a]	302
b. Parapsychology conflicts with current physical or biological theories.	58	36	25	40	= – .23[a]	299
c. Scientists want to avoid any association with "occult" phenomena.	57	37	47	33	= + .15[a]	302

continued

d. There is insufficient evidence for psychic ability.	14	71	44	80	$= -.41$[a]	305
e. The complexity and elusiveness of psi makes it extremely difficult to research.	44	62	65	62	$= +.10$[a]	289
f. Scientists are simply unfamiliar with the present evidence for psi.	73	18	38	10	$= +.37$[a]	278
g. No adequate theory has been produced to explain psychic ability.	44	57	59	56	.00	293
h. Scientists feel that, on the whole, parapsychological research has not been conducted in a competent manner.	68	68	60	71	$= -.12$[a]	267

[a]Significant at the .05 level, but see caveat, table 5-8.

important by the elite scientists. The argument that parapsychological research is not being conducted competently was considered to be of high importance by 68% of the elite scientists (this argument was suggested by numerous professors during the pretest process).

The elite scientists' evaluation of the importance of most of these arguments was found to be correlated to belief in ESP. This seems to reveal the rhetorical dimensions of the controversy over psi. Even the consideration of why parapsychological research is neglected by science is directly related to the respondents' suppositions regarding psi. Evaluating the validity of parapsychological evidence and the competence of parapsychological researchers is part of the political and rhetorical process that seems to be an inherent aspect of science. These findings support those of Collins (1976), which were reviewed in chapter 2.

Analysis of Open-Ended Questions

Response to the open-ended questions regarding attitude toward parapsychology can be classified into four categories. The most typical response indicated open-minded skepticism. A second, lesser body of response argued against the legitimacy of parapsychology. A third body of response supported greater research in this field, and a fourth (and smallest) category expressed belief in ESP but also doubt in the value of scientifically exploring the phenomenon.

Open-Mindedness. The main body of response expresses curiosity, general lack of knowledge of parapsychology, and open-minded skepticism. These scientists believe that (a) methodological problems exist within parapsychology, (b) the evidence they are aware of is not particularly satisfactory, (c) anything is possible, and (d) it is important to keep an open mind. A listing of direct quotes from the questionnaire responses will reveal a sampling of the opinions that were expressed:

> Until there is much more in the way of reports to laymen based on scientific study, I have no "attitude" except curiosity.
>
> Interesting area—I am highly skeptical but feel it should be explored by the scientific method.
>
> Don't care about it one way or the other. Irrelevant. It's fun (like reading the horoscope in the daily hometown paper) but not to be taken seriously.
>
> Although I regard parapsychology as a legitimate field for scientific inves-

tigation, that investigation must be performed in a more scientific manner than has usually been the case. True double-blind experiments, appropriate statistical methods, replicability of main results—these are missing from most attempts to explore parapsychology. Without scientific rigor, the results can only be an interesting but non-scientific curiosity.

I would not vote against it dogmatically, although I am skeptical.

Rejecting of the Legitimacy of Parapsychology. A second group of elite scientists judges parapsychology far more harshly. This group tends to a priori reasoning and feels that only incompetently generated evidence exists supporting psi. The fact that a social conflict exists (especially noted in chapter 4) irritates some individuals and indicates to them the poverty of ideas that parapsychology represents. Others desire a mechanistic explanation for psi or feel that these phenomena, by definition, are outside the realm of science. Some feel that parapsychology attracts fakery and has a negative effect on society. A sample of their reasons for rejecting parapsychology follows:

Scientific reasoning, known laws of physics, common sense!

No concrete scientific evidence.

My reasoning concerning how ESP could take place (this constitutes grounds for rejection of it).

I studied the reports in Rhine's journal some years ago, and decided that the research designs were inadequate.

Personal experience via physical principles.

I do not accept such an idea unless there is at least a possible mechanism. I see none.

Sensitivity and picking up sensory clues—ok—beyond this, it's nuts!

I have looked at parapsychology in my efforts to study the sciences in the past to understand what characterizes them. It is not a special interest of mine, but it seems to me that it lacks certain characteristics that other behavioral sciences have: (1) a well articulated series of theories that can be extended to new cases (i.e., poor theory articulation in detail), (2) the data are not clear cut, even as presented in public, (3) too much of a cult, i.e., if the results are not what is expected, you can blame the audience! This is not an option in other sciences—ever.

Rather skeptical—do not foresee any practical value.

Support of Parapsychology. A smaller segment of elite scientists believes in the probability of ESP and wishes to see a continuation of the research endeavor, though sometimes with modificatons. These scientists often express a cautious optimism, a feeling of the revolutionary potential of the field, and suggestions that new methodologies may be required.

Worth pursuing. Any breakthrough would be a colossal event.

It is a legitimate field that needs to be carefully examined with the same kind of care and objectivity as in dealing with phenomena that do not easily replicate but are extremely important, if real.

There are too many unexplained events described and documented to shrug this off as a pseudo-science.

I find it exciting, tantalizing, very interesting, intriguing, puzzling.

Perhaps, just as astronomy lept beyond rudimentary positional measurements with the invention of the telescope, so may psi studies leap ahead when some new tool (physical or mental) becomes available.

I believe that there is a strong possibility of a sixth sense operating on low frequency electric and/or magnetic fields which can confuse the issue—that is, what may actually be a sensory perception might be interpreted as extrasensory. Needs research!

Belief in ESP but Doubt in the Value of Exploring Phenomenon. A small segment of the elite group feels that although ESP may be likely, certain aspects of it preclude the possibility of scientific explanation and, consequently, the value of scientific exploration in this field is doubted. The possibility exists that psi may be forever beyond human understanding or that there are other forms of "understanding" besides scientific "understanding."

Parapsychology may well not lend itself to the rigors of classic scientific investigation. Social engineering also does not lend itself to "pure" scientific procedure. When all the parameters cannot be determined, there is a tendency to cry "unscientific." Different procedures may well be required.

Heisenberg uncertainty principle may apply to efforts to demonstrate psi.

Although it is legitimate for science to investigate psi, given our present prevalent paradigm, such experimentation cannot lead to understanding, only to documentation that something extrasensorimotor can take place.

The so-called hard sciences have attempted to confine descriptions of reality within a frame of widely accepted guidelines. Psi, in large measure because of its evanescent character, cannot, in my judgment, be described adequately by the usual guidelines of science. Reality has many faces, but I would like to think that any description of it would minimize its subjective character by an attempt to hold it to criteria of reproducibility and predictability.

I don't think parapsychology should be so worried about being a science.

Belief in psi is associated with anomalous experience rather than familiarity with research results. A review of selected responses to one question can shed light on this relationship: "If you have had what might be considered a paranormal or psychic experience, would you describe it briefly?" Forty-two scientists (12% of the entire group that responded) wrote descriptions of their experiences. Many wrote evaluations of their experiences. The phrase in brackets following each description signifies the individual's response to the "opinion of ESP" question. Some scientists gave unique answers to this question by modifying the possible responses to it. A sample of response to the "request for psychic experience" question follows:

My wife awoke in the middle of the night, calling out the name of a friend she hadn't seen in years. Soon after, we learned that at about the same time, he had undergone a profound spiritual experience while doing yoga medita-tion. A coincidence? As infants, my children sometimes appeared to antici-pate my unspoken thoughts. [ESP: a remote possibility]

For example: a feeling of "spiritual" contact, and a desire to communicate physically has occurred from time-to-time over the years, i.e., (1) just yesterday, I phoned my father—his immediate response was "I have been thinking about you all day." I normally phone him about six times per year. (2) Last year, I had a special urge to go visit my Ph.D. advisor over a period of about 3 months. At the end of that period, I received word of his death, following 3 months of serious illness (I had no tangible communication for 9 months before). (3) A few years back, I had a yearning to see an old friend and colleague—only to learn shortly thereafter that he had been killed in an accident, etc. [ESP: a likely possibility]

Many telepathic experiences, both spontaneous as well as in experiments. [ESP: an established fact]

I have had several, including a kind of "predictive" clairvoyance on several occasions. Most frequently, I find myself anticipating who calls on phones well before I have seen them or heard their voices, or (and I suppose this is most frequent) knowing exactly what my wife or other very close family members are about to say or do before they do so when they are not far away. . . . I have seen, heard, felt, and spoken to both deceased parents within one to three months after their deaths, with a full realization that it was impossible to do so yet an overwhelming conviction of the "reality" of the contact (this I attribute to my own brain states under stress). Some of these phenomena are undoubtedly internal, individual and psychological phenomena. But a small residue is almost certainly parapsychological as you use the term. (I have also seen one case of purported telekinesis.) [ESP: an established fact]

Recently, at dinner (7:30 pm), I "knew" that an ill friend of friends (whom I knew only casually) had died. Two days later, we learned that he died that evening when I had the "feeling." Similar "feelings" have occurred occasionally before. [ESP: a possibility]

On several occasions, all occurring during a several month span, I had remarkable experiences in very ordinary situations. I would suddenly know precisely what was about to occur, what people were going to say, what movements they would make, and even what would be occurring in the background. During the time that the "pre-known" events took place, I had a sort-of hollow feeling in my stomach and chest, and was very light-headed. I also had the idea that I was in two "places" simultaneously, taking part in the scene and also observing it as though watching a very well-known stage play. I never, however, saw myself in the way some people describe out-of-body experiences. These incidents lasted from perhaps as short as 5–10 seconds to as long as several minutes. It required some time and some effort to return to my normal state after the "pre-known" events were complete, greater time and effort the longer the experience. [ESP: a likely probability]

The normal Christian life experiences supernatural events which are the works of God. In particular, the gifts of the Holy Spirit are manifested in visions, prophesy, etc. [ESP: a likely possibility]

Experienced events in a dream two or three days before the event happened. [ESP: a likely possibility]

1. On my way to work each morning during the summer of '60, when I was nineteen years old, the same plane flew over as I walked from the subway to the lab. One morning, I "thought" or "knew" that the plane would crash. It did in Arizona. It was a flight from Philadelphia to California. 2. I felt it when my grandmother died. Again, I was about nineteen. 3. My husband and I often find ourselves thinking about a subject not under discussion previously that day. [ESP: a likely possibility]

Experiences such as these are not at all unusual in the para-psychological literature (except that because of the scientistic orientation within parapsychology, there is a tendency to note only cases that are highly documented, verified, witnessed, etc.). What might surprise skeptics is the frequency with which these types of experience occur within this elite scientific group.

There is irony in labeling these experiences as deviant. A large percentage of those who have not had an anomalous experience tend to belittle the importance of the experience. Others seem willing to accept another's reports on the significance of such experience and regard these reports as evidence of the possibility of paranormal phenomena. A sampling of replies from skeptics (and from a few believers who have had no experiences) to the "request for psychic experience" question illustrates the variety of response of those who do not have a specific personal experience to relate.

Personally, I like to separate "spiritual" experience from other "psychic" experience. The former, to me, refers to belief in God or a superior force. I also believe that science or scientific logic as we know it cannot study "spiritualism." However, "extrasensory perception or communication" between people can perhaps be studied by scientific method. [ESP: a likely possibility]

I haven't. All the above experiences are perfectly understandable as matters of imagination, conscious or unconscious states of mind. [ESP: an impossibility]

I have interviewed many MZ [monozygotic] twins who seem to have unusually close rapport. [ESP: a likely possibility]

Because I am not—or try not to be—misled by wishful thinking, dreams, and illusions, I have never in my life had such an experience. Randi has a $10,000 prize to anyone who can prove paranormal powers under controlled conditions; in 17 years, he has only collected interest. R. Steiner has a similar, but smaller, outstanding award. I assert (but only as a strong opinion) that there *are no* paranormal or psychic experiences. [ESP: there is no convincing evidence for it]

While I have had no such experiences, I am acutely aware that some of these experiences have taken place in others. [ESP: an established fact]

I find this difficult to answer. Is a spiritual experience of God in prayer considered paranormal or psychic by parapsychologists? Is there a difference in attitudes among parapsychologists regarding prayer? I feel close to people who have died and in the Communion of Saints take it for granted that I can communicate with them; I have never "experienced" in the sense of "felt" or "otherwise perceived by my senses" their communication with me. [ESP: a likely possibility]

I have not. Please note that these [the responses to the "anomalous experience" questions] are not meant to indicate anything like a psychic experience—simply that I, like many people, sometimes think "what would my
Father or Mother have said or thought about this? . . . and I think [of] their
views and values. A less sophisticated person could well think that this is a
"conversation" or that they "hear voices." . . . I am simply glad that their
values live on in my memory. [ESP: A *very* remote possibility]

Since I personally don't believe in them, it is unlikely that I'd have one.
[ESP: a remote possibility]

Some of these responses indicate the disparaging attitude of nonexperiencers toward experiencers. Anomalous experiences are
deemed "perfectly understandable as matters of imagination" by
people who are "misled by wishful thinking, dreams, and illusions."
People who accept the validity of their own experiences are probably
"unsophisticated." One respondent explained such experience as due
to "minor malfunctions of the brain" (see Appendix B).

Because journal editors sometimes harbor these attitudes, it is not
unknown for them to accept articles that attempt to explain all paranormal experience following this line of reasoning. Singer and
Benassi (1981:49) attribute belief in the occult to "media distortions,
social uncertainty, and deficiences of human reasoning." Psychic
experience may spring from "faulty cognitive apparatus" (p. 53). The
solution to belief in the occult, they believe, lies in correcting "defi-
ciencies in science education" (p. 53). The stereotype being suggested
is that the individual who has mystical experiences tends to be irrational, neurotic, and perhaps oppressed. Such a person gains reas-
surance and release from believing in a delusionary experience.

Most available research reveals this stereotype as false. McCready
and Greeley (1976) found that psychological well-being (using the
Bradburn "happiness scales") was closely correlated with degree of
anomalous experience (using the same anomalous experience scale as
was administered to the elite scientist group). Those having frequent
anomalous experience in this national sample tended to be over forty,
male, college-educated, and making over $10,000 a year.

Belief in ESP has generally been found to be associated with positive personality attributes whereas skepticism has been linked to
negative traits. Carpenter (1971) reported that skeptics scored significantly higher on Mosher's sex-guilt scale (Mosher, 1966) than did

believers. Thalbourne (1981) used a scale combining belief in ESP and history of psi experience and found scores on this scale to be significantly correlated to extraversion as measured by the Minnesota Multiphasic Personality Inventory, Cattell's 10PF Questionnaire, and Eysenck's Personality Inventory. One could make a case that degree of anomalous or mystical experience and belief in ESP are more closely related to psychological adjustment and well-being than to negative psychological aspects. At the same time, Singer and Benassi (1981) may be correct in viewing belief in the paranormal as negatively related to science education. This present study predicts that the tacit ideology of science taught as an aspect of science education may result in lower reporting (and belief in) anomalous experience.

These elite scientists were also given the opportunity to add extra reasons for the "resistance of scientists to the work of parapsychologists." Because this present study may not analyze all the factors that thwart the work of parapsychologists, we should note additional ideas suggested by these prominent scientists. A sample of some of the forty-five responses to this invitation to list "other reasons" reveals the variety of attitudes on this issue:

Research easily perverted by media, especially when encouraged by psuedo-scientists.

Believers have promised too much and expect miraculous explanations.

Potential for fraud and evil.

Too much like "witchcraft."

There is no reliable evidence to be explained. Please note: I find the pervasive rhetorical purpose and bias of these questions offensive. In my view, parapsychology is rejected because it is unable to make a reasonably persuasive case to reasonable and rational open-minded skeptics. That is the true essence of the "scientific method."

If mechanistic tests are used, then mechanistic answers are all that can result. Parapsychology cannot use the methods of chemistry and physics and come up with anything other than chemistry and physics, which proves nothing concerning the validity of parapsychology. It would be like analyzing an oil painting by figuring out the chemicals in the various colors and the thickness of the paint, etc.

Scientists are rightly skeptical about claims for processes or capacities which (a) only occur in a few gifted individuals, and (b) cannot be replicated by other investigators.

Many scientists are rejecting the epistemologies of the 60's and 70's, but there is not a generally accepted epistemolgy to replace the rejected.

It's plain silly.

It implies a whole other order to the world. It implies a spiritual nature at loose in the world.

Seems to support religion.

Some of these comments might be classified among the reasons listed in the questionnaire (for example, the idea that parapsychology is "occult" or that there is insufficient evidence to support the field). Some comments point out "unscientific" qualities (silliness, unreplicability, perversion by media, etc.) that exist in parapsychology. Other comments seem to point out a transcendental nature in psychic phenomena that may require a new "megaparadigm."

Conclusion

The population of elite scientists surveyed in this study demonstrated the highest level of skepticism over ESP of any major group surveyed within the last twenty years. This doubt in the probability of ESP is positively related to denying the legitimacy of parapsychology. In that this population of scientists constitutes an "administrative" elite, these results shed light on the reason parapsychology has failed to gain full legitimacy within the scientific community even though its proponents attempt to adhere to all the norms and canons of science. Within this group of elite scientists, belief in ESP is more closely related to personal experience than to familiarity with the research literature on psi. There is a tendency for those who doubt the existence of ESP to cite a priori reasons for this opinion. The frequency of anomalous experience reported by members of this population is highly and positively correlated to their belief in ESP. A far lower percentage of these elite scientists report anomalous experience than is reported by the American population. This suggests that such experiences violate aspects of the scientific world view and that aspects of the scientific education and socialization process reduce the value placed on these experiences. These findings are similar to those reported by Gallup (1982). He found in a national survey that leading scientific and medical authorities tend to dismiss, disparage, or explain away the reported findings dealing with "near-death experiences." While 67% of a national sample endorsed a belief in life after death, only 32% of physicians and 16% of scientists in Gallup's sample did.

Elite scientists can be expected to defend the scientistic world view more vigorously than non-elite scientists because part of their role as an elite is to define the nature of science. This leads to their tendency to stigmatize scientists who investigate anomalous experiences (or who attempt to induce such experiences under laboratory conditions) as silly, incompetent, or fraudulent.

6

The Reaction of Parapsychology to Deviant Labeling

The resistance to the research conducted by parapsychologists has had a profound impact on the field. This resistance, actually a form of deviant labeling, has caused parapsychologists to increase their own vigilance and skepticism regarding possible methodological flaws in their research. Since they have increased their allegiance to the "scientific method," their actions tend to support indirectly the scientistic orientation. This reaction has had effects on the recruitment, socialization, methodology, and theory associated with parapsychology. These effects have tended to restrict the field's impact on the larger cultural processes of science. A latent effect of this reaction is that the scientific cultural process has been allowed to continue unaffected by the possibility of psi's existence, and a stable relationship has evolved between parapsychology and science.

Sociologists have found that labeling of deviants often leads to these individuals accepting their deviant role. Ironically, labeling of deviance can have a latent or hidden effect of contributing to its continuance. Deviant behavior that occurs as a result of labeling is referred to as "secondary" deviance as opposed to "primary" deviance which consists of the originally labeled acts (Lemert, 1951). The reaction of parapsychologists to their labeling can be considered a form of secondary deviance that consolidates their role within science.

The recruitment, socialization, methodology, and theory associated with parapsychology have taken a form that reflects the process of labeling the field as deviant (a form of secondary deviance). A latent effect of the field's reaction supports the ideology justifying this label. The evidence presented in this chapter is based on participant observation, a reading of parapsychological journals, and attendance at parapsychological conferences from 1979 through 1982. During 1979, I visited each of thirteen "parapsychological research centers" on a list furnished by FRNM and interviewed over forty-five parapsychologists. A "parapsychologist" is defined as a member of the PA. During my visits to these centers, I located and interviewed other parapsychologists (and former researchers). Over one hundred interviews were conducted. The questions I asked are listed in Appendix D. Direct quotations that are not associated with a citation have been derived from these interviews.

Before I began this investigation, I had assumed that the field of parapsychology existed as a form of scientific "cult." I assumed that a latent function of the social interaction of parapsychologists was to maintain their belief in psi in the face of a hostile scientific community. I hypothesized that parapsychologists who failed to produce signs of psi through their experiments would have a greater tendency to proselytize outsiders. This expectation was drawn from Leon Festinger's concept of cognitive dissonance as a reaction to seeing the failure of prophecy (Festinger, 1957; Festinger, Riechen, and Schachter, 1956).

This hypothesis was not supported. Visits at two parapsychological research centers in North Carolina, three in Texas, talks with various researchers in California, and visits to two other centers in New York and Virginia revealed that parapsychologists act, think, and feel much the same about science. The most typical opinion is that proselytizing is unnecessary. They believe that, in the end, owing to the scientific method, truth will be revealed. This assumption, which is basically positivistic, permeates many aspects surrounding parapsychology.

Recruitment

The major patterns of recruitment in the field of parapsychology reflect the deviant status of the field. Although the "Kuhnian" model (accepted by many parapsychologists) presents the image of innovative, mainstream scientists turning their attention to exciting anomalies, this does not coincide with the case of parapsychology. The

majority of parapsychologists focused attention on psi before establishing careers as scientists and before the age of twenty-five.
Although recruitment of mainstream scientists is considered highly
desirable, numerous social factors seem to block the Kuhnian revolution that such recruitment might bring. Although the few mainstream
scientists who have been attracted have generally been granted high
status within the field, the legitimacy gained from this recruitment
has drawbacks. Even though this is the case, the desire and need for
the legitimating and integrating qualities gained from attracting mainstream scientists with established careers gives this form of recruitment the greatest priority.

Because parapsychologists have generally been denied access to
the system of scientific communication, most scientists who later turn
their attention to the field first learn about it through the popular
media. Professors have had their attention brought to the field by their
students who request aid with special projects that involve parapsychology. This initial interest is generally continued only if the
scientist successfully demonstrates and observes psi under his or her
own control.

The concept of "interest" is of critical importance in attracting
individuals to a new field. Ideas that violate an individual's assumptions too greatly are thought absurd. Ideas that coincide with an individual's assumptions are deemed mundane, dull, or boring. A limited
degree of violation of the assumptions used by the individual in his
or her daily work is important in generating interest.

Consequently, the potential parapsychologist's assumptions must
be only minimally violated by the ideas inherent within parapsychology in order for interest to develop. Because of the nature of
modern quantum theory, physicists who work with subatomic particles sometimes fall in this category. Psychologists who study hypnosis
or altered states of consciousness also occasionally show interest.
Scientists who find that the phenomena they investigate are not easily
replicable (behavioral bioassay phenomena, for example) might be
attracted to parapsychology. The number of established scientists who
have devoted attention to parapsychology has been small, owing to
general a priori assumptions inherent within science. Parapsychology
violates these assumptions too much and its ideas are consequently
deemed absurd by many. It would seem that there is far greater
interest in parapsychology among the public than among scientists.
Training in science seems to narrow the range of an individual's

assumptions so that these assumptions are violated to a greater degree by parapsychological ideas.

The attempt to attract the attention of mainstream scientists creates difficulties when combined with the need for increased caution in producing "exceptional proofs." The dictum that "exceptional claims require exceptional proofs" necessitates a great deal of training for the potential parapsychologist. Parapsychologists feel that only skilled individuals have the special expertise to produce "exceptional proofs," a skill that has evolved after more than a century of research into the nature of psi. Seventy percent of the PA membership agreed with the statement "Special training is essential for successful, high quality research in parapsychology, today. No regular academic program is sufficient" (Allison, 1973). Schmeidler (1977:131) notes that "parapsychology, like other specialized fields, has developed a variety of distinctive techniques. It uses built-in controls, methods of eliciting an appropriate instructional set, and ways of examining the data which are unfamiliar even to most psychologists." Because skeptics have severely scrutinized parapsychological research, many "tricks of the trade" have evolved that would not occur to the average researcher (special care in selection and concealment of ESP targets, for example).

A latent effect of attracting established scientists into the field of parapsychology is that they may make methodological errors in research. Their ability to get this research published compounds the problem for parapsychology. These publications stimulate controversy and focus attention on the established scientists' research. Other research, which is considered to be more valid and sound by those within parapsychology, is largely ignored by the mainstream scientific community. One parapsychologist noted during my interview with her that "the best parapsychological research isn't found in mainstream scientific journals. It can't get published there. The editors reject it because it was conducted by people within the field of parapsychology. If you collected all that was published in the mainstream journals about parapsychology, you would find it was not representative of the work done in this field. The editors of most journals aren't that knowledgeable about parapsychology. They don't know what to look for in a piece of research."

The tendency for skeptics to seek out established scientists' reports and to ignore the main body of psychical research published in parapsychological journals contributes to the oblivion to which this body of information has been committed. It should be noted that of the seven experiments selected by Beloff (1980) as representing the best evidence of psi, only one gained brief mention in a mainstream scientific publication. This irony should be considered a latent effect of the process of deviance labeling.

Examples of established scientists who turned their attention to parapsychology illustrate this point. Harold Puthoff and Russell Targ began their parapsychological experimentation as a result of their laser and quantum theory research. This led to their eventual testing of the psychic entertainer Uri Geller, and to a remarkably successful remote viewing experiment (a type of ESP experiment). After publishing their results (Targ and Puthoff, 1974; Puthoff and Targ, 1976) in *Nature* and in the *Proceedings of the Institute of Electrical and Electronic Engineers*, critics alleged various flaws in their methodology. The defense of Puthoff and Targ's experimentation has become part of the political and rhetorical struggle between parapsychologists and their critics (for an example of a critical analysis, see Marks and Kammann, 1978, 1980; for examples of defenses, see Tart, Puthoff, and Targ, 1980a, b). Some of the controversy might have been avoided by slight modifications in the methodology of research and data analysis if Puthoff and Targ had been more fully integrated into the parapsychological community. A certain amount of controversy probably springs from the high reputation of the Stanford Research Institute (SRI) where the studies were conducted, and which gave the research more visibility. Various parapsychologists, like Charles Tart and Stuart B. Harary, have aided Puthoff and Targ in more recent research. Although they continued to report highly significant results supporting the existence of psi (for example, Puthoff, Targ, and Tart, 1979), this research has not drawn criticism. Their more recent (and more tightly controlled) work seems to be ignored while critics refer to their earlier (and more vulnerable) studies.

The controversy surrounding Puthoff and Targ's earlier publications seems to reflect negatively on parapsychology since accusations include both fraud and incompetence. The problem is compounded by the vehemence and renown of some of their critics. Some critics have published articles that Targ and Puthoff (1977:177) consider to be "substantial and deliberate misrepresentation of the facts." James Randi, a prominent member of CSICOP, alleges that a segment of SRI's film of a dice box experiment was a reenactment (Randi, 1980).

The SRI parapsychologists have resorted to circulating "Documentation Reports" by direct mail or handout to correct what they consider "misinformation" (Puthoff, 1981a, b). It is very doubtful that this information will reach the wide readership gained by Randi's original allegations. On my questionnaire sent out to elite scientists, the one instance in which an elite scientist mentioned a living parapsychologist involved a derogatory comment concerning Uri Geller's ability to "fool Puthoff and Targ."

The controversy over Puthoff and Targ's research seems to negate evidence that they have generated demonstrating psi, illustrating the difficulty any mainstream scientist has in producing the "flawless" research demanded by parapsychology's critics. Puthoff and Targ's reevaluation of their original remote viewing (RV) research reduces the significance level they claim from $P = 10^{-4}$ to $P = 3.9 \times 10^{-4}$, still a quite significant result. "We recognize that our original RV studies are not without flaw, and the potential effect of possible cues deserves critical examination. However, in our continuing re-examination of this work we find that the suggested cueing artefacts, although providing some potential for confounding, are yet well below the magnitude necessary to account for the strength of the results" (Puthoff and Targ, 1981:388).

Later, replications of remote viewing experiments by parapsychologists (for example, Dunne and Bisaha, 1979; Schlitz and Gruber, 1980) appeared only in parapsychological journals and, consequently, seem to have been ignored by mainstream scientists.

Even though this controversy may have reduced many of the benefits that parapsychology has derived from recruiting these established scientists, other benefits were gained. Puthoff and Targ have made major presentations regarding their research before the Electro 1977 National Convention of the Institute of Electrical and Electronic Engineers (IEEE) and the 1976 and 1977 IEEE International Conference on Cybernetics and Society. Other established scientists, such as Robert Jahn, the Dean of Engineering/Applied Science at Princeton University, have also benefited parapsychology through their research and support. These individuals justify the field's continuing interest in attracting established scientists.

John Taylor is another illustration of the recruitment of a mainstream scientist. Taylor holds a chair of mathematics at King's College, London, and is a reputable physicist and mathematician. The witnessing of a demonstration by Uri Geller profoundly influenced Taylor and he began a personal investigation of Geller-like effects in his own laboratory. His controversial book *Superminds,* which appeared in 1975, presented incredible claims concerning the effects of metal benders similar to Geller. Both the parapsychological community and the fraternity of conjurers and magicians were unimpressed with Taylor's methodological expertise. Although some of his descriptions of phenomena seemed to indicate the existence of psi, many felt Taylor was gullible, given the exceptional quality of his claims. After meeting with James Randi and others, Taylor again became highly skeptical. In his book *Science and the Supernatural* (Taylor, 1980), he explains away many (but not all) of the effects he observed during his previous life as a "believer." His explanation for this change in attitude illustrates the essence of the scientistic orientation. He was unable to find an electromagnetic explanation for psi; consequently, he now doubts its existence. Certainly, the field of parapsychology has not benefited from Taylor's change of heart.

Helmut Schmidt presents an example of the benefits that can accrue for the field of parapsychology through the recruitment of a mainstream scientist. Schmidt, a physicist, became interested in parapsychology after noting that his children seemed to demonstrate psychic ability when he tested them under his own informal conditions. After a long apprenticeship under J. B. Rhine at the Foundation for Research on the Nature of Man, Schmidt established one of the major innovative paradigms of parapsychology. He has devised machines that test a subject's ability to influence psychokinetically a random process (for example, radioactive decay). Since the subject's scores are mechanically recorded, this method virtually precludes the possibility of explaining data that indicate psychokinesis as a result of recording errors. His quantum mechanical models for psi are a major advance in the attempt to integrate physics and parapsychology. Like Puthoff and Targ, Schmidt has called a certain amount of positive attention to the field of parapsychology through his interactions with established physicists. His machines for testing PK show how psi experimentation may be virtually invulnerable to fraud on the part of the subject. Skeptics have been confounded somewhat in their attempts to dismiss his evidence. They tend to use the fraud hypothesis (as noted in chapter 3) or to take a wait-and-see attitude. For a critical discussion of Schmidt's work, see Hansel (1981) and Hyman (1981).

Even though serious drawbacks exist in recruiting mainstream scientists, parapsychology is forced by its deviant role to spend energy continuously seeking established researchers. Younger individuals who enter the field are quickly dismissed as incompetent by the mainstream scientific community and, consequently, ignored. One parapsychological informant stated, "It's important not to become too interested in parapsychology early in one's life. It's best to get into this later on."

Even though this is the case, recruitment of established scientists has not been the norm. Allison (1973) noted that 40% of PA members first decided to become involved in parapsychology after they had already entered another field. Individuals who may be potential scientists, but have not been trained as such, seem more likely to develop interest in the field. McConnell and Clark (1980) noted that 69% of the members of the PA became familiar with the field before age twenty-five. Although the average age of the entire membership was fifty in 1975, the mean age at first familiarity with the literature was twenty-two. "Bearing in mind that the pool of potential members is large and roughly constant for all ages, we conclude that there is little hope of attracting to the field those who have completed their education and almost none at all of gaining new members among older scientists from other fields" (McConnell and Clark, 1980:253).

The popular media play a primary role in the recruitment of these younger potential parapsychologists. Parapsychologists cited various means of introduction such as newspaper articles, popular books, science fiction, and even comic books. Books and articles about Rhine were cited with great frequency. A minority cited paranormal experience as a key to triggering their interest.

The American Society for Psychical Research reports that a great many individuals request information on how to become a parapsychologist. Parapsychologists consider it important that these individuals receive special training, but they face a dilemma in recommending how one is to receive it. The problem is that parapsychology has no professor/graduate-student training like that which exists for the rest of science. This is because parapsychologists are often discriminated against in academic circles and find it difficult to gain legitimate teaching positions, promotion, and tenure. Consequently, few parapsychologists have the academic positions required to train graduate students. One tenured faculty member informed me that he has decided not to work with any graduate students who might be interested in parapsychology, owing to the intense hostility that has been expressed before against such students by other faculty members.

The recruitment process begins when an aspiring student first contacts a parapsychological research center. Usually this is through the mail. Some parapsychologists use form letters to respond to such requests. One such letter is by Gertrude Schmeidler, a former president of the PA, who writes:

> In the first place, no college in the country offers good training in parapsychology with a reasonably large competent faculty and good sequence of courses. Don't look for it; you won't find it. Next, even when a single course is offered the person who teaches it may not be well trained in parapsychology. In the third place, a college degree isn't usually enough for professional competence. The phrase you hear is: "The Ph.D. is the union card." Keep in mind the possibility of eventually doing graduate work which will lead to a doctoral degree.

Since Schmeidler wrote this letter, the situation has changed slightly. One accredited institution, John F. Kennedy University (JFK), offers an M.A. in parapsychology. The first degree was awarded in 1980. Yet, some members of the PA are distressed that the graduates of this institution have no real job opportunities and, in fact, are not qualified to become full members of the PA (a Ph.D. is generally required). JFK does not confer upon the graduate a position of high status among parapsychologists. In fact, quite the opposite is the case; some parapsychologists have privately criticized the program, though they applauded its existence as a milestone toward legitimization.

Dr. Schmeidler also states in her letter:

> Since parapsychology is not a recognized college major, you must major in some other field. But this is good because the skills you learn will almost surely be applicable to parapsychology. Almost everything is, from psychology and biology and physics to computer programming or anthropological field studies or mathematical theory. The general advice here is to study what interests you! It will be relevant.

The parapsychologist-to-be is advised to become something else. Schmeidler concludes by describing the process of attaining a role within a field that exists only on the margins of science:

Now let's come back to the first question: how do you become a para-psychologist? Answer: by working in parapsychology. And if you say, "No. that's no answer!" I can respond only with a question of my own: how did any of us become parapsychologists? I'll tell you how I did: took a doctorate in psychology which trained me in research methods, audited a course with Dr. Gardner Murphy, and began experimenting. How did Dr. Murphy? He took a doctorate in psychology and did a lot of reading on his own. How did Dr. Rhine? He took a doctorate in biology and worked with Dr. McDougall. How did Dr. Osis? He took a doctorate in psychology and worked with Dr. Rhine. A final suggestion: read the *Journal of the ASPR* or the *Journal of Para-psychology*, see in their pages who is working in parapsychology and where they are located, then write to appropriate ones, asking what study opportunities they offer.

Various parapsychologists have informed me that they advise potential parapsychologists as follows: Conceal your interest in para-psychology. Get a doctorate in whatever subject interests you. Then you can be of value to the field.

This is not to say that individuals without doctorates (and indeed without any college degree) have not contributed to the body of para-psychological research. However, the required degree of expertise for researchers has become extensive and training opportunities are limited. Professional credentials seem to be highly valued in this field, which is trying to shed the stigma associated with the deviant label.

One form of training has been instituted by the Foundation for Research on the Nature of Man. Since 1966 this group has held summer training sessions in which a few students (thirteen in 1966) pay to take part in an intensive period of lectures, study, and research directed by senior staff members. Among Allison's (1973) PA survey respondents, 58 percent of the forty-eight full PA members had received their training or had been on the staff at the FRNM labora-tory, demonstrating the importance of the Rhine group as a train-ing center.

Other potential parapsychologists have sought out professors who can support and advise them. For example, various graduate students met weekly with Gertrude Schmeidler while she held a professorship at the City University of New York. There they discussed their interest in parapsychology and received her guidance in planning research projects. Their general goal was to receive a doctorate in psychology while gaining expertise in the methods and theory of parapsycholog-ical research.

Parapsychologists react to deviant labeling by creating a professional association that is highly restrictive in its membership policy. A major role of the PA is to present the image of a professional and competent group to the mainstream scientific community. Full members generally hold a Ph.D. All potential members must present evidence that they have "provided tangible evidence of contributing to parapsychology as a science. Such tangible evidence might include, but not be limited to, published or unpublished written work of a scientific nature (empirical, methodological, or theoretical) related to parapsychology" (PA Council Resolution, 1979). One parapsychologist noted, "The PA is one of those organizations that was founded with the intention of keeping people out rather than letting them in."

The high level of public interest and low level of public finance means that many people are attracted to the field but that there is little money to pay them. This means low salaries for researchers. It is not unusual for people to begin as volunteers or work for less than minimum wages (i.e., working long hours on fixed pay). Career security is nonexistent in that the private benefactors who support parapsychological research may reduce their funding during periods of economic downturn. As one informant stated humorously during a discussion of factors that seem to produce psi phenomena, "If hunger among researchers produced the effect we would be OK, we would get it all the time!"

An added difficulty for younger researchers is the lack of a structure for careers within the field. A person rarely "starts at the bottom and works up" (the parapsychologist Charles Honorton is an exception). Often younger researchers work at a center as part of their learning process. The individual is expected to leave eventually in order to earn a doctorate in another field.

Some younger researchers idealistically seek to make a contribution to science yet later realize that their future advancement within parapsychology is blocked. Status and respect given within the field often reflect what an individual has achieved within mainstream science. One older parapsychologist noted, "The surprising thing isn't that so many leave the field but that so many stay so long without being able to earn a decent living. It requires an astonishing degree of interest and dedication." Those who do continue to do parapsychological research gain a certain status merely because researchers are so few, but their efforts are ignored by established scientists.

Researchers I interviewed who had left the field cited a variety of reasons and attitudes toward parapsychological research. Only one rejected the field as invalid, but many were glad to be on a career path that would lead toward financial security. "I know what it is like to be carried away by an idea," one noted. "Only later did I realize that science is a political game." Various former researchers expressed a belief in psi yet a hostility toward the "political games" they felt existed within the field of parapsychology. The field is hostile to innovation, they claimed, and is overly concerned with establishing its legitimacy.

The field seems to have no difficulty in recruiting younger researchers (they are attracted by the media, which stimulates their interest). The problem seems to lie in supporting these individuals after their recruitment. During the period of my participant observation various younger researchers dropped out of the field. They did so not for any lack of belief in psi but because the field lacks a career structure. The private benefactors who fund parapsychological research generally wish to support established scientists.

A few individuals have been granted doctorates in parapsychology. This has generally been the result of special programs that the individuals have put together with the aid of academically established parapsychologists. It is too early to predict the career structures of these individuals although it would appear that most have successfully found employment at parapsychological research centers.

The difficulties of attaining the role of parapsychologist have restricted the growth of the field. This has caused the PA to grow arithmetically rather than exponentially, a result that can be partly attributed to parapsychology's being labeled as deviant. PA members numbered 126 in 1958, 170 in 1965, 221 in 1973, and 285 in 1981 (White, 1982). In 1983, 306 individuals were members of the PA. "Parapsychology has both survived and grown, but its growth has been extremely slow—certainly not the exponential growth that Price (1963) attributes to science as a whole, and which Crane (1972) found in several specialty groups" (Allison, 1973:96).

Socialization

Individuals who are recruited into the field of parapsychology tend to adapt to the common needs of the group. This adaptation or conformance involves not only understanding the special methodologies and theories associated with parapsychology (which will be briefly discussed as an aspect of socialization) but also accepting special values that are unique to deviant science. Some of these special values reflect the process of labeling the field as deviant and have latent effects that thwart the appearance of scientific progress within the field. Other special values have resulted from the process of argumentation that has occurred within the field over the last century. These values constitute the form that the "knowledge" generated by the field has taken. Parapsychologists are socialized in such a manner that they tend to adhere more strongly to the scientistic orientation. This response to being labeled as deviant has latent effects that ironically tend to consolidate this realm of inquiry as a deviant science. When I asked how they had been changed by becoming parapsychologists, most researchers said they had become more cautious. As a group, parapsychologists tend to be cautious, careful, and conservative in their claims. They seem intent on trying to gain acceptance for the field as a legitimate science. One major aspect of working toward this goal is to become more skillful in the art of skepticism than even the critics of the field. My question "How has socialization into the role of parapsychologist affected you as a researcher?" received the following representative responses:

I've become more cautious by working in the field. It's difficult to determine the genuine cases from the ungenuine. It has not changed my attitude, which was positive. Now I'm just cautiously positive.

If anything it has made me a bit more skeptical of paranormal claims, more critical of them. A person is guilty until proven innocent. Before I didn't really question things so much. Before I had had minor psychic experiences that I didn't question. The telephone rings and I knew who was calling, or I was thinking about a thing and then someone talks about it. Now I'm far more skeptical. Maybe these things are merely coincidence.

Alertness to fraud has also increased skepticism within the parapsychological community. This skepticism, although most frequently ventilated against the occult belief systems of the general public, also affects the field itself. One parapsychologist notes, "An essential requirement for the investigator is knowledge plus the ability to suspect deception from every possible angle—a kind of objective paranoia in the service of science" (Hastings, 1977:134).

This "objective paranoia in the service of science" can be considered an exaggeration of the norm of skepticism that Merton considered inherent in science. This skepticism is directed against claims of experimental subjects, the general public, and other investigators of the paranormal.

Skepticism About Experimental Subjects and the Public

Since no subject can be trusted not to engage in fraud, some parapsychologists consider that the only valid research occurs under tightly controlled laboratory conditions. This attitude creates a demarcation between laboratory and field research. Although the vigorous and active cases of alleged paranormal phenomena (e.g., poltergeists, hauntings, paranormal healing, etc.) occur outside the laboratory, priority within the field has been placed on quantified laboratory research. Phenomena obtained (or elicited) within the laboratory are generally weak, sporadic, and of little emotional significance. This illustrates a latent effect of the scientistic orientation on the field, that it is separated from the *actual* phenomena it wishes to investigate. Some parapsychologists distinguish between parapsychology, a field that conducts controlled experiments under laboratory conditions, and psychical research, a realm of inquiry which investigates experiences that occur outside of the laboratory. Parapsychology is considered to have higher status than does psychical research.

Parapsychologists tend to reject as evidence most of the experiences that lead the public to belief. The psychic experiences that over half of a sample of the American population report (McCready and Greeley, 1976) are granted an inferior status within the body of parapsychological evidence.

The canons of research in parapsychology require us not to favor a paranormal explanation for a case unless we have eliminated—either completely or as nearly so as makes no difference—all possibilities for the subject to have obtained through normal means the knowledge shown in the experience. This rule applies whether we are concerned with a telepathic dream, a death-coinciding apparition, a mediumistic communication, a claim to remember a previous life or any other experience in which the paranormal communication of information appears to have occurred. (Stevenson, 1983:1)

This means that parapsychologists cannot "favor a paranormal explanation" for almost all the apparent cases of "psi" that people experience.

Even the most remarkable anecdotal and observational evidence is often dismissed unless it occurs in a manner that cannot be duplicated by fraud. The magician and parapsychologist Arthur Hastings (1977) notes, "In the investigation of psychics, if an apparent psychic effect can be duplicated by sleight of hand under the same conditions, or can be reasonably explained by the principles of magic, then any conclusion as to its paranormal nature must be put aside. This is not a judgment on the event, but on the nature of the report as evidence for scientific conclusions. Anecdotal and observational evidence is important, but we do not yet have adequate ways of processing it into scientific knowledge" (Hastings, 1977:136).

A latent effect of this "paranoia in defense of science" is an extreme, often unchecked skepticism. This form of "unpacking" involves devising a scenario in which fraud could have occurred and then assuming that it did occur. Some critics who assume that fraud must have occurred within an investigation have slipped into *saying* that it *did* occur. Arthur Hastings (1977:134) cites an example that occurred during the SRI's investigation of Uri Geller: "In another experiment, Geller successfully ascertained the number on a die shaken in a metal file box. Randi and Gardner both assert that Geller handled the box and lifted the lid slightly, enough to see what face was up. The SRI film shows clearly that Geller does not touch the box. It is shaken by one of the experimenters, who simply sets it on the floor. Geller then writes a number on a pad. The box is opened and Geller's number is found to be correct."

James Randi has accused SRI of producing films with staged re-enactments. Puthoff and Targ at SRI have denied this accusation. A latent effect of this dialogue is to focus attention on an event that is actually a minor part of the SRI parapsychological research (Puthoff, 1979).

This form of bias does not occur only among skeptics. The parapsychologist Harry Price also claimed to detect fraud without evidence that fraud had occurred (Gregory, 1977). This form of bias has the latent effect of reducing psychics' desire to be investigated by parapsychologists.

A latent effect of methodological advances made by parapsychologists hoping to preclude fraud is that some critics demand that *every* possible precaution be used to prevent fraud even when it seems inappropriate in the experimental design. For example, a parapsychologist conducted an experiment using fairly simple methods, in accordance with normal psychological experimental procedures. All usual precautions were taken against bias, recording error, and so on. He submitted his research evidence (which supported the existence of psi) to *Science* for publication. It was given an unfavorable review by a referee, who stated, "The (currently not unusual) practice of having an expert conjurer present and an active participant was not followed. Such an expert might have asked that Swan, a professional psychic, be searched and that the hypothesis of non-paranormal means for affecting the results be investigated" (Zimmerman, PA Files). In this particular experiment, it is difficult to understand how searching the subject might affect his ability to commit fraud. The demonstrations of psi in most modern laboratories are statistical. They are not the sort in which a magician would have any expert ability, nor could a magician duplicate these demonstrations through conjuring.

Parapsychologists do not actively resist scientistic criteria but, like other scientists, seem to apply it selectively in demarcating allowable from unallowable practices. Like other scientists, they label individuals as deviant who investigate phenomena deemed to be too "extraordinary." Some consider the study of macro-PK to fall in this category. Macro-PK is psychokinesis that violates the "laws" of physics to such a degree that it can be detected by the unaided eye, such as the purported metal bending of children tested by John Hasted (1981). Some parapsychologists consider Hasted to lack sufficient "skepticism." Macro-PK research seems to deviate too far from the "mainstream" paradigm established by J. B. Rhine. Consequently, there is a tendency to assume that those who demonstrate macro-PK are cheating, and researchers who fail to detect fraud are often assumed to be incompetent. It appears that labeling some forms of inquiry as deviant fulfills functions for parapsychology just as it does for science as a whole. The latent effects of adhering to this attitude are similar for parapsychology and science. Innovative claims are restricted.

Skepticism Toward Fellow Researchers

Various respondents among the elite scientists (sixteen instances) mentioned fraud as a reason for resistance to the work of parapsychology even though no evaluation of fraud was asked for on the questionnaire. Various cases of fraud have occurred within parapsychology and have been revealed by the parapsychological researchers themselves (Rhine, 1973, 1974; Markwick, 1979). Most parapsychological researchers believe that fraud is no more prevalent in their field than in any other. The resistance of mainstream scientists, however, has led to great emphasis on fraud as an explanation for psi phenomena. Methodological advances in proof-oriented research and efforts to train researchers in these methodologies have increased the critics' need to cite fraud as an explanation for psi effects. Margaret Mead (1977:xvi) notes, "I think it may be fair to say that as the experimental methods to investigate so-called psychic powers have improved, so have the violence of controversy, the proclamations of disbelief, and the accusations of either conscious or unconscious fraud."

Parapsychologists themselves view the problem of fraud in a different light. Although they are always aware that acts of major fraud by their colleagues are possible, minor forms of fraud are viewed by some to be more of a problem. One form occurs through poor statistical techniques, such as improper data selection, manipulation, and reporting. Some parapsychologists point out that such (often unconscious) fraud is highly prevalent within the social and biological sciences and, since many researchers have been trained within these fields, such poor techniques tend to intrude into the realm of parapsychology. The emphasis on fraud has increased parapsychology's vigilance for even minor forms of statistical sloppiness. This reaction to deviant labeling will be discussed later in this chapter.

In some cases, parapsychologists have attempted to produce more convincing "proofs" through experimental designs that require multiple researchers. This often occurs when a "gifted" subject is located who reportedly can demonstrate psi under highly controlled conditions (two examples: Kelly, Kanthamani, Child, and Young, 1975; Morris, Roll, Klein, and Wheeler, 1972). In order for fraud to occur, the various researchers would need to conspire with each other. A latent effect is that many research hours are tied up in producing the multi-experimenter "proof."

Another latent effect of this "paranoia" is restriction of theory development. Science requires both trust and skepticism to operate. Scientists must trust their fellow researchers since they cannot replicate every experiment. The low rate of replicability within parapsychology often leads to a suspension of this trust. The argument that a particular confirmation of an experimental hypothesis supports a particular theory is negated when the audience refuses to believe that the result is replicable. One parapsychologist notes, "People don't believe what they can't do themselves. That holds for this field also. Parapsychologists don't take each other's work seriously."

This form of skepticism sometimes causes parapsychologists to use personal factors in evaluating others' research. Personal contact becomes highly important. One researcher notes, "Not even everyone within the PA is okay. Some that they let in at the beginning may not be that good. I can only be sure of the people I have worked with in the past."

The ability to "seem scientific," to inspire trust in one's professional bearing, takes on greater importance. The scientist's standing outside the field of parapsychology also has great bearing. This factor, which is also inherent in mainstream science, has increased importance within parapsychology.

The distrust of colleagues' claims thwarts theoretical development within parapsychology since the perfect proof of any hypothesis, although desirable, is impossible in practice. The deviant status of the field makes the "unpacking" strategy seem appropriate when parapsychologists critique each other's work.

Charles Tart conducted various experiments which seemed to indicate that immediate feedback after ESP success aided some subjects in increasing their predictive ability (Tart, 1976). The study seemed to draw increased criticism owing to the high levels of statistical significance that were claimed. Other parapsychologists used the "unpacking" strategy in examining his research. They noted it was possible, in at least one case, that an assistant researcher may have psychokinetically influenced the generation of the random number pattern, since this pattern was not "random." This could have produced the appearance that "learning" had occurred. This and various other efforts to "unpack" Tart's study have discouraged efforts to develop a means of teaching ESP that otherwise might have been stimulated. This observation is somewhat speculative, in that controversy still surrounds claims of learning ESP through any particular method.

Effects of Skepticism on the Methodology of Parapsychology

Within the larger historical context, Rhine's establishment of the parapsychological paradigm can be seen as a result of his own and others' skepticism. His early observations of mediumship phenomena led him to believe that fraud could easily occur within the conditions required for a séance. Indeed, he believed that he had witnessed fraud during a séance conducted by a medium who was accepted by many of the psychical researchers during his era (Tietze, 1973; Mauskopf and McVaugh, 1981). He eventually went on to devise standardized laboratory procedures, which, when followed, would seem to preclude fraud on the part of the subject as an explanation for any ostensible paranormal results. The skeptical orientation has given parapsychological research a higher status than psychical research could achieve, though the distinction is not always clear. The *Journal of the Society for Psychical Research* and the *Journal of the American Society for Psychical Research* publish articles that could be classified in both categories. The *Journal of Parapsychology* sometimes publishes social-psychological surveys regarding spontaneous experiences associated with psi, but not investigations of haunting or poltergeist cases.

Owing to the interaction between parapsychologists and their critics, the methodologies involving proof-oriented research within the laboratory setting have evolved a great deal over the years. Methodologies used by parapsychologists include major aspects of "symbolic hardware" of science (double blinds, control groups, statistical techniques, precautions against experimental bias, precautions against recording errors, complex randomization processes, etc.). Because of the requirement to produce "exceptional" proofs (corresponding to the "exceptional" claim that psi exists), use of this symbolic hardware (a term devised by Collins and Pinch, 1979) often goes beyond that of normal scientists.

One reaction of parapsychologists to their critics is the manner in which the field attempts to prevent selective data reporting. The *European Journal of Parapsychology* advises potential contributors to submit the design of a planned study before it is carried out. The rationale of the study and all the related hypotheses must be stated, as well as the planned number of trials, subjects, and statistical tests to be conducted. This precludes selective reporting of those hypotheses that achieve statistical significance. The acceptance or rejection of a manuscript takes place prior to the phase when the experimental data are collected. Thus, the temptation of a researcher to engage in selective data reporting in order to get his or her work published is removed. The *Journal of Parapsychology* requires that every statistical analysis be clearly labeled as preplanned or post hoc. Research that is deemed methodologically valid will be published in full or in abstracted form whether the results indicate the existence of psi or not. A latent effect of this reaction to deviant labeling is that parapsychological researchers may lose the spontaneity that some investigators believe is important in producing psi.

The PA has made every effort to support and encourage the publication of nonsignificant results (no other scientific group or organization has publicly taken such a stance). Parapsychologists are accused of selective reporting very frequently, particularly when successful lines of research are involved, such as the ESP Ganzfeld experiments (ESP seems to increase through this particular type of sensory regulation). Special efforts have been made to detect selective reporting. Blackmore (1980) sent a questionnaire to "any person who it was thought might have been associated with Ganzfeld studies" asking about studies not completed or not published. On the basis of the number and the proportion of significant results in the unpublished studies which she uncovered, she concluded that selective reporting could not account for the overall success occurring in this line of research. Selective reporting is generally ignored in other scientific fields.

Other "exceptional" methodologies involve extreme precautions against sensory cueing. Certain practices have become second nature in parapsychological experiments that would not even be considered in other fields. For example, any individual aware of target information cannot be allowed to come into contact with any person or object that might later enter into the presence of (and possibly bias) the subject in the experiment. The subject can never be trusted not to seek out these forms of bias, and parapsychologists have often gone to extreme lengths to preclude them. Construction of special shielding devices, continuous supervision of both subject and agent, and even having an agent "transmit" from one continent while the subject "receives" the message on another continent are some of the precautions that have been used.

Critics of parapsychology have at times developed complex scenarios in order to explain psi as a form of sensory cueing. Other fields such as sociology and psychology ignore this problem, although Rosenthal may be bringing it to the forefront with his demonstration of interpersonal expectancy effects (Rosenthal and Rubin, 1978). Some parapsychologists have turned their attention to research in precognition, since the hypothesis of sensory cueing cannot be used to explain these phenomena. Sensory cueing is impossible when the targets are selected after the calls.

The need to produce "exceptional" proofs often requires that the modern parapsychologist use devices which generate random sequences from atomic decay or electronic noise. Many contemporary investigators consider J. B. Rhine's use of cards and dice to be outdated when compared to more modern methodologies. Modern "proofs" are considered more "exceptional" by some parapsychologists than those produced by Rhine. A latent effect of this advance in methodology is the dependence on expensive electronic hardware. The computer has become an important tool for conducting psi research. Some physiological studies on psi produce large quantities of data that would be impossible to analyze without a computer (for example, Heseltine and Kirk, 1980). This struggle to emphasize quantitative procedures has placed many types of parapsychological experimentation beyond the reach of poorly funded researchers.

Just as the methodological advances cited earlier, which were designed to prevent fraud, have led to critical dismissal of some experimentation, so have critics pointed to methodological innovation preventing recording error as grounds for dismissing other research. For example, a researcher submitted his experimental report to a mainstream scientific journal for publication. A referee replied, "It seems incredible that results are still being recorded by hand. In an experiment with this degree of electronic sophistication, to have added this well-recognized safeguard should have been easy" (Zimmerman, PA Files).

Parapsychology's struggle with its critics precludes the possibility of a "perfect" experiment proving the existence of psi, since in principle it is always possible to require a further degree of exactitude or precaution. Methodological advances in research oriented toward producing proofs merely evoke new rhetorical strategies for critics to use in rejecting any particular parapsychological study. The executive secretary of the PA wrote this rebuttal to the referee's comment: "Recording results by hand is currently not unusual, particularly in lightly-funded laboratories. 'It seems incredible' that it would be offered as a reason for rejection" (Zimmerman, PA Files).

Researchers who devise highly proof-oriented procedures, such as Helmut Schmidt (1969), are generally either ignored or accused of fraud. The philosophical orientation of the critical argument makes this stance seem logical to the skeptics. Consequently, the increase in methodological rigor in proof-oriented research has merely forced the critics of parapsychology to use the fraud hypothesis more frequently.

One effect of skepticism on the methodology used by parapsychologists has been the distinction within the field of two broad goals within the research effort. "Proof-oriented" research has the purpose of producing evidence to convince the critic that psi is real. "Process-oriented" research is basically a search for mechanisms explaining psi. Various respondents reported that during the 1960s and 1970s the field tended to shift its emphasis from proof- to process-oriented research.

Part of the reason Rhine's paradigm became so established was that it is proof-oriented. Rhine wanted to prove that psi was real and convert his critics. He invited criticism and made every attempt to comply with critics' demands (for example, he frequently used two people separately transcribing any verbal call at a target to reduce the possibility of a recording error). Although Rhine attempted to determine correlates of ESP, one result of his effort was his claim that ESP was unrelated to distance, a claim considered by some to be astonishing. Rather than discovering any underlying process associated with ESP he merely "proved" that it was more "extraordinary" than many had thought. When Rhine turned his attention to psychokinesis and precognition and claimed to have demonstrated the existence of these phenomena, mainstream scientific rejection merely intensified. Precognition is considered especially extraordinary, since sensory cueing cannot be used to explain the effect. Rhine claimed to have proved the existence of these phenomena but not to have explained them. Skeptically oriented critics were forced to conclude that Rhine was either a charlatan or a fool.

Rhine felt that the best defense against such charges lay in process-oriented research: ". . . perhaps the most telling reason for the failure of the evidence to secure public confidence is that it has shown merely that these phenomena do occur, and almost nothing more. None of the work had gone far enough to show what might be the nature of such unorthodox phenomena, to find their relations or laws, or even the conditions under which they might be demonstrated" (Rhine, 1937:25). Yet, at the same time, the intensity of the criticism surrounding his work caused him to remain methodologically orthodox. Some parapsychologists whom I interviewed considered Rhine inflexible in his methodological approach due to his "proof-orientation." Certainly many of Rhine's experiments involved searching for correlates of psi and it seems arguable that they were totally "proof-oriented," though the reaction of his critics may have caused him to lean in that direction.

A closely knit group within Rhine's research laboratory eventually reacted against his orthodoxy and left en masse during the fall of 1967. Some parapsychologists I interviewed referred to this as the "Great Leaving." Most maintained close contact with one another and have developed lines of research oriented more toward understanding the processes associated with psi. As much irony seems to exist in this orientation as in proof-oriented research. Seeking processes explaining psi seems in tune with the scientistic, mechanistic orientation some feel is inherent in science, even though parapsychology has an antiscientistic tradition (chapter 2). Process-oriented research is basically a search for mechanisms involving psi. The search seems to be intensified by parapsychologists' recognition that proof-oriented research has only limited impact on the mainstream scientific community.

Quotations from various parapsychologists illustrate a common orientation:

In parapsychology, for the last few years, they've been saying "let's stop reproving it and really begin investigation."

I've long ago given up collecting evidence. I'm more interested in the mechanisms.

We must uncover the mechanisms that govern the interaction between human consciousness and the environment. I feel certain that we will some day understand those mechanisms more fully.

The search for mechanisms associated with psi is part of what the parapsychologist Stanford (1977b) labels the "psi-conducive syndrome." Basically, the scientistic assumption prevails within this dominant paradigm of parapsychology. Many parapsychologists I interviewed support this orientation. The assumption is that, through diligent investigation, factors conducive to psi will be uncovered, replicability of experimentation can then be increased, and a valid theory explaining the factors which are psi-conducive will emerge. Some parapsychologists might argue that this process is indeed occurring (e.g., Honorton, 1977). Basically, this orientation hypothesizes that psi will eventually either be integrated within mainstream science through this uncovering of its physical mechanisms or else science will be changed by the parapsychological research effort. Some parapsychologists explain:

I still don't think these things are paranormal. I don't think they're any different from anything else, but I do feel they're just as important as anything else. I see from physics [quantum mechanics] that the thing is possible and I see that this thing holds up under lab conditions. It's really the physical aspects that I find fascinating. . . . I never had any intention of becoming a parapsychologist. Each step along the way has grown by itself. My main interest is quantum mechanics.

My world view is actually rather materialistic. I feel certain that the phenomena studied by parapsychologists will eventually be integrated into physics. There's nothing inherently mystical about psi. Mind is probably an epiphenomenon of brain activity.

There has to be some underlying structures to this phenomenon. By using the methods of science, we have found some and will be able to find more. There's electro-chemical processes which need to be uncovered. It may be incredibly complex, but we have to start somewhere.

Ironically, a high percentage of the parapsychologists that I interviewed believed that the major advances in the field during the last fifty years have been methodological rather than theoretical. Some said that no true theoretical advances have occurred. One stated:

Parapsychological methodology is a derivation of a certain way of thinking that occurs within psychology. . . . It's a web of methods but it's not catching anything.

Others see a new methodological orthodoxy emerging that restricts creativity. For example:

What's been discovered? Very little. . . . The methodology is better because it's more automated. What could you do with just cards and dice? Now you can do whatever you can imagine. There have been some advances . . . but . . . the present approach hasn't gotten us that far in the last forty years. But when you do things differently, it puts you in conflict with others.

Even though some parapsychologists see little or no progress, the process of debate within the field has produced a limited consensus about psi. Ironically, this consensus contributes to the process of labeling the field as deviant.

Scientism and Theory Within Parapsychology

The forms of theory within parapsychology reflect the process of labeling the field as deviant and of parapsychologists' attempt to shed that label. Parapsychologists have tried vigorously to create theoretical orientations which would fit the scientistic mold. A latent effect of these unsuccessful attempts is that the field is further stigmatized. The factors that they claim to be psi-related are antiscientistic because they hint that it may be impossible to investigate and understand psi in a scientific manner. Second, these factors make the field seem similar to deviant realms of inquiry which have failed in the past. Third, some of these factors associate the field with religious or occult belief systems and their rituals (prayer, meditation, chanting, etc.). Even though researchers in the field continuously struggle to create scientific theories, their failure to generate an acceptable theoretical orientation has contributed to the covert antiscientistic nature of the field.

Parapsychologists claim that certain "factors" related to, or aspects of, psi are emerging through their experimental efforts (Stanford, 1977b). Other factors are being ruled out. Because the ontological status of psi is still in doubt, the status of each of these "factors" is also uncertain. My interviews uncovered a pattern of response in researchers' tendency to mention these factors as evidence of parapsychological "findings," although many claims are still tentative. The evaluation of these factors has become part of the rhetorical and political process that is occurring within parapsychology. Since uncertainty clouds much that occurs within this field, the list below is presented as a form of "folklore" which has emerged from parapsychological research. These claims are presented (unreferenced) as sociological interview findings, since this present study claims to be sociological rather than parapsychological. The validity of each claim is not at issue. It will be argued that the form which this "folklore" has taken has affected the field of parapsychology by contributing to its role as a deviant science. These "factors" or claims constitute elements that parapsychological theories hope to explain some day:

1. ESP is not related to distance, time, or complexity of the task.
2. Certain "signs of psi" are related to the statistical demonstration of it. One finding is that psi performance seems to "decline." It has been found to decrease within the run, within the experiment, and within the subject's experimental career.
3. Psi is related to expectancy. If a person believes in or expects psi to occur, its probability of occurring is increased.
4. ESP is related to personality in that extroverted people seem to manifest ESP more often in the laboratory. This factor may involve just the testing situation, in that the extroverted person may be more suitable for creating the "harmonious" social situation that some parapsychologists believe facilitates psi.
5. Laboratory ESP is facilitated by deep relaxation, sensory restriction, or hypnosis. Spontaneous psychic experience, which occurs in actual life situations, is often associated with emergency situations. Psi is said to be related to altered states of consciousness.
6. A general assumption of many (but not all) parapsychologists is that everyone has at least some potential to demonstrate psi. Some feel that psi may be acting continuously in an unconscious manner.
7. Psi is related to specific researchers or perhaps the social situations surrounding specific researchers. Some researchers cannot produce psi consistently. Some produce psi fairly regularly.

The general thrust of many of these claims is that scientists who disbelieve in psi are incapable of creating proper conditions. As presented by these claims, psi does not seem equivalent to "normal" methods of communication, psychological variables, or means of affecting the physical world. The unusualness of these claims contributes to the stigma associated with the field.

Parapsychology, like sociology, has many theoretical orientations. Because of the low rates of replicability within parapsychology, no theoretical orientation has been granted high status. Some theories are granted higher status than others, owing to their ability to generate testable hypotheses (for example, Stanford's PMIR model [1974] and conformance model [1978]) or their ability to coincide with theoretical orientations within mainstream science (such as various "observational" theories described by Millar, 1978). None of these theoretical orientations can be said to explain fully the empirical findings of the field, and their failure to do so allows critics to use the "lack of a valid theoretical orientation" argument.

The "experimenter" effect, "expectancy" effect, and the relationship to unconsciousness and altered consciousness make theories dealing with parapsychological claims appear extraordinary. For example, White (1977:298) states:

A favorable subject-experimenter relationship favors psi test results. . . . It is hypothesized that successful experimenters are able to pose questions in their research which are of great personal importance and that the possibility that that question might be answered in a particular experiment may induce an altered state in the experimenter which in turn affects the subject(s). In other words, experimenter expectancies may be necessary in order to induce psi results, and the more unconscious they are, the more effective they may be.

This orientation makes parapsychology different from other fields, since no chemist or biologist could resort to such a claim. An equivalent situation exists in Rosenthal's hypothesis that "expectancy effects" can intrude into experimental results (Rosenthal and Rubin, 1978). Although this claim is controversial, it is basically psychological and somewhat limited. First, it does not hypothesize that the effect can occur without any sensory contact. Second, the parapsychological "experimenter effect" has such large possible scope that *any* result could be attributed to it. A radical version of the experimenter effect might lead to the conclusion that theory building within parapsychology is pointless; replicating any specific hypothesis would depend merely on the experimenter's motivation regarding that hypothesis.

Some parapsychologists have sought to limit the experimenter effect by hypothesizing that researchers who are psi-conductive have different personality traits from ones who are psi-inhibitory. Indeed, Schmeidler and Maher (1981) found psi-conductive researchers' body language elicited higher ratings from a panel of judges in regard to positive adjectives (such as "flexible," "free," "friendly," "relaxed," "warm"), while psi-inhibitory researchers elicited higher negative ratings ("rigid," "cold," "overconfident," "tense," "irritable"). This conclusion is tentative but holds the possibility of leading parapsychological theory out of the experimenter-effect dilemma.

The prospect that some experimenters will be incapable of replicating certain experiments is still unusual within science and is often associated with what Langmuir (1953) has termed "pathological" science. Pathological science produces invalid knowledge derived from errors owing to the neglect or violation of methodological canons. Proponents of phenomena later deemed as pathological science often claimed an experimenter effect. For example, N-ray researchers claimed that only some researchers could produce the effect under certain (vaguely specified) conditions.

The list of parapsychological "findings" described previously (psi is beyond space and time, involves an expectancy and experimenter effect, tends to decline, etc.) gives the field many features of pathological science:

(1) The maximum effect is produced by a causative agent of barely detectable intensity, and the magnitude of the effect is . . . independent of the intensity of the cause.

(2) The effect is of a magnitude that remains close to the limit of detectability.

(3) Nevertheless, "claims of great accuracy" are made.

(4) "Fantastic" theories contrary to experience are used to explain the phenomena.

(5) Criticisms are met by *ad hoc* excuses.

(6) The ratio of supporters to critics rises up to somewhere near 50% and then falls gradually to oblivion. (Langmuir, 1953; quoted from Zuckerman, 1977:112)

A latent effect of the research results generated by parapsychologists has been that some of the field's critics label it as a pathological science. The "psi" found by parapsychologists under laboratory conditions is "of barely detectable intensity" and the magnitude of the effect is only sporadically related to the intensity of the cause. This magnitude of effect remains close to the limit of detectability even though parapsychologists conduct sophisticated statistical analyses of their data. The existence of psi is considered contrary to experience by many and might be deemed a "fantastic" theory. The experimenter effect might be deemed as an ad hoc excuse since no parapsychologist can predict exactly when psi will occur. Although a majority of American scientists currently believe in the existence of psi, this level of belief could decline should parapsychology universally be deemed as a "pathological science." The theoretical orientation presented within this present study (figure 2-1) suggests that as long as psi experiences occur within the general public and their investigation is supported by lay groups, belief in it will not decline to zero.

Many parapsychologists are aware of this dilemma. The results of over a century of scientific inquiry into the nature of psi have not brought about the scientific revolution that had originally been sought and expected. To some, parapsychology appears to be a protoscience which may never become legitimate. One parapsychologist expressed his opinion of research into the processes of psi, "I don't think parapsychology will ever become legitimate. I think that ultimately we will not learn very much about psi. I base my opinion on my reading of 100 years of formal research. I doubt that we'll get any more replicable results than we have today."

This attitude is frequently supported by respondents through their discussion of the history of parapsychological "progress." In outlining the history of research findings of the field, some parapsychologists noted that the results seemed to indicate that psi has a nonmaterial nature which conflicts with assumptions inherent within science. The conflict might be so severe that legitimacy may be beyond the reach of parapsychological inquiry. The issue is beyond resolution within science. One parapsychologist noted:

To me, there have been three phases of progress: the demonstration phase ended in the late 50s. This involved the statistical demonstration of psi. Then, we moved into the process-oriented research phase. It looked as if we were making progress, but if we take the experimenter effect seriously, it means a third stage where we're not ever sure of the focus of psi. Any psi could be an effect of the investigator working behind the scenes psychologically. Suppose psi occurs sometimes. We must ask, why does it fail? Or perhaps the investigator is fulfilling his own process-oriented theories through his own psi ability. This isn't to say that process-oriented research can't give the appearance of progress. Honorton's internally deployed attention states orientation, when taken as a whole, have a pretty good replication record. But my own guess is that it will not be very well understood scientifically. Maybe it will be understood in a more personal sense—as a religion or a philosophy. That might be better anyway.

Although this is not a dominant theme in parapsychological discussion, it is not unusual to hear parapsychologists argue that parapsychology seems to reveal the limitations of science. The two parapsychologists quoted previously agree with the twelve elite scientists who said that although psi may be real, parapsychology may never become a legitimate science since it seems to exceed this limitation. The scientific method may be unsuitable for exploring all realms of human "understanding."

An alternative means of "understanding," which might be more suitable, lies within religious mysticism. All major religious traditions have devised means of explaining paranormal experience, and many of these explanations coincide with the belief that psychic phenomena may defy scientific or logical analysis. Some explanations even claim that attempts at such analysis may be detrimental to the researcher; for example, during the pretest phase of the questionnaire, some scientists said that psi should not be investigated because it is the "work of the Devil." A second example of a religious orientation that would support the reality of psi but not its scientific exploration exists in various Eastern traditions. For example, although a meditator is believed to acquire psychic ability as a result of practice, many sects warn that this can be detrimental rather than beneficial. The Buddha did not encourage his disciples to strive after psychic powers, since the possession of them might distract the monk from his original purpose of reaching nirvana. The Buddha also prohibited even demonstrating these powers: "You must not show the miracles of the *iddhi* [psychic powers] to the laity, O *bhikku* [monk], miracles that surpass the power of the common man. He who behaves in such fashion will make himself guilty of an evil deed" (Vinaya, II, 212, and Vinaya Texts, III, 81, quoted by Eliade, 1969:174, 175).

The clash between the Western orientation and Eastern mysticism is illustrated by offers of money for demonstrating psychic powers. Eliade (1969:102) presents a poster (apparently from the British colonial era in India) in which 1,000 rupees are offered to "anyone who, by yoga powers, will raise himself three feet from the ground, and remain suspended for ten minutes." The magician James Randi has made a modern offer of $10,000 to anyone who can produce a paranormal phenomenon to the satisfaction of a committee under conditions that he accepts as suitable.

Some parapsychologists would suggest that although psychic phenomena are real, efforts to "prove" them (especially by using money to gain such evidence) will not succeed. The nature of psi is claimed to be such that it defies such demands for "proof." This "nature," uncovered by parapsychologists' research, has an elusive quality that contributes to labeling the field deviant.

An additional latent effect of efforts by parapsychologists to uncover the processes behind psi has been the support their findings give to occult and religious belief systems. The rituals of various religions could also be said to gain justification from evidence generated by parapsychological research. Effects from prayer could be deemed a form of psychokinesis. Fervent prayer may be considered as self-hypnosis which may be associated with psi. Meditation, rhythmic chanting, and altered states of consciousness, which occur within some religious rituals, have been found to be associated with psi under experimental conditions. A general assumption of the ideology of science is that religion and science are mutually exclusive, yet parapsychology hints at a fusion of these two ways of "knowing."

Religion is also supported by parapsychological *theory*. Some parapsychologists (Honorton, 1977; Whiteman, 1977) point out the value of Eastern mystical philosophy as an aid in formulating parapsychological theory. Others (LeShan, 1969) point out the striking similarity between statements made by modern quantum physicists (whose findings many parapsychologists feel are supportive of their field) and various mystics. The body of information assembled by parapsychologists (apparition studies, out-of-body experience, mediumship phenomena, near-death experience) is regarded by many as supporting life after death. Stevenson (1977) has assembled and analyzed numerous cases suggesting reincarnation.

The prevailing attitude toward life after death among parapsychologists is basically scientistic. Theorists have gone to great lengths to explain all life-after-death experiences through ESP and psychokinesis. This explanation, known as the "super-ESP" hypothesis, attributes all apparitions, poltergeists, mediumship phenomena, and so on to vast extrasensory powers possessed by persons still alive. The majority of parapsychologists seem to support this hypothesis, though they generally recognize that it cannot be tested today within the scientific framework. Although some critics consider (perhaps rightfully so) that a tacit goal of parapsychology is the scientific verification of religious belief, the scientistic orientation of the field prevents it from actually working toward this goal.

Even some of the most scientistic parapsychologists recognize the unique role of parapsychology: "This isn't like other sciences. There's something we're missing about it. There's a 'spirit' thing we're missing. The mystics say that once you get to the place where you can do it [psi] you don't want to."

Others view the parapsychological realm of inquiry as merely ahead of its time: "It bothers me that we are unable to convince our critics. Although psi is real, this field may never become a legitimate science in the sense that word holds today; maybe it's more of a proto-science or some form of future science. Our present scientific methodology may not be appropriate for the actual goals that we have, the goal of understanding psi."

Ultimately, it would seem that the covert goal of parapsychology is to change, not just science, but the entire society. The name that J. B. Rhine chose for the organization that he founded hints at this objective: the Foundation for Research on the Nature of Man. One parapsychologist illustrates the careful scientistic nature of the field while also expressing the tacit goal: "We are revolutionists but we don't reject scientific methodology. The revolution will be in the way mankind conceives of himself. But this will be very difficult. We must be careful not to exceed the actual meaning of our data."

It is paradoxical that while parapsychology attempts to adhere to the scientistic orientation, its experimental data are viewed as invalidating certain aspects of the metaphysical foundations of science. Some parapsychologists consider modern physics as a pathway or bridge that will lead to legitimacy. Whiteman (1977) views quantum mechanics as having devised an outline for this new world view. He believes that as this new ontology gains greater acceptance, parapsychology will be granted legitimacy.

This new world view, associated with a new image of human nature, must permeate the scientific establishment as well as the general society. The view of the person as a machine, composed of economic, political, social, and psychological fragments, will be replaced by a concept of the inner unity of human nature; the person in this image will be seen as autonomous, self-healing, and free-willed (Young, 1981). This concept transcends present empirical data generated by the field, yet is internally consistent with the mystical orientations assumed in some parapsychological theories.

This tacit goal has a latent effect. Parapsychology is visualized by many as antiscientistic and is rejected, partly for that reason. It is felt that science should be "value-free."

To overcome this rejection, parapsychologists have continued attempts to generate "better" scientific proofs and to gain a "better" understanding of the processes behind psi. This is not new. Psychical researchers have always hoped that the logic of experimentation would force acceptance of psi. For example, in his second presidential address to the SPR, Henry Sidgwick (1883:67) stated: "If they will not yield to half-a-dozen decisive experiments by investigators of trained intelligence and hitherto unquestioned probity, let us try to give them half-a-dozen more recorded by other witnesses; if a dozen will not do, let us try to give them a score; if a score will not do, let us make up the tale to fifty." Today hundreds of experiments by researchers of "trained intelligence and hitherto unquestioned probity" claim to have demonstrated psi effects, yet critics have not "yielded."

Rather, the latent effect of this increased acceptance of scientific method and ideology by parapsychology has led to increased resistance by scientists. The number of elite scientists who have been attracted to parapsychology has declined since Sidgwick's declaration in 1883, despite the field's increased adherence to rigid scientific methodology.

This is not to say that parapsychology has chosen an incorrect strategy. On the contrary, parapsychologists have chosen a strategy leading to lasting social relationships that insure the continued existence of their field as a science. Yet, legitimacy eludes them.

By adhering to the ideology of science, parapsychologists contribute indirectly to the stigma their field has gained. These latent effects, revealed in the recruitment, socialization, increased skepticism, concern with problems of fraud, and theory development, have contributed to restricting progress in the field. The world view associated with the field also contributes to its present problems, tacitly exposing the possible limitations of science.

At the same time, parapsychologists aid science by demonstrating the limits of activity that are acceptable within the scientific domain. Just as "deviant" behavior defines the meaning of "normal" behavior, so does deviant science demarcate the domain of mainstream science. The process of labeling parapsychology as deviant and its reaction to that label creates this scientific borderline. The manifest and latent effects of parapsychology's reaction to its labeling contribute to the stability of social situations surrounding the field and its longevity.

7

The Interaction Between Parapsychology and the Public

Parapsychology's adherence to the scientistic orientation has produced latent effects within its interaction with the general public. Scientists wish to avoid professional association and affiliation with nonscientific groups. The wish to differentiate insiders from outsiders is natural for any profession. With the success of science as a problem-solving endeavor, certain forms of etiquette have evolved regarding scientific interaction with lay groups, and especially with the media. It is considered improper, for example, for the scientist to make his or her findings excessively available to lay publics (especially through the mass media) before members of the relevant scientific community have assessed the work. This would violate the norm of skepticism, since it would bypass qualified peer appraisal. Scientific journals generally prohibit releasing news of discoveries until the scientific article concerning the discovery has been published. Even after publication, scientists are expected not to seek publicity actively. This form of scientific etiquette places scientific knowledge in an elevated position, since special means have been used for its production.

Various latent effects result from the parapsychological attempt to participate in this process. In reaction to being labeled as deviant, parapsychologists attempt to adhere strictly to all the forms of etiquette that are appropriate for scientists. This means restricting their interaction with the media and with lay groups. A latent effect of this reaction results from the different values held by media elites, the general public, and the scientific community. Some members of

197

the public who have psi experiences find difficulty integrating them with their everyday life. Elites within the media consider psi a source of popular entertainment appealing to a large segment of the public. Scientific parapsychologists consider psi an anomaly requiring explanation. These value differences and the limited interaction of scientific parapsychology with the public give psi a distorted public image. This image pictures psi as an "occult" phenomenon that has little possibility of being integrated into mainstream science.

The result is a paradox for the field of parapsychology. If parapsychologists use the media, they are accused of seeking improper publicity. If they do not use them, they risk losing the public support required for the field to survive.

The belief that the media and public are of little importance in the scientific search for truth has had a latent effect on parapsychology. Parapsychologists who seem to devote too much time to seeking publicity are regarded as poor scientists. Status within the field tends to be inversely related to interaction with the media. Scientific reputation is gained through research and acknowledgment by other scientists.

The media's ability to damage the parapsychologist's professional reputation has led the average parapsychologist to view the press negatively. He or she feels that there is little personal benefit from interacting with the media. Consequently, the public image of psi has developed through media presentations that have little to do with the results of scientific research. One parapsychologist, who has been in the field for over three decades, notes the basic changes in public and media attitudes since her early association with Rhine's laboratory:

The science editors of the newspapers—Waldemar Kaempffert, of the *New York Times*, for instance—used to write very professional, objective types of things. One of my jobs would be to send out simplified abstracts of experimental reports pointing out what was new in the research to the science editors. But gradually, parapsychology became less newsworthy and the older writers moved on. Now you have the Jeane Dixon type of thing. Just last Friday, I saw a big headline: "Psychic Makes 50 Predictions." We didn't used to have much of that. The nearest we came was a relatively conservative layout in *Life Magazine*. A lot of sloppy business has come up in the last ten years or so. The number of books on the market by non-lab-type people has proliferated tremendously. They claim to be parapsychologists and the public is taking all sorts of dubious stuff to be parapsychology. Years ago, people who knew me used to ask: "Parapsychology—What *is* that?" Recently, I went back to a college reunion and one of my former classmates said: "Oh! I remember you. You're the one who's into the weird stuff." I think this is because so many people associate parapsychology with the uncontrolled sensational material being published now.

A second parapsychologist describes the media image of psi and counterposes it with his own image that has evolved from his research.

The media is doing a great deal of harm. They emphasize an aspect of psychic phenomena that corresponds with images that people are comfortable with. These types of images enable people to put a distance between themselves and the psi phenomenon. It seems scary, but also safe and fun. It's like finding diamonds or oil or some other precious entity. But psi is viewed as some entity, a thing outside of ourselves.

If the phenomenon of ESP actually occurs, it places a great burden of responsibility on us. It could be occurring all the time without our realizing it. One way of running away from this responsibility is having the media tell us how fun or safe this phenomenon is.

But psi is probably not like that. My immediate mind activity could become part of your environment. My anger or my wish to manipulate you may affect you whether you are physically present or not. We have a great responsibility dealing with this and with ourselves. . . .

We need to correct the image of the subject matter we are dealing with. It needs a revolutionary shift of emphasis. . . . The real shift comes with a shift of experience for ourselves. It's like considering whether the sun moves around the earth or the earth around the sun. If we don't see ourselves cut off from other entities, we can better experience ourselves—we can experience that connected web that is ourselves. . . . The experimenter must become aware that he and others can become aware of this connection.

But generally, newspapers are no help and most often, something is misquoted.

The distorted public image of psi springs partly from the inability of scientific parapsychology to communicate clearly its findings to the public. This is due, in part, to the "etiquette" of science and to the media's desire to entertain the public. Parapsychologists have found that most experiences called "psychic" are somewhat mundane and that even poltergeist phenomena are rarely harmful. The descriptions of anomalous experiences given by the group of elite scientists polled in this study are typical of possible cases of psi (see Appendix B).

Generally, they startle only the individual who experiences them. The statistical correlations demonstrating psi in the laboratory usually bore the public. Yet, psi's media image is of phenomena that are demonic, malevolent, and beyond the possible concern of science since they are apparently fantasies. For example, in the film *Scanners* a character uses psychokinesis to make someone's head explode. In *The Exorcist* paranormal phenomena are associated with the devil. The film *Carrie* shows PK's potential for murder since scores of people are destroyed by Carrie's psychokinetic ability. *The Amityville Horror* portrays a modern haunting case in which a family is driven out of its house by malevolent entities. One parapsychologist noted, "The real horror of *The Amityville Horror* was that they allowed people to think that it was true even when major aspects of the movie are almost certainly very distorted."

Stephen King (1981), author of numerous paranormal thrillers (*Firestarter*, *The Shining*, *Salem's Lot*, *Carrie*), analyzed the function of this form of entertainment. He feels that psychic horror stories appeal to strong and universal archetypes, that they aid people in coping with real problems through observing fantasy terror. He feels his books are popular because they help people understand their own taboos and fears, allowing a therapeutic catharsis. King (1981) believes, for example, that the film *The Amityville Horror* "allows people to touch the unknown in a simple, uncomplicated way" (p. 133), which is beneficial in relieving homeowners' real anxieties. A latent effect of this public image is that psi is associated with ridiculous topics. King (1981) reviews not only *The Amityville Horror* but many other nonclassics such as *The Giant Spider Invasion* and *Godzilla vs. the Smog Monster*, which he feels fulfill the same functions.

Because of these types of distortions, parapsychologists interact cautiously with the media.

You have to be careful of public relations in this business. Frequently, you'll find there's a normal way to explain this phenomenon [ostensible psi] when it is reported outside of the laboratory. . . . We're very skeptical.

Many parapsychologists have been burnt by the media. The qualified are very cautious, but it can be used as a technique to get funds. I'm very ambivalent . . . we have never sought out the media.

This researcher then went on to describe a paper he had presented before the AAAS. He reviewed the actual scientific evidence concerning psi phenomena, alpha levels, and a specific course that is reputed to teach the use of psi.

I said some very explicit things about the danger of those types of courses. But, a major press service came out with a release saying I said those courses drive people crazy. That's not what I said. I wrote them and got back a snide letter. They said they don't normally retract articles. With a little change, they can make things very controversial. . . . Last summer, I was interviewed by telephone for a major news magazine. The reporter had his own ax to grind; he wanted to believe that the socialization process caused psi to disappear in children. We had not pursued publicity at all, but some people I respect told me he was a good man, so I gave him the interview. The article was pretty good, but he did put the socialization idea into my mouth.

A large percentage of parapsychologists I spoke with use the same cautious method for dealing with newspaper reporters. They demand the right to edit the final version of whatever is to be published. This policy could not and did not protect them from editors who would create sensationalistic headlines above the edited version. A consensus is that parapsychologists, in general, are not dealing with the media very effectively. A second consensus among parapsychologists is that the Committee for the Scientific Investigation of Claims of the Paranormal, a group generally dedicated to debunking purported psi phenomena, is highly adept at presenting its case to the media. The difference seems to be that parapsychologists, as scientific researchers, wish to adhere to scientific etiquette, while the Committee, which is not particularly research-oriented, is primarily interested in "educating" the public.

Although many parapsychologists believed that the Committee has unfairly attacked legitimate psychical research, many others supported the Committee's aims:

We should have formed the Committee ourselves.

I'm kind of for the ideals that the Committee has set up for themselves. I think scientists should look into claims of the paranormal and evaluate them.

Yet, such activity is beyond the competence of many parapsychologists because of their orientation toward laboratory research. One noted:

The Parapsychological Association has not publicly criticized presentations on TV. If we don't take responsibility for that, they [the Committee] will. We in the PA could play a role if we would make an effort. We need to find someone who is willing to be a spokesperson, someone who knows how to deal with the media; scientists just don't know how to do it. Maybe it shouldn't be up to the PA. We don't easily agree about anything; we too often can't agree what kind of press release to give. Some time back, the PA wanted to give out a press release; I was against it. The media ought not to be the one that hears the blow-by-blow struggle of science. They wanted to use my studies. My reaction was—it's ridiculous. The stuff hasn't been replicated in someone else's lab. So nothing happened, but the PA is moving in the direction of press release, perhaps of a different kind.

Later, in fact, the PA appointed a public information committee with Robert Van de Castle as chair. In July 1980, a factual press release was issued describing the "Psi Lab of the 80s." In a cover letter sent with the release, the PA admits,

In the past, the P.A. has been reluctant to invite news coverage, for the subject often seems to attract sensationalized and distorted treatment. However, because much misinformation continues to reach the public through some of the media, there seems to be no alternative. If it is to be properly informed, then we must provide the public with information that we know is acccurate, reliable, and scientifically sound.

Thus, on a quarterly basis, the P.A. will provide news feature and background materials, similar to the enclosed "Psi Lab of the 80s." We hope that you will be interested in receiving and using this information.

At the 1980 PA conference in Reykjavik, Iceland, Van de Castle noted that the press release program needed to balance conflicting orientations, since the releases had to "sound reliable but also be juicy enough to go over with the newspapers." The conflict between "reliable" versus "juicy" material illustrates the dilemma faced by parapsychologists in dealing with the public. The same dilemma is illustrated by the response of a former president of the PA when asked if he gave lectures to public organizations: "Occasionally, I do. But that's not really my thing. There's a generally perceived need to do it, but there's also a sense of caution. It raises suspicion of other scientists. You might find a negative correlation of esteem from fellow scientists in parapsychology and the extent to which a person goes out for public lectures."

My informant then discussed one individual who was very active publicly but held in low esteem scientifically. Later, in visits to other research institutes, I noticed that other informants agreed with this perception. One institute had even crossed off the name of the researcher in question from a list of recommended lecturers. The original informant then discussed a researcher who went to great lengths to avoid media exposure, even though his field of research was especially titillating for the media. This researcher became the next president of the PA.

The conflict between parapsychology and the media has a certain "Catch-22" aspect. The reputable media in which parapsychologists most desire coverage are least willing to report on parapsychological research. Conversely, the type of media least desirable for parapsychology are the most willing to present their own version of present research. Some parapsychologists point out specific editors of major periodicals who block unbiased coverage of psi research: "I was surprised at the lack of impact of this work. In 1977, I gave a paper at [a major scientific conference] and what happened? Nothing happened. We expected some impact. The *New York Times* did not take note of it. The East Coast media are pathologically negligent on the whole field. I lectured at [a second major conference] banquet. It was a nonevent in the newspapers." Targ and Puthoff (1977) have presented various examples of media bias. They cite a case in which they were attacked by *Time* (March 12, 1973) on the basis of hearsay even before they published their findings in an appropriate scientific forum. Such negative experiences with reputable media seem to be an aspect of deviant science.

The *National Enquirer* evokes the most hostility from parapsychologists. Many described incidents in which they had been misquoted and even had entire incidents virtually fabricated, printed, and attributed to their research.

The *National Enquirer* is quite a pest. . . . Sometimes you get entrapped by them. I tell them I'm working with a conservative research organization and can't have my work put in their paper. It's not that all *National Enquirer* articles are lies, it's that the editors sometimes put in terms, adjectives, and headlines that are so outrageous. I have had cases in the *National Enquirer* though, and have also called up and got cases. Once a psychic was giving info about a police case and a sheriff hired the psychic. It's an extremely risky business, dealing with the media. . . . The difficulties with the press are not only with the *National Enquirer*. Some others can be even more distorting, even *Time* magazine. At Duke, a local reporter once interviewed Rhine, and it came out funny. The editor slanted it. Sometimes it's not a good thing, dealing with journalists. You can't sell to them what you want. They already know what they want.

As part of my research, I systematically examined issues of the *National Enquirer* in order to determine what qualities so deeply troubled the parapsychologists. In no case did I find an example of blatant falsehood, though parapsychologists have told me that many such cases have occurred in the past. But I did observe numerous examples of what might be considered the distorted public image of psi. Descriptions of psi phenomena in the *National Enquirer* tended to use adjectives such as "incredible," "amazing," "unbelievable," "mind-boggling." On May 26, 1981, the *National Enquirer* described what might be considered a typical poltergeist case. Parapsychologists have observed that such cases often have central figures, typically pre-adolescent children, and generally do not last for extended periods. The *National Enquirer* referred to the thirteen-year-old in this case as "an incredibly powerful psychic who just can't control his amazing powers." Descriptions of the typical phenomena that often surround these cases (rocks flying, furniture tipping over, and dishes crashing to the floor) were framed so as to increase their dramatic and frightening quality.

One sequence of events illustrates what I often observed in my reading of the *National Enquirer* and in my interaction with parapsychologists. During the summer of 1979, I casually talked with a parapsychologist at a research institute. He described a series of experiments with a famous psychic in which statistical significance at the .05 level had been achieved under various different experimental conditions. He cautiously considered the entire series a success in that the chance for these results occurring "by luck" was less than one out of twenty in most of the experimental series. The research report, which was later published in a parapsychology journal, carefully specified the test conditions and the experimental results (many, but not all, of which demonstrated psi ability in the famous psychic).

Later, the *National Enquirer*'s description of some of the successful experiments centered on extraordinary quotations from subjects who claimed they could feel the psychic affecting their emotions during the experiment. In contrast to the journal article's dry report of the measured physiological effects, the *National Enquirer*'s account, quoted from selected subjects, created a strikingly powerful article.

The parapsychologists also were directly quoted giving a cautious but positive appraisal of the experimental results. Within the context of the article, their quotes added weight to what was described as "impressive," "incredible," "amazing," "startling," and "dramatic." This tendency to inflate and distort research findings is the facet that most troubles parapsychologists. The media are more interested in personal human experiences than in laboratory findings.

One parapsychologist shared his views:

It's naive to say we can educate the general public—we can't. All we can do is educate the media. This field has such bizarre roots that anyone can go before the media and seem to represent the field. The problem is that the most colorful things get the most attention. . . . The *National Enquirer* calls once a month. I refuse to talk to them, though I recently got quoted not too long ago. They want to write the quote and attribute it to you.

A second factor that troubles parapsychologists is the media's tendency to blur the distinction between parapsychological research and other investigations of anomalous phenomena. This nullifies parapsychology's effort to demarcate its realm of inquiry from fields with less status. Just as in orthodox research it is necessary for scientists to demarcate science from nonscience, parapsychologists similarly draw a line between their field and ones less respectable. Publicly, parapsychologists strive to clarify and amplify this distinction. Some parapsychologists attempt to conceal their UFO experiences from their colleagues. One parapsychological journal editor noted that until the UFO issue is scientifically settled, she cannot allow the question to intrude into the journal. Privately, many parapsychologists realize that the distinction may be merely a reflection of their scientistic orientation.

Journalists who represent publications that report personal UFO experiences, monster sightings, or other anomalous situations are often shunned by parapsychologists, since the reporting will tend to lump psi research with these other deviant belief systems. Parapsychologists who write books that reveal similarities or relationships between psi and these less accepted phenomena are also criticized.

The disadvantages of parapsychological interaction with the media might be listed as follows:

Manifest

1. Prestige of individual scientist is damaged through excessive interaction with the media.

Latent

2. Media tend to present distorted image of psi owing to desires of public and elites within media.
3. Mainstream science rejects field of parapsychology on the basis of distorted public image.
4. Media tend to blur distinctions between parapsychology and other fields investigating anomalous claims.

At the same time, the field of parapsychology is dependent on the media for survival. Catering to these forms of dependency can be viewed as advantageous for the field:

1. Media aid in locating sources of recruitment and funding for the field.
2. Media can act as means of educating the public.
3. Media can aid the parapsychologist in locating new "cases" or subjects who ostensibly have paranormal ability.

A few quotations from parapsychologists illustrate these advantages:

I haven't been burnt in the past. Maybe I can get a little advertising in. Maybe get subjects to come here. I'm not totally opposed to it. Otherwise, I'll have to stick up signs.

TV shows can shift attitudes. The very fact that it's on Channel 4 causes it to shift attitudes even though it's hokey. . . . The media often makes gross mistakes, but they're not scientists; it's almost expected. Everything is progressing at its own limping pace.

Although these advantages are apparent to most parapsychologists, the general tendency is to ignore the media and the social phenomena involving psi that most interest the media. Parapsychological research tends to focus on laboratory studies rather than spontaneous human experiences: "Although nonrecurrent psi experiences have been reported in practically all cultures, they have not figured directly in modern parapsychological research, which has been devoted to experimental methods almost exclusively" (Rhine, L., 1977:59).

This tendency reflects the intrusion of the scientistic orientation. The general scientific criteria during the 1880s permitted use of anecdotal material, and psychical researchers collected a large number of cases (e.g., Gurney, Myers, and Podmore, 1886). Yet with the evolution of science, modern scientism placed a lesser value on anecdotal information. Moreover, most of the investigations of mediums conducted by the SPR were not scientifically fruitful since so many were caught cheating. Although a few parapsychologists have continued to collect anecdotal cases, the paradigm established by J. B. Rhine seems to allow the scientifically oriented researcher to engage in a legitimate process of experimentation that is confined to the laboratory. The scientistic ideology supports the belief that progress should occur through a program of carefully controlled research occurring only under laboratory conditions. Interaction with the media or lay public should be unnecessary.

By choosing to serve the needs of the scientific community, parapsychology neglects the needs of the lay public. A latent effect is not only the distorted public image of psi but a consolidation of the stigma surrounding numerous forms of psychic experience occurring within the public.

The actual incidence of psychic experience among the public is far greater than might be expected. This has been noted by various researchers (Green, 1967; McCready and Greeley, 1976; Palmer, 1979; Prasad and Stevenson, 1968). In one survey, Palmer (1979) mailed a questionnaire to a representative sample of adult residents of Charlottesville, Virginia. He found that:

A substantial percentage of the respondents considered themselves to have had interactions with their environment that cannot be accounted for by known physical laws. More than a third of our sample, for instance, responded affirmatively to the items concerning waking ESP experiences and ESP dreams. These figures are comparable to those reported by McCready and Greeley (1976) based upon similar questions. We calculated that 51% of our T sample [respondents living in the town of Charlottesville, Va.] and 55% of our S sample [students at the University of Virginia at Charlottesville] claimed either a waking ESP experience or an ESP dream. (Palmer, 1979:248)

These experiences can be considered "sociologically" real in that they have "real" effects on the people who report them. Many respondents to Palmer's (1979) poll indicated that psychic or psi-related experiences affected their attitudes toward themselves, their life-styles, and the meaning of life.

It is not surprising that some of those whose experiences could not be explained by known physical laws should feel troubled or disturbed by the event. The scientistic mind-set holds that such experiences are invalid and, hence, demonstrate a form of insanity or at least mental instability. Since science is the dominant ontology in Western society, it is quite natural that many individuals, both curious and troubled, contact parapsychological research institutes seeking information about the phenomena they have experienced.

Contact by the public with scientific parapsychology illustrates the irony of parapsychology's strain toward scientism. The reaction of the field to its critics has had the latent effect of alienating those who have experienced psi most frequently. Parapsychologists, adhering to the norm of skepticism, generally cannot validate any particular psychic experience. They often neglect cases that are suspect or lack supportive evidence. The report of the Society for Psychical Research concerning its census of hallucinations (Sidgwick and Committee, 1894) was selective. Only more "evidential" cases were presented. Louisa Rhine (1956) also developed a classification system of psychic experiences that illustrates this latent effect. Owing to the stigma that skeptics attach to such experiences, it is generally expected that anyone who has had a psychic experience will make every attempt to invalidate its ontological reality. The experiencer is expected to attempt to find a "normal" explanation for his or her "paranormal" experience. Two example cases illustrate this point.

One man wrote to a research institute that he had dreamt his wife had five twenty-dollar bills concealed in a red fold in her purse. In the morning, he checked her purse and, to his surprise, he found the money. Although the letter did not reveal his wife's reaction, or if she knew about the money, the experience constitutes an alleged form of psi in that information apparently, or possibly, could have been received by the man through nonsensory means. The man reported he received the nonsensory information through his dream and testified that this information is correct. By sending this piece of intelligence to a parapsychological research lab, he apparently hopes to (a) contribute to the advancement of science; and (b) legitimate his own personal experience, demonstrating the possibility of its validity (rather than his own insanity). The scientistic orientation of most parapsychologists prevents the field from firmly legitimating the man's personal experience. The man's dream could easily have been caused by sensory cues derived from his wife (the parapsychologist uses the skeptic's rhetorical strategy of "unpacking" the man's statements). Consequently, the man's hopes to legitimize his personal experience are thwarted by the scientistic orientation of the para-psychologist.

A second example reveals an experience that the scientistic orien-tation would classify as psychotic. A person writes, "My problem is that I have an involuntary problem of transmitting thought. . . . I also absorb feeling and thought." Because the individual makes no attempt to establish the ontological reality of his experience through skeptical analysis, his problem cannot be included among examples of alleged psi. If parapsychology were a completely established science which could demonstrate that certain individuals do indeed involuntarily transmit and receive thought (some parapsychologists believe this could be the case), then this man might be taken more seriously, especially if scientific parapsychology had some theoretical explanation or practical solution for his dilemma. As it stands, the man describes features that are widely held to indicate mental disorder.

Most of the parapsychologists I interviewed felt that they could easily distinguish between normal individuals, who report ostensible psychic experiences, and individuals who suffer from mental disorder. Some individuals who suffer from mental disorder incorpo-rate idea systems associated with the paranormal into their fantasies. Parapsychologists generally feel that there is little evidence demon-strating a relationship between mental disorder and psi. On the contrary, the laboratory demonstrations of ESP show a vague relation-ship between positive personality attributes and ESP. That a form of pathology seems related to reports of psi (and the inability of para-psychologists to deal with that pathology) may contribute to the stigma associated with psychic phenomena.

Often, parapsychological research institutes receive requests for references to psychic healers or to fortune tellers. No institute makes such references, since they cannot be certain that any particular healer or clairvoyant is legitimate. Sometimes, the research institute will direct inquiries to a lay organization interested in psychic phenomena.

Many researchers voluntarily counsel people who have had fright-ening psychic experiences. To do so, they must step out of their role as scientific parapsychologists. Pragmatic orientations are often stressed. One informant explained:

All the glorious, marvelous fantasies people have! The people tell me a ghost is chasing them in their house. They're terrified. Now I don't know whether a ghost is chasing them or not, but they somehow have to cope with the situation. Are you going to put the groceries on the table and change the baby? If the person can integrate it into their life, it's OK, but if not, they have to seek help. Many psychics are not enlightened enough to use psychic experience to aid anyone. . . . It's not going to help you unless you use it rather than let it use you.

Some of the problems parapsychologists face in counseling those who seek help are illustrated by another respondent's remarks:

Not too many people are actual kooks. Many times, people just want psychological counseling. Once a woman called saying she was having poltergeists in her apartment, so I went to talk to her. I couldn't verify anything, but it was clear she was having severe guilt feelings. People who complain of psychic problems often have other underlying problems. People have dreams that come true. That can lead to terrible guilt when it means an accident for a loved one. They wonder: "Could I have prevented it?" My basic approach is to stress that it's a normal phenomenon. Perhaps the person shouldn't worry about getting rid of the ability, but should try to gain control over it. It's not as pathological as other people might diagnose it.

Another parapsychologist is less encouraging of psychic experience:

Some people who call here are disturbed; they're upset about something that has been happening. I give them a reading list about the field and also a lot of support and encouragement. Once a woman came in and described a form of out-of-body experience. She was absolutely not crazy; she was just having this experience which some people obviously have. I questioned her about her background and the patterns of occurrence of her out-of-body experience. Her experiences could have had something to do with her rapid-eye-movement periods which occur while she sleeps. That's affected by many things, such as alcohol and diet. I suggested that by eating more protein in her diet, she might stop having the unusual experiences.

This may have been the solution (or have acted as a placebo leading to resolution) since the problem seems to have ended. The parapsychologist continues:

I don't see any reason to encourage OBE's. Maybe I disagree with many parapsychologists on that point. I'd like to see a pooling of resources in the field concerning psychic experience and counseling. She might have been diagnosed as a schizophrenic. It could have ruined her life. Some persons should devote themselves to counseling. Only a certain percentage of these people who come in to see us about experiences are crazy. People have precognitive dreams concerning some future bad event, and think, "Could I be causing it?" Often people have an apparent psi experience and their friends say, "Are you crazy?" We have no reason to believe that insanity is intrinsically connected to psi experience. We need a much more systematic way of dealing with persons who come to us with problems. They're running to these quacks—commercial rip-of artists. They're led to certain unrealistic ideas about the psi phenomena.

These quotations illustrate the discrepancy between the needs of scientistic parapsychologists and the needs of those who have had frightening psi experiences. Only by stepping out of his or her role as a skeptical scientist can the parapsychologist be of service.

Nonlaboratory phenomena are often too bizarre to quantify scientifically. Parapsychologists know they cannot handle some alleged paranormal events in a quantified, qualified scientific manner: "Did my colleague tell you about the lady whose back turns black? [He had not.] She appears to feel third-degree burns on her back. She's been to numerous doctors. It seems to be some form of psychic chain of events. It happens two or three times a week and causes her a great deal of pain. One of her physicians told her to consult a 'bruja.' That's more of a kind of witch around here. I don't know what he expects."

The public propensity to experience strange and unusual events reaches even the well-known skeptics of paranormal phenomena. One individual who is famous for debunking macro-PK demonstrations told me this story:

People usually call the University Psychology Department. The secretary refers anyone who has a strange request to me. I sometimes try to put them in touch with a parapsychologist involved with counseling or try to get them to come to our clinic. It's a tricky situation. Some are very weird. There's one lady who claims that no one listens to her—not even her doctor. An object, for example, her hair, will fall in her toilet bowl. Then the object will do all kinds of strange things, floating around. Her hair may try to give a message, trying to make letters of the alphabet.

"Did you go out there and check it out?" I asked.

"No. It's just too strange," he replied. "I can't imagine myself leaning over her toilet and watching her hair."

This example illustrates how experiences among the public exceed what is conceivable as normal behavior, even by parapsychologists. A science that holds physics as the ideal model cannot deal with hair spelling messages in a toilet bowl. When I asked permission to quote the above, his reply showed the puzzlement that psi experience seems to evoke: "I'm not sure what to make of the quote. I know the situation that it refers to. I think my point was that there might be a question of propriety and sanity if my colleagues heard that I was spending my time looking in this lady's toilet bowl to see if her fallen hairs wiggle around in the water in patterns conforming to letters of the alphabet. However, if you want to use the quotation, go ahead."

There seems to be a philosophical question of rationality in conducting these forms of investigation. Consider these possibilities: (1) The skeptic visits the woman's house, does not see any messages and, consequently, wastes his own time and raises questions of propriety. (2) The skeptic visits the woman's house, sees various messages, and, consequently, raises questions regarding his own sanity or reliability. (3) The skeptic is quite rational in ignoring the case.

The parapsychologist might feel obligated to investigate this case and, consequently, questions of sanity or propriety would be raised. Paradoxically, although the field deals with the paranormal, parapsychologists tend to doubt the authenticity of much that the public attempts to tell them about psi. Each researcher generally selects phenomena for his or her concern that seem possible. "We get countless people who have their minds under control of UFOs or the CIA. Some have ESP like you catch a cold. In general, I don't see any of these people. People who have the kundalini experience call often; perhaps a call a week at least is involved with psi experience." "Kundalini" refers to the feeling of energy flowing up one's spine that is associated with some forms of yoga meditation and exercise. The experience can apparently occur spontaneously and may be frightening when it occurs unexpectedly.

Researchers gain little scientific data in their role as counselors. Owing to the emphasis and focus on controlled laboratory research, few parapsychologists see much value in their interacting with lay groups, especially those that are occultism-oriented.

People who feel they are psychic are often disappointed when they cannot demonstrate their ability in the statistical manner required in the laboratory. One researcher reports, "It's not that easy to find people who can use their ESP in the way that we require." Another states: "All these people who think they're witches, or the astrologers, or those believing in the occult—they don't just *think* they'll be successful, they know it. I don't like to work with them. They're never any good."

A particularly interesting example of deviance labeling's latent effects is how the parapsychologist is affected personally by interacting with the public. Allison's (1973) research results hinted that this interaction was related to a decline in the professional's adherence to orthodoxy within parapsychology. The causal relationship between these variables could not be specified. This evidence might support the argument that orthodoxy within parapsychology causes latent effects which spoil interaction with the public.

Some researchers describe a tedious boredom and occasional hostility when they are with social acquaintances. At one extreme are people who want to unburden themselves of their own or relatives' personal experiences. At the other extreme are the hostile skeptics. "I was reaching a point of burn-out. I was sick to death of the regularity of the same old pattern. I would meet someone who learned I was a parapsychologist, and they would begin with 'well, my own Aunt Ethel . . . ,' and I would have to listen to the whole story. If the person was positive, it was just too naive and anecdotal. It was really no help to me, and I didn't want to deal with this kind of admiring attitude. If the person was negative, I didn't want to fight."

Through interaction with those who perceive the parapsychologist as having a special attribute, the researcher acquires a special role. As noted by Goffman (1963), the stigmatized individual often integrates his or her personality around the attribute in question.

One researcher describes attempting to slide past that critical moment when a stranger finds out what the parapsychologist does for a living. Her description of a conversation:

Neighbor: What do you do?
Parapsychologist: I'm a researcher in a lab. (*evasively*)
Neighbor: What kind?
Parapsychologist: Parapsychology. (*spoken quickly*)

Then the person must tell their stories. It's like meeting a doctor and describing symptoms. They want to describe their personal experiences.

In a way, many encounters are a form of counseling. The lay person wants an evaluation of his or her experience.

The parapsychologist's inability to harness the high level of popular interest in psi is a result of the field's scientistic orientation. By adhering so strongly to the norms of science, the parapsychologist loses public support yet consolidates his or her role as a deviant scientist.

Another latent effect of the field's scientistic orientation is the parapsychologist's difficulty in counseling those who are troubled by their psi experiences. Counseling for people who contact parapsychological research institutes is so important that a special round table concerning it was held during the 1980 convention of the PA. It was estimated that, nationwide, about sixty people per week were seeking some form of psi counseling (information that might aid them in integrating their psi experiences into their lives). Because some do not regard their experience as paranormal and others cannot contact a parapsychological research institute, the level of paranormal experience is estimated to be much higher. A goal of counseling seems to be to normalize the paranormal. It was suggested that the counselor should accept the individual's description of an experience and then attempt to integrate the anomalous experience into that person's everyday life.

The round table also discussed a phenomenon referred to as the "battered recipient syndrome." This occurs when a person experiencing an ostensible psi phenomenon becomes even more anxious after being labeled as insane by a "mainstream" counselor. The round table was also concerned about fraudulent claims of psychic ability and the tendency for the elderly to be exploited by charlatans. The parapsychologists generally felt that although a researcher must maintain a scientific orientation, some format or procedure was needed for dealing with those who claimed "psychic" problems.

The scientistic orientation can also enter into the counseling process. I was curious about the methodology used by a counselor who was highly sympathetic to the parapsychological research program. He described the need for caution in dealing with clients who claimed "psychic" ailments: "There's a lack of authority and consensus in the field. I don't want to take the responsibility for increasing or decreasing belief in psi in a person I'm counseling. . . . I could send someone off on such a tangent. So many people are already so much off the deep end. . . . I don't believe in providing people anything but a scientific base." The counselor went on to tell how he might counsel a person who complained of other people interfering with his thought. After gaining enough relevant background information, he would try to steer the person in a healthy direction:

Sometimes when people are heavily into drugs and have no real personal relationships, strange things can happen. I'm trying to begin support groups, discussion groups. . . . Psi has to be treated as something real. It has to be treated with the utmost respect. It's a very, very serious dilemma. . . . Perhaps what could be occurring is that a person's will, when operating on a minimum level, is susceptible to bizarre thoughts. . . . Sometimes my recommendation, when people are experiencing bizarre thoughts or perhaps just normal psychic experiences, is to ignore it. In the support groups, you can talk about it. But outside, in society, you have to be careful what you say to people. You have to deal with that limitation; leave it at that. Don't develop problems for yourself by telling about your psychic experiences. Be cautious. Don't share your deepest experiences with people who can't understand them. That's my advice.

Ehrenwald (1948) has attempted to relate the telepathy hypothesis to understanding paranoia and schizophrenic psychoses. The occurrence of unwelcome telepathy may show impairment of a filtering mechanism designed to prevent it. Although Ehrenwald's hypothesis has stimulated a great deal of criticism, it has also stimulated an interest in the possible relationship between mental disorder and psi. Yet the empirical evidence seems to indicate that the best laboratory subjects are well adjusted. This creates an ambiguity between the parapsychological theories devised to explain laboratory results and those devised to explain mental disorders. Psychiatrists who are interested in psi seem to have reached little consensus regarding the meaning of laboratory research, since many of them find that psychic experiences intrude into their clinical practice.

It would seem that counseling evolving from the parapsychological approach does not differ radically from mainstream counseling except that, in the former, the counselor takes the person seriously when he or she complains of a "psychic" ailment. The counselor tries to bridge the gap between the client's personal experience and a reality defined by everyday life.

The scientific base from which the counselor attempts to draw his "knowledge" actually has little to say about what causes "psychic" disorders. Often counseling consists of telling a client the frequency of others' personal psychic experiences, which thereby helps normalize the experience of otherwise isolated individuals. The contradiction is that, scientifically, the parapsychologist is concerned with "proof" of paranormal phenomena, yet proof from lay informants is impossible in the skeptical framework within which the parapsychologist is socialized.

Visitors at parapsychological research centers often have specific questions regarding occult systems of belief. The parapsychologist counsels while trying to avoid any nonscientific judgments. For example, an elderly couple from Indiana were talking with a parapsychologist at a research laboratory:

Man: We've sat in these places where they have these materializations, you know. So many of them are just frauds. When they do readings, they keep asking—how am I doing? Always asking leading questions. But at this place, they would bring out people from your family. There was a boy there and they had his father come. They form right in front of you. You can see them. Next thing you know, this chief forms right in front of this Indian boy. Later, the chief said to me, "Now you watch me. I'm going right down between your feet," and he went right down like smoke swirling. You can touch them, but they tell you not to touch them unless they touch you first. I touched him; he seemed real! I don't know if I'm hoodwinked or not.

Parapsychologist: Well, it seems funny to me; if you can touch them and they seem real, I would say they are real. Maybe there's something—a door or something in the floor.

Man: First time I was there, they told me my mother's name. It isn't known by many, but they knew it. My father came down spiritually, and we talked.

Then the "spirit" described various anecdotal incidents that only his father would know about. The spirit also knew his wife's maiden name.

Wife: How could they have found out my maiden name?

Parapsychologist: I don't know what to say. I've never experienced such a strong case myself. I've talked with many people who say they have. Basically, I'm suspending my judgment.

If past experience with such cases is any guide, we would expect that until the Indian chief appears in a laboratory under controlled conditions, the parapsychologist must keep his judgment suspended. Even then, the chief would be required to demonstrate his ESP or PK ability using some tightly controlled experimental design devised by the parapsychologist himself. After that, the parapsychologist's colleagues might point out ways of strengthening the experimental design. Finally, the skeptical community would dismiss any conclusions. Fraud could have occurred, since a skeptical magician was not present during the entire experiment (or if one was, he or she might be labeled as incompetent). This scenario illustrates the tension between scientific parapsychology and types of psychic experience occurring among the public. The parapsychologist resists fulfilling the antiscientistic or religious role the public wishes him or her to play. It behooves the parapsychologist to do so, especially in regard to spiritualistic phenomena, which generally can be explained by fraud.

The sharpest contrast illustrating the divisions between parapsychologists and the public occurs within parapsychological field investigations. Here, claims tend to be labeled most extraordinary while proofs are deemed to be least adequate. The latent effect of this dilemma is that the phenomena which constitute the driving power and most exciting aspect behind parapsychology's existence are consigned to the edge of parapsychological research. It would seem that some realms of inquiry, although clearly involving alleged cases of psi, are considered to be so extraordinary that even parapsychologists tend to label their investigation as deviant. When field investigators are stigmatized, the latent effect of their reaction tends to lend authority to orthodox parapsychology and to mark the borders of the field. Within the field investigation, the process of deviance labeling can be observed in miniature.

One aspect of my participant observation study involved the conduct of a long-term parapsychological field investigation of an alleged haunting in Baltimore (McClenon, 1980, 1981a, b). Each aspect of the case illustrates an effect of deviant labeling on the participants.

During the summer of 1980, a family in Baltimore began experiencing disturbances such as apparitions; knocking on walls; unexplainable voices, lights, shaking beds; and unusual tactile sensations on the face and legs. After months of deep anxiety during which they were afraid that they were all going insane, they contacted the Psychical Research Foundation in North Carolina. Through this interaction they were able to label the phenomena as paranormal and their anxiety was alleviated to a degree. This incident demonstrates the effect of the interaction of scientific investigators and anomalous claims that was described in chapter 2. Scientific investigation can reduce the stigma attached to claims that might be labeled insane.

As the researcher assigned to the case by the Psychical Research Foundation, I attempted to maintain all the norms inherent within science. My attempts to borrow equipment from various departments within the University of Maryland (to measure electromagnetic radiation, create a fraud-proof test, design an energy-related experiment, etc.) were treated by academics with amused scorn. I had hoped to use the hardware of science in order to legitimate my investigation. I ceased attempting to interact with physical scientists because I feared I might damage the reputation of the Sociology Department at my university. I decided to conduct the investigation merely as a sociological participant observer. This interaction demonstrates the restrictions that deviance labeling places on those who attempt to conduct these types of investigations.

Although I observed various instances that could be regarded as paranormal (unexplainable raps, light, vibrations in a bed), I carefully stated in my report to the regional parapsychology affiliate that I could not exclude the possibility of fraud. They considered skepticism appropriate.

Because of my report at the regional parapsychology meeting, parapsychologists have brought other ongoing cases to my attention. To a certain extent, I was labeled (and stigmatized) as a field investigator and have played that role. As predicted by the theoretical model developed in chapter 2, my activity increased the number of reports of this type of experience. Apparently many people have experienced apparitions yet have no means to report these experiences to a scientific authority. My "scientific" activity labeled me as a collector of such reports.

My interaction with the media also illustrates the dilemma faced by psychical researchers. Various sensationalistic tabloids wanted to interview me following my report to the Southeast Regional Parapsychological Association. One reporter even called from London on various occasions seeking an interview. Following the advice of various parapsychologists, I refused to cooperate. I could gain nothing from such interviews and I could be stigmatized as an incompetent investigator if the newspapers failed to stress my cautious conclusions. This need to keep the investigation discreet illustrates how deviance labeling reduces reports of anomalous experience.

Even after two years of the continuing "haunting-type" phenomena, the latent effects of the process of deviant labeling have prevented any complete investigation. As it became apparent that investigating the phenomena could not stop their occurrence, the family realized that "science" could not really help them. They were concerned that neighbors, friends, or relatives would find out about their difficulties and they wished to conceal the problem, especially from professional people, such as a physician they knew. They realized that such authorities had the power to "lock them up," to judge them insane. As of 1982, they have somewhat adjusted to the disturbances, yet plan to sell the house as soon as mortgage rates fall lower.

Although this case at first seemed quite unusual, I came to realize that the experiences the family members reported occur with surprising frequency. Palmer's (1979) random sample of residents of Charlottesville, Virginia, and of University of Virginia students revealed a surprisingly high percentage of anomalous experiences of this type. When asked, "Have you ever lived in a house you believed to be 'haunted'?" 7 percent of the town sample and 8 percent of the student sample replied affirmatively. When asked, "Have you ever 'communicated' with the dead or believed yourself to have been controlled or 'possessed' by a 'spirit'?" 8 percent of the town sample and 5 percent of the student sample replied affirmatively. Seventeen percent of both samples replied affirmatively to Palmer's question concerning experience of apparitions. Considering the large percentage of the public who have experienced haunting-type phenomena, one is led to believe that deviant labeling effectively restricts the communication of this information.

The Baltimore case might be considered somewhat typical in that: (1) when a case occurs under uncontrolled conditions, it is always considered suspect and, consequently, dismissed by skeptics; (2) the parapsychological reaction is to increase the level of skepticism required to investigate such cases; (3) the latent effect of this reaction is a limitation of the distribution of information and a restriction of the normal freedom allowed in science.

It is apparent that the parapsychological attempt to be more scientific in the face of criticism has produced various latent effects with regard to interaction between parapsychology and the general public. These effects are associated with a distorted public image of psi, special difficulties with media interaction, and special problems with relationships with lay individuals. These problems are illustrated by the counseling role undertaken by parapsychologists both with visitors to the research centers and with individuals experiencing phenomena during field investigations. This latent effect of parapsychology's adherence to scientism contributes to the process of labeling the field as deviant.

8

Conclusions

The central question is, Why, after over a century of inquiry, has science not resolved the issue concerning paranormal phenomena? Most coherent social groups undertaking innovative activities within science survive less than fifteen years (Griffith and Mullins, 1972). They either solve the problem they address or else pass out of existence. Why has parapsychology survived for over a century without either achieving legitimacy within or rejection from science?

In response to this puzzle, a theoretical model based on concepts of scientism and deviant behavior was developed (figure 1-1 in chapter 1). This model explains parapsychology's longevity as part of a process of rejecting certain types of anomalies. The past ideologies associated with scientific advance, coupled with the needs and desires of present scientific elites, create criteria for rejecting various anomalies. People who investigate these anomalies are labeled as deviant through a process of argumentation that occurs within science. A stable social process occurs when the scientists investigating a set of rejected anomalies react by demonstrating greater allegiance to the ideology of science. Various latent effects result when these people react to their being labeled as deviant. The deviant researchers are prevented from having an impact on the mainstream scientific process, yet because of their commitment to the ideology of science, they nonetheless keep on trying to make such an impact. This tends to stabilize the process.

A second theoretical model demonstrates the role that lay groups can play in aiding researchers of rejected anomalies. This model (figure 2-1 in chapter 2) presents two processes associated with the treatment of rejected anomalies. Rejected anomalies that cannot attract the attention of lay individuals or groups are generally reported and investigated less with the passage of time. Without the support of these groups, long-term investigations of such anomalies rarely continue. Lay groups can use rejected anomalies that have been experienced by a sufficient number of people as a means for supporting nonscientific ideologies or for reducing the stigma associated with experience of the rejected anomaly.

Propositions, Evidence, and Findings

The propositions generated by these theoretical orientations were supported by the evidence gathered in this research. A review of these propositions and the evidence that has been collected in regard to them will constitute the major conclusions of this study.

Proposition 1: *Scientism aids scientists in differentiating anomalies that can be rejected from those that can be granted legitimacy.*

Science exists as a community of individuals who must establish boundaries and methods of demarcation to continue existing as a social group. The intellectual progress and social institutionalization of science attest to the capacity of scientists to regulate themselves. Development of a general ideology and means for labeling certain behavior as deviant is required of any long-lasting community.

Scientism consists of the body of ideas used to legitimate the practice of science. These ideas are used to evaluate anomalous claims in terms of attitudes that exist within institutionalized science. There is a tendency for proto-sciences (realms of inquiry that are labeled unacceptable by institutionalized science) to be evaluated as unacceptable in terms of methodology (Collins, 1976). This view was held among the elite scientists surveyed within the AAAS. Seventy-one percent of those who might be called skeptical about the existence of psi considered it "very" or "extremely" important that "scientists feel that, on the whole, parapsychological research has not been conducted in a competent manner." Elite scientists' evaluation of parapsychology's legitimacy is closely related to their evaluation of psi's ontological status.

Truzzi (1977) differentiates anomalous variables (facts) from anomalous relationships (processes), thereby defining cryptoscience, parascience, and crypto-parascience (see table 2-3). The concept of a claim being "extraordinary" is central to these definitions. This concept derives its meaning from the criteria, historically derived within science, which are deemed to be associated with the scientific body of knowledge. Scientism legitimates the practices used to generate that knowledge and is central to the definition of the idea of "extraordinary." Chapter 2 argued that criteria associated with past ideologies of science are used by scientific elites to demarcate science from nonscience. Criteria such as appearance of replicability, susceptibility to laboratory experimentation, and the ability to devise a mechanistic explanation for the phenomenon are used to generate reasons for rejecting anomalies. Mechanistic explanations are suitable only if they are compatible with existing bodies of knowledge. Since the resources of science are limited, the cost/benefit ratio of investigating anomalous claims must be considered. Explanations that are not mechanistic, or that interfere with orientations which have produced many benefits, hold little promise of justifying the cost of their development. Criteria for the rejection of claims which seem to require such explanations must continuously be developed and used.

One might conclude that science cannot exist as a community without some unifying ideology. The rejection of certain anomalies, a consequence of scientism, requires a process of labeling some investigators as deviant. Scientism furnishes criteria that justify and rationalize this process. It exists as a set of ideas that legitimate the present practices of science.

It might be argued that the claim that scientists use a scientistic ideology in differentiating anomalous claims is tautological. Since rejection of some claims is a scientific activity, any justification of that activity can be labeled scientism (by definition). The proposition that states this is of sociological interest, since it reveals an irony within this ideology. Science is supposed to be "free of suppositions" except for limited assumptions on the worth of the scientific endeavor, belief in the rules of logic, and the value of the "scientific method" (Weber, 1962). One aspect of the ideology of science (belief in the worth of the scientific endeavor) claims that all phenomena in nature can be better understood through investigation using the scientific method. Scientists should be free to investigate whatever phenomena they wish. The irony arises from the need of scientists to function as a community. Certain aspects of scientism have evolved with the success of science as an ongoing process. The need of scientists to reject some anomalous claims and to label some investigators as deviant creates contradictory suppositions. It is the role of sociological analysis to reveal and analyze such ironies (R. H. Brown, 1977).

This irony is an aspect of what Kuhn (1977) refers to as "the essential tension" between conservative and innovative elements within science. In the border areas of science this tension is associated with the process of deviant labeling and, therefore, is not necessarily related to scientific progress.

Proposition 2: *Scientists engage in a rhetorical and political process by labeling certain belief systems as deviant.*

Science can be viewed as a process of argumentation in which qualified speakers present evidence before scientific audiences within the context of specific situations. The evidence presented in the study reveals that this process does indeed occur. Various rhetorical strategies have been developed to attack and defend the claims regarding the existence of psi. The presentation of these strategies is associated with a political process within science, the educational system, and the media. The political struggle between parapsychologists and their critics is not on equal footing. Those who have been labeled as deviant are generally at a disadvantage. Consequently, the parapsychologists, although they use the methodology of science to present their empirical claims, are at a disadvantage in refuting the philosophical positions of their opponents. Since the scientistic orientation deems psi as highly improbable, proponents of the phenomenon who claim to have verified its existence are labeled as (probably) incompetent or fraudulent. Parapsychologists are often unsuccessful in getting their work published in mainstream scientific journals (though cases of articles being published do exist). Courses presenting parapsychological evidence in the academic setting are also somewhat rare, though the presentation of evidence within the format of philosophy of science or philosophy of religion may be increasing. Parapsychologists have been more successful in retaining their access to the popular media, especially television. This allows the field to continue its "guerrilla warfare" against the stigma attached to psi experience, a movement supported by lay groups within the general population. A latent goal of this movement is the establishment of a new world view of the nature of humanity.

One aspect of the process of rejecting some anomalies seems to be the prevention of dysfunctional conflict. Elite groups within science play a primary role in determining which anomalies are rejected and the types of scientific activity which are labeled as deviant. Evidence generated through polling a group of elite scientists within the AAAS reveals the percentages of this group that accept the various rhetorical strategies surrounding the issue of psi. Scientific empirical evidence seems to have had little effect on the formation of their opinions about psi. The rhetorical orientations themselves, coupled with personal experience, are of primary importance in attitude formation. The decision to accept evidence depends on scientific opinions that have been previously internalized.

Proposition 3: *Scientists labeled as deviant can create a stable social situation through increasing their adherence to the scientistic orientation, and will tend to do so in response to the process of deviance labeling.*

This proposition was supported through evidence generated by participant observation of the field of parapsychology. This evidence supports the theoretical model presented in figure 1-1 in chapter 1. Those labeled as deviant tend to accept the orientation of their labelers. This reaction was portrayed as having various latent effects. These effects tend to thwart the metamorphosis of parapsychology into a fully legitimate scientific field.

Numerous ironies exist in this process. Those labeling parapsychologists as incompetent or fraudulent generally do so without full access to scientific information on parapsychological work, since the process of deviance labeling restricts the publication of this evidence. Proponents of parapsychology, reacting to the stigma of deviant labeling, have chosen the scientific methodology as their primary guide. A result of this decision, the acceptance of scientism, has been the tendency of the field to develop criteria in research that are more rigid than in most other fields. This rigidity tends to restrict the dissemination of information concerning the work in the field. Parapsychologists tend to shun interaction with the media and refuse to accept much of the evidence for psi accepted by lay groups. Only the most carefully and rigidly controlled research is accepted for publication within the parapsychological journals, all of which have low circulation. The majority of scientists remain unaware of this reaction on the part of parapsychologists, or of the latent effects of this reaction. The evidence indicates that most elite scientists who were polled do not consider the research efforts of parapsychologists convincing. A poll of their opinions reveals numerous stereotypical remarks on the low quality of parapsychological research. These attitudes allow the process of deviance labeling to continue. Consequently, only token legitimacy has been granted even though a sizeable percentage of the general and academic population "believes in" and has experienced psi phenomena (Gallup, 1979; McCready and Greeley, 1976).

Weaknesses of the Theoretical Model

The theoretical model presented in chapter 1 might be criticized for being inherently tautological. In a way, scientism has been defined by both its historical development and by its present effects rather than by the absolutist epistemological claims made by some for science. It might be argued that this manner of definition ensures the generation of evidence supporting the propositions. Although this criticism harbors a degree of legitimacy, the model redeems itself through its explanatory power and predictive capacity. It also might be argued that the model is more explanatory than causal. This is of course correct. Many formulations within the sociology of science have this quality since they seek to explain both the rational and irrational qualities within science.

Laudan (1977) has addressed this issue through his discussion of rationality and the sociology of knowledge. What may seem like rational criteria in one era may seem irrational in a later one. Anomalies often gain full acceptance only after the problems that they have generated have been solved. If parapsychologists are able to devise suitable mechanistic or physicalistic solutions, the resistance of present elite scientists may be deemed irrational. If a consensus is reached that the phenomena investigated by parapsychologists do not exist, this resistance will be deemed rational. Regardless of that possibility, the longevity of the parapsychological research effort constitutes a puzzle within the sociology of science, since no such consensus or solution has yet been developed. This present study suggests that the field will continue to survive as long as lay groups give it support and it maintains a scientistic orientation.

One conclusion of this study is that the decision as to whether a solution had been found for any puzzle would depend on the community of science itself and, consequently, on the process of decision making within science. Future elites within science using modified ideological criteria may select other anomalous phenomena for rejection than those presently used. This study cannot speculate on the rationality of present ideological criteria as viewed from the future (although historically all eras have aspects that have been deemed irrational when viewed retrospectively). I can only conclude that the modern community of scientists *does* use scientistic criteria to reject certain anomalies and that at present these criteria have numerous rational aspects (for example, attention to rejected anomalies may result in the scientist investigating problems that he or she has little chance of solving; consequently, the thwarting of such investigation is rational).

In response to the charge that the theoretical model is merely explanatory and tautological a discussion of the predictive aspects of the model is in order. Although a totally descriptive model should be considered to have value within the sociology of science, it can be argued that the model has *some* predictive aspects.

Predictive Aspects of the Model

The theoretical models developed in this study indicate that within this border area of science the ontological reality of the phenomena being investigated has limited and unknown impact on the survival of the field. Parapsychology can continue to flourish as a form of "proto-scientific" ideology engaging in a form of guerrilla warfare against some aspects of scientism without completely demonstrating the authenticity of the anomaly it investigates and without gaining complete legitimacy within the scientific community. The field at present can gently rock the boat of science in a mildly threatening manner. This contributes to the resistance of scientists who perceive the admittance of this deviant system of belief as an act that would upset the rationality of, and possibly swamp or sink, the boat.

The model has some value in pinpointing changes in the process that might lead to greater acceptance or rejection of the field of parapsychology. The model is weak in that it does not sufficiently detail the means for entrance into the scientific process of factors existing within the general society. The theoretical models presented in this study point to three factors that should be important: (1) the means of selection of elite scientists (since these individuals have a role in the formulation of scientistic orientations), (2) the scientific/cultural process, and (3) the power and resources available to individuals or groups who support deviant science. Possible means for the increase or decrease in the acceptance of parapsychology will be discussed by considering first those processes occurring within science and later those occurring within the general society.

Scientific Change Affecting the Legitimacy of Parapsychology

A major conclusion of this study is that changes in the legitimacy of a deviant science generally are detemined, not through the efforts of the deviant scientists, but through changes occurring within established science. Parapsychologists may make major claims concerning discoveries about psi, yet, if their relationship with science remains the same, these "findings" will be ignored. The claims of experimental replicability may be increased (as some parapsychologists believe has occurred) with no apparent reaction from mainstream science. Deviant scientists may accept the scientistic orientation but this acceptance does not grant them legitimacy. Their status is determined through a process of argumentation that occurs within mainstream science and is controlled by elites within the scientific establishment.

Changes in the scientific/cultural process may lead to the evolution of a mega-paradigm that is more (or less) accepting of paranormal claims. The seeming "advance" of science without uncovering any verification of psi might lead to a future mega-paradigm in which parapsychology would be totally rejected. On the other hand, some parapsychologists believe that ideas developed within quantum mechanics point to greater acceptance of their field in the future. For example, an article published in the *Scientific American* by Bernard d'Espagnat (1979:158) states, "The doctrine that the world is made up of objects whose existence is independent of human consciousness turns out to be in conflict with quantum mechanics and with facts established by experiment." This idea and the idea that human consciousness *can affect* the physical world without sensory contact (psychokinesis) are somewhat similar. The "extraordinary" quality of many formulations derived within quantum mechanics leads some observers to hypothesize that the acceptance of psychokinesis would be a logical next step. It is possible that the various quantum mechanical models of consciousness developed by parapsychologists which mathematically model psi effects might be empirically supported by established scientists' research. This would tend to authenticate psi since a solution to its occurrence would then exist. With the development of such a solution, psi would be regarded as an accepted anomaly and the search for more answers to the puzzles of psi could take place within the scientific/cultural process.

In all probability only some of the anomalies that parapsychologists investigate would be granted legitimacy. It is conceivable that laboratory investigation of ESP and PK might be granted greater respectability, while investigation of other psychic phenomena would continue to be stigmatized. This division would reflect the historical distinction between parapsychology and psychical research, a demarcation that reflects the scientistic orientation. Parapsychology might then be granted a similar ontological status as hypnosis. It might be accepted, but not "understood." Psychical research could then constitute the "deviant science" and act as a means of demarcation between science and nonscience.

It is also conceivable that psychical research (as distinquished from parapsychology, which is more scientistic) might gain legitimacy as a form of social science. Psychical researchers might collect and compare cases that are considered folklore without demanding that psi be accepted as "real." Such a field would probably not be granted high scientific status but perhaps be considered equivalent to realms of inquiry within the liberal arts. Colleges might find that courses in this field attract sufficient student interest that they are deemed economically justified.

An interesting study has been conducted along these lines that could guide future research of this type. Hufford (1982) uses a methodology he refers to as an "experience-centered approach" in studying nightmare-paralysis experience. He refers to his topic as the "Old Hag," a name derived from Newfoundland folklore. Hufford found that this experience has central elements which are *not* culturally determined. Primary features include the impression of wakefulness, paralysis, and the ability to perceive the real setting accurately. Secondary features include such aspects as the sensation of an "evil" presence and hearing footsteps or voices. The research takes the form of what Hufford refers to as "applied folklore." He notes that various psychologists' attempts in the past to explain these experiences have become hopelessly muddled in preconceived notions of what is theoretically probable. Hufford concludes that although cultural factors heavily determine the ways in which the experience is described, the contents of this experience cannot be satisfactorily explained on the basis of current knowledge. This leads to the speculation that many experiences "may in fact also be *causes of* belief rather than being *caused by* belief" (p. 251). "A major advantage of the experience-centered approach for carrying out this task is that it does not require presuppositions about the ultimate nature of the events investigated, although it can provide some information relevant to investigations of that nature" (p. 256). Such an approach, if applied to psychical research, might remove it from the realm of crypto-parascience and allow it to be included beside Hufford's highly legitimate study, which might be classified as "applied folklore."

Numerous other possible scenarios exist. For example, mainstream scientists might decide that some fields have been "mined out." Some scientists might decide that the rewards for solving puzzles in their paradigms are insufficient. This could lead to increasing interest in more marginal fields, such as parapsychology. At the same time, if these scientists could not produce the psi effect and no explanation existed for their failure, the field might not gain legitimacy.

The attitudes and opinions of future elite scientists have special importance for the future legitimacy of parapsychology. The evidence generated by this study indicates that future elite scientists might be only slightly more accepting of the field. It is highly probable that future elite scientists, selected to replace those who retire or die, will tend to be more resistant to innovative claims than the general scientific population. Elite groups can be expected to defend the system which gave them their elite position. On the other hand, the gradual increase in belief in psi that has occurred over the last few decades within the scientific and general community may affect future elite attitudes. This change in belief makes it probable that future elite scientists will be more accepting of parapsychological research merely because they will be selected from a population whose acceptance seems to be increasing.

The policies of elite scientists can be affected by the public's attitude toward science. A science held in high esteem might allow different policies than a science which seemed counterproductive or valueless. The model does not predict how the interaction occurs though it would seem that lay groups do have a vague effect on the policies of elite scientific groups. Elite scientists have the power to change administrative policy in response to criticism that they deem to be valid.

The degree to which science is associated with the military, industry, and the government may have an effect on the policies of scientific elites. A science which is less attracted to these institutions might be more willing to allow innovative (and possibly fruitless) research that has little practical application. A science that has greater attachment to these institutions might tend to reflect the goals and needs of the institutions to a greater degree and engage in highly applicable forms of research.

The military use of psi would, of course, have a major impact on its acceptance. Speculation as to the probability of this occurring is beyond the scope of this study. Parapsychologists are divided regarding this probability. Various U.S. Defense Intelligence Agency reports express concern about Soviet capabilities (Ebon, 1983).

Factors Affecting the Future Legitimacy of Parapsychology That Exist Within the General Culture

Although the theoretical models developed within this study might be considered weak in relating the general culture to the rejection or acceptance of parapsychology, various factors derived from the general culture do enter into these models. These factors are: (1) the level of psi experience existing within the general populace and (2) the resources available to supportive lay groups and individuals. Both of these factors could have an effect on the future legitimacy of parapsychology.

Little research has been conducted on fluctuations in the level of psi experience within the general population. It might be expected that the *observed* level of this form of deviant behavior is a function of the process of deviance labeling. Scientific investigation can be expected to lend authenticity to such experiences and increase their reporting. The evidence generated in this study reveals that such experiences are the major factor leading to belief in ESP and acceptance of parapsychology. The frequency and form of psi experience, although having some constant qualities throughout the ages and cross-culturally, tend to correspond to the culture in which they are reported. For example, cases suggestive of reincarnation are reported more frequently in cultures supporting belief in reincarnation (Stevenson, 1977). Certain phenomena (such as observation and interaction with werewolves) have failed to survive the age of witchcraft, whereas other reported phenomena (such as telephone calls from the dead) have evolved during the last century. The resources of supportive lay groups and individuals are presently of critical importance to parapsychology. These groups allow the collection and documentation of psi experience (both inside the laboratory and out), an activity that tends to legitimate the field. Socially, their activity increases the belief that "psi is real" since psi has real consequences for those who experience it.

The model predicts that some of the products of deviant science may be incorporated into the scientific/cultural process. More components of the "parapsychological tradition" may gain legitimacy in the future. ESP might eventually become as accepted as hypnosis, a phenomenon that is poorly understood yet legitimate due to its practical applications. Various police departments already attempt to use professional and amateur psychics, and "therapeutic touch" (a form of psychic healing) is taught within some nursing programs. "Applied psi" might join other social methods used by established but nonscientific groups that have never been fully evaluated and retain a degree of controversy.

A primary factor that may determine the future legitimacy of psi has been only briefly mentioned in this study since it involves a form of hidden agenda within the parascientific ideology. As with previous megarevolutions that have occurred within science, numerous parapsychologists expect that the acceptance of psi will lead to the development of a new image of human beings. Previous revolutions (Copernican, Newtonian, Darwinian) have had similar effects. Successful megarevolutions within science lead to the abandonment of any world view that seems incompatible with the new research tradition. A new world view eventually evolves that is compatible with the new paradigm. Conversely, a new scientific paradigm might evolve from future world views.

Revolutions that occur totally within the scientific process seem to lack this capacity to modify the cultural image of the nature of reality and of people. Neither quantum mechanics nor behavioristic psychology has caused massive change in most people's beliefs about the world or themselves. Laudan (1977:101) notes, "Contrary to quantum mechanics, most people still conceive of the world as being populated by substantial objects, with fixed and precise properties; contrary to behaviorism, most people still find it helpful to talk about the inner mental states of themselves and others."

On the other hand, innovative scientific orientations that involve support from individuals and groups outside science have the capacity to generate new world views, images that overthrow the previously held perceptions. These ideological idea-sets tend to be revolutionary since they explain anomalies that have been rejected by the ideology in vogue.

Groups using these idea-sets might benefit from the changing public conception of science. The image of science held by the average person is now less favorable than it has been in the past. Modern science has become highly bureaucratic and closely associated with government, industry, and the military (Barnes, 1974). Groups attempting major modifications of these institutions might use parapsychological "knowledge" as an aspect of their ideology, based on a new image of humanity. It would seem that parapsychology's legitimacy may depend not so much on empirical success in verifying psi as on the rhetorical and political skill of those who feel the need to develop this new image. This image of humanity might picture an individual more suitable for living in an atomic, yet ecologically sensitive, age. Such an individual might be conceived as unconsciously connected on a psychical level to all other individuals and, consequently, as being less self-destructive and more humane. Parapsychology might be only a minor aspect in the development of this new image. Although the field is only peripherally involved with the "occult explosion" (Freedland, 1972) that has occurred in America during recent years, parapsychology exists as a legitimating aspect for various "new age" belief systems.

Proponents of "proto-scientific" ideology might choose to portray the world in dramatic images rather than the logical, physical, or causal conceptions of present dominant ideologies. This would not mean that "logical" scientific processes would be rejected, but that other ways of "knowing" might be granted greater importance than they are at present. More aesthetic or dramatic images of the world may be deemed as more "valuable" to humans who regard peaceful existence on the ecologically balanced earth as more important than scientific "progress." At present it would seem that the scientific image of the world excludes other "dramatic" or "mystical" images

(Fingarette, 1963). These dramatic world views are considered a portrayal of the imaginary. For those who harbor dramatic images, the scientific or physical world is, to a degree, an illusion and an obstacle that must be transcended in order to grasp the greater "reality" of existence. Greater acceptance of the dramatic images of reality might increase the legitimacy of parapsychology.

Yet various factors make the widespread acceptance of dramatic images based on psi seem unlikely in the short term. Not only does the theoretical model developed within this study present a means for the continuing resistance to parapsychology (no matter how "socially real" that psi may be), but certain historical aspects of psi reduce the probability of its acceptance. Historically, psi has been feared and stigmatized by numerous societies. The public image of psi places it beyond the realm of scientific exploration. A synthesis of the scientific image and the dramatic image seems, at present, impossible since, almost by definition, they are mutually exclusive.

Yet as noted by Fingarette (1963), it is possible to use dramatic images in some aspects of life and scientific images in others. It is a sign of a more flexible and adaptive cognitive orientation to be able to do this. Scientists seem to be using dramatic images in their selection and rejection of paradigms. Humans seem to be highly adaptable in their ability to compartmentalize their systems of belief and to ignore contradictions inherent within these systems. Future scientists may modify the ideology that guides their practices to such a degree that the appearance of complete replicability within parapsychological research will no longer be required to legitimate the field. The role of "faith" or "belief" may be recognized as a factor within scientific "progress" and scientists may attempt to "understand" this factor. Dramatic and scientific images of life may become fused to a degree.

Until then, parapsychology seems certain to flourish as a scientistic methodology harboring proto-scientistic metaphysical assumptions. Public and media interest insure its continuing existence. The resistance to its proto-scientistic nature can be considered rational within present scientific frameworks but may not always be considered so. The assumption that "society cannot, in principle, determine the contents of scientific knowledge because these are to be determined by observations of nature" (Richter, 1972) is less valid than has been assumed previously. Scientific knowledge associated with defining human nature is dependent on social processes unrelated to scientific methodology. Although scientific progress *seems* to occur when successive scientific theories show an increasing degree of effectiveness at solving problems (Laudan, 1977), evaluating such effectiveness requires a rhetorical and political process which is dependent upon ideology.

The problem-solving effectiveness of the parapsychological paradigm might be evaluated more favorably if the problems associated with physical paradigms were deemed as less important. Until then, we can expect resistance to proto-scientific paradigms that are less oriented toward physical solutions. Parapsychology may continue to investigate phenomena that are "socially real" but scientistically rejected. Until the "problems" that are considered "worth solving" deal more with the world inside human consciousness and less with the world outside, parapsychology may remain a deviant science.

Appendix A
Elite Scientist Questionnaire

1. Sex: _____ Male _____ Female

2. Current Academic Field _____

3. Birthdate: _____ month _____ year

Extrasensory perception is defined as experience of, or response to, a target object, state, event, or influence without sensory contact.

Psi is a general term to identify a person's extrasensorimotor communication with the environment. Parapsychology is a branch of science that deals with psi communication, i.e., behavioral or personal exchanges with the environment which are extrasensorimotor—not dependent on the senses and muscles.

4. In your opinion is extrasensory perception:
   a. An established fact
   b. A likely possibility
   c. A remote possibility
   d. An impossibility
   e. Merely an unknown

5. Is this opinion based on: (Choose as many as are applicable)
   a. Reports in newspapers and magazines
   b. Books by Rhine, Soal, or other parapsychologists
   c. Experimentation as reported in scientific journals
      Which journals?
   d. Television
   e. Hearsay
   f. *A priori* grounds
   g. Personal experience
   h. Other (summarize briefly)

6. Do you consider the investigation of extrasensory perception a legitimate scientific undertaking?
   a. Yes
   b. No
   c. Not sure

7. Additional comments concerning your attitude toward parapsychology:

8. How familiar are you with parapsychological research?
   a. Not at all familiar
   b. Slightly familiar
   c. Somewhat familiar
   d. Fairly well familiar
   e. Very familiar

How much do you agree or disagree with each of the following statements?

9. It is possible to distinguish science from nonscience.
   a. Strongly disagree
   b. Disagree
   c. Uncertain
   d. Agree
   e. Strongly agree
   f. I cannot make a judgment

10. Success in science depends not only on rational argument but on a mixture of subterfuge, rhetoric, and propaganda.
    a. Strongly disagree
    b. Disagree
    c. Uncertain
    d. Agree
    e. Strongly agree
    f. I cannot make a judgment

How often have you had any of the following experiences? Read each item and circle one code for each.

	Never in my life	Once or twice	Several times	Often	I cannot answer this question
11. Thought you were somewhere you had been before but knew it was impossible. (déjà vu)	1	2	3	4	5

	Never in my life	Once or twice	Several times	Often	I cannot answer this question
12. Felt as though you were in touch with someone when you knew that it was impossible. (ESP)	1	2	3	4	5
13. Seen events that happened at a great distance as they were happening. (clairvoyance)	1	2	3	4	5
14. Felt as though you were really in touch with someone who died. (communication with the dead)	1	2	3	4	5
15. Felt as though you were very close to a powerful, spiritual force that seemed to lift you out of yourself. (out-of-body experience)	1	2	3	4	5

16. If you have had what might be considered a paranormal or psychic experience, would you describe it briefly.

17. Many reasons have been suggested to explain the resistance of scientists to the work of parapsychologists. Several possible reasons are listed on the next page. Please rate each according to your opinion of its importance.

	Extremely important	Very important	Somewhat important	Slightly important	Not at all important	I do not know or cannot answer
a. Parapsychology threatens the established mechanistic world view of scientists.	____	____	____	____	____	____
b. Parapsychology conflicts with current physical or biological theories.	____	____	____	____	____	____
c. Scientists want to avoid any association with "occult" phenomena.	____	____	____	____	____	____
d. There is insufficient evidence for psychic ability.	____	____	____	____	____	____
e. The complexity and elusiveness of psi makes it extremely difficult to research.	____	____	____	____	____	____
f. Scientists are simply unfamiliar with the present evidence for psi.	____	____	____	____	____	____
g. No adequate theory has been produced to explain psychic ability.	____	____	____	____	____	____
h. Scientists feel that, on the whole, parapsychological research has not been conducted in a competent manner.	____	____	____	____	____	____
i. Other reasons: ____						

_____

_____.

Owing to my oversight, this questionnaire was originally labeled as an "AAAS Questionnaire." All recipients were informed of this error.

Appendix B
Additional Comments from Elite Scientists

Item 7 on the Elite Scientist Questionnaire requested "additional comments concerning your attitude toward parapsychology." Additional responses, not contained in chapter 5, are listed below:

Open-Mindedness

I found Rhine's early results on ESP interesting, perhaps plausible. But when he obtained similarly positive results on everything he tried, including precognition, I became more skeptical.

It would be nice if there really were a solid body of parapsychological experiments. But more than anything else (except perhaps UFO's), the field is messed up by carelessness, incompetence, and plain dishonest fakery (e.g., Uri Geller). Good scientists can easily be fooled, and should have the assistance of a professional magician before testing subjects in this field. Thus, I remain very skeptical.

I know too little about it to say more.

I would be interested if carefully controlled data supported the demonstration of such phenomena.

Science deals with and is based upon facts. Facts are gained through the senses. Therefore, extrasensory phenomena (if real) are beyond the realm of science. Unless the parapsychologists can bring the proposed phenomena into the arena of verifiable fact, parapsychology can't be considered science. This objection, on the other hand, does not imply that the subject should not be investigated. It should if there is any reasonable theory or evidence for extrasensory phenomena.

Seems reasonable that there may be, as yet, undefined senses. If so, extrasensory perception becomes simply sensory perception. Seems to me that looking for other sensory modes is a legitimate scientific endeavor (although it might not be very fruitful). I can think of many more interesting and promising scientific studies, though.

While I see no reason why extrasensory phenomena cannot occur, I am not convinced that it is a significant aspect in general behavior.

Rejection of the Legitimacy of Parapsychology

I have never known, or know of, any one active since 1940, whom I respect, who did credible research on the so-called phenomenon.

Why can't you guess my answer? Even the most scientific investigations are almost invariably very insensitive to possibilities of fraud or self-deception. If even one proven instance of intentional fraud is discovered, in *any other scientific field* not only the deceiver but his associates are essentially discredited from that time on; yet, people continued to work with Uri Geller long after it was clear he was a charlatan. I have literally *never* seen any attempt to investigate these phenomena on a truly scientific basis (such attempts are usually opposed by the practitioner).

Reports I have read, and specifically those about Rhine's work, indicate that many investigators in parapsychology have used sloppy experimental techniques and have drawn conclusions that cannot be verified by more careful work. . . . Many of the experiences covered by your questions 11-16 [déjà vu and mystical experiences] can be explained simply as minor malfunctions of the brain, and if more complicated explanations are offered, Occam's Razor requires that they be proved, and not merely asserted. . . . Parapsychologists apparently continue to assert the correctness of their results even when no one else can repeat them except another "believer."

We do not improve the ability of individuals or of society to deal with reality by diverting our attention to a "world" that can be neither shared nor perceived by more than one person.

I believe in God and religion but think this should be regarded as faith, not provable, not scientific.

Even if extrasensory perception exists, it has more potential for evil than good because it is always susceptible to fraud and quackery.

It has had an adequate run for its money. Put it on the shelf until some evidence of the "remote possibility" is found.

It impinges on religion and the supernatural. To believe in any such phenomena is to accept all. It immediately becomes impossible to place limits and say: we accept this and not that. Intellectually, it is a regression to a culture that believes in magic. . . . It is not susceptible to objective analysis. No other person can prove or disprove my personal subjective experience of, for instance, communication with someone who died.

I am probably biased by the fact that I never hear anything from this field of research except the complaints of its proponents that nobody wants to listen to. I find it easier to get interested in scientific controversies when they are about some substantive scientific issue rather than being different groups' attitudes toward each other. I suspect you [the author of this questionnaire] of bias or mischievous intent, since there is little opportunity given by the specific questions for answers reflecting the opinion that seemingly paranormal or psychic experiences may be purely subjective, that parapsychology really doesn't have anything to say scientifically, and that that is the reason for its problems.

There are too many charlatans who have been attracted to the field.

I would put it in the same class as astrology. It is even more conceivable that the positions of stars influence us by gravity, etc. than that communication without sensory exchange can take place.

PSEUDOSCIENCE—a dangerous challenge to true science

I'm tired of the subject.

NOT INTERESTED

Support for Parapsychology

This is important to be studied to lend credibility to consistently repeated experience.

More research is needed to better understand the subject, e.g., what are the limits? What are the facts and what are the nonscientific perceptions?

It is a potentially revolutionary field—difficulty in performing research is due to the often uncontrollable nature of the phenomena, but [it] could provide new insights into the natural world if adequately described, explained, and controlled. We should keep our minds open to all controversial explanations of reality, but remain vigilant for charlatans and fakes, at the same time. The culture seems to accept parapsychological phenomena on an anecdotal basis and historical accounts go back to the Bible—but controlled experimental proof is difficult. The anecdotal accounts tend to be spectacular (such as ghostly visions, out-of-body experiences, premonitions that save lives, etc.), but the lab evidence is mostly statistical. What the lab needs to show is a verification of the more spectacular psi phenomena which are claimed—not merely statistical proofs on the basis of card games. etc.

On a priority scale of 1 (high) to 10 (low), I would allocate this at about 7.

It appears to be a fruitful area of research and probably will have many interesting breakthroughs.

Important to continue research in area. Also need to educate public more.

I feel very strongly about the fact that parapsychology has not been treated as a "new" or emerging arm of science. However, there are problems on both sides of the fence.

Parapsychology needs a new experimental method. Neither the direct manipulation of Newtonian mechanics nor the statistical averages of epidemiology is appropriate for phenomena dependent on factors that are rare within *Homo-sapiens*. Since many disease phenomena also depend on such factors, medicine also needs such a method.

Paranormal or Psychic Experiences Described by Elite Scientists

Additional responses to Item 16 on the questionnaire are listed below. Item 16 reads, "If you have had what might be considered a paranormal or psychic experience, would you describe it briefly." The phrase in brackets following each statement is the individual's response to the "opinion of ESP" question.

When I was moving out of my apartment after graduate school, I thought I saw an apparition in the living room as I lay in my bed. I had rented the apartment furnished and the lady who rented it to me recently died. It appeared to me that the apparition might have been of this deceased lady checking to see that I did not take any of her possessions when I left for a new residence. However, I would not swear I saw a ghost as other explanations are possible. My wife, who was sleeping with me, was not awakened by the apparition and saw nothing when I woke her to tell her about it. Thus, I would *not* rule this as a highly psychic or paranormal experience. [ESP: a likely possibility]

I felt the presence of my mother-in-law the evening after her burial. During the brief period, her dog went almost wild. [ESP: a likely possibility]

On three occasions in my life (early, not recently), I dreamed of events that occurred in advance of their actually happening. Two of the events involved the deaths of individuals—one expected, but not imminent; the other, unexpected. One event was an accident. On the other hand, not long ago (about 1 year ago), I dreamed of the death of an individual and, fortunately, he is still healthy and active although over 80 years of age. [ESP: a likely possibility]

With certain people (some friends of both sexes and my mother), I am aware of times of great trauma even though we might not have communicated in months. Examples: knew day and approximate time (recorded and witnessed) friend in London received eye injury. Called friend in Illinois to ask wife what was wrong with Charlie—no contact for about 9 months—she replied he had been out of surgery for about two hours at that time and all seemed O.K. after the emergency operation. Then she asked, "How did you know?"

Another friend in England contemplating suicide—no contact in nearly a year—I wrote a long letter which she felt was a turning point. I am a receiver but apparently am not picked up the other way except by my mother. She receives me better than I get her. After years of hiding this, I have talked to my friends about it and they know of each other. One in Ohio has had several emergencies—we never write (sometimes we call or visit)—I missed just one emergency. Lately, I have not had the "white mind" time to check on my friends so may have missed something. Obviously, except to those involved, I don't talk about this as it would be viewed as screwy to all my allegedly professional colleagues and I have really let my "contacts" know rather recently. I have not learned to control what comes in nor do I receive something every "white mind" time. Am interested how many others have comparable experiences. [ESP: an established fact]

When my father suddenly died, I was very upset. He was "waked" at our home, and late that night, as I was settling down to sleep, and grieving, he spoke to me. He said, "Don't be upset, Barbara. It's all right. I am going away now. You will be all right." He appeared before me for some time as if in a haze as he was speaking, and then he went away. When I looked at his body in the casket the next day, it was as if nothing were there. The spirit of my father had been present, as if he were really with me, during the wake and until he said goodbye. After that, there was nothing. My father speaks to me sometimes now (20 years later), when I want to reach out to him. But I don't want to that often now. I love him no less, and I know he is aware of all that I do, but I don't need to contact him so often. [ESP: a likely possibility]

I had a phone call at a time when I needed support that I am convinced came from a recently dead support source—the manner of approach, the times and content of the call absolutely convinced me . . . and achieved the support needed. I have a witness to the fact of the call and my reaction but not to the content. [ESP: a likely possibility]

A family member was ill and hospitalized. I "kind of went into a trance" as a result of continued thinking of the person. I "traveled" in my mind 400 miles to the hospital where I had never been, looked down into the operating room, saw her there at the beginning of the surgery. As the surgeon prepared to make the incision on the right side, I said to him (in my mind) "no—it's on the left side." The surgeon changed over, made the incision. At that point, all went black. I was frightened and came out of the trance. When I received information about the surgery, I asked, "Which side was involved?" I was told, "they finally decided it was on the left side." I understand that this kind of ethereal travel is possible. [ESP: an established fact]

My wife, who was dying of cancer, was post-operative and drugged in a hospital room. She read several cards (about 7 in sequence) as to suit and number which I placed on her back. Situation prevailed for perhaps 2 minutes, then rapidly deteriorated. *A priori* probability 10^{-12}. [ESP: a remote possibility]

Additional Comments from Elite Scientists Regarding Parapsychology

Many refuse to recognize that an experience can be a-rational, in a different sense of values, without being irrational, i.e., opposed to reason.

I have found a similar resistance in the field of hypnosis—too many physicians and scientists avoid getting involved with areas exploited by stage performers and charlatans.

Psi has no rational, physical, scientific basis and diverts attention from reality and real problems of world concern.

Parapsychologists seem to exaggerate the resistance and increase it by making it their cause instead of letting the scientific chips fall where they may. This makes me doubt they really have anything.

Belongs in the world of arts, not of the sciences.

Psi often threatens personal identity (fear of insanity).

It is uninteresting, i.e., has not led to an interesting research field or set a series of problems that can be investigated as a matrix of problems leading to further problems and research.

More important and pressing issues exist in other disciplines.

Few scientists have had or accept that they have had psi experiences.

Appendix C
Parapsychological Research Centers

Foundation for Research on the Nature of Man
Institute for Parapsychology
College Station, Box 6847
Durham, NC 27708

William Roll, Ph.D.
Psychical Research Foundation
P.O. Box 3356
Chapel Hill, NC 27514

Ian Stevenson, M.D.
Division of Parapsychology
Department of Psychiatry
University of Virginia Medical Center
Charlottesville, VA 22901

American Society for Psychical Research
5 West 73rd Street
New York, NY 10023

Gertrude Schmeidler, Ph.D.
Department of Psychology
City College of the City University of New York
New York, NY 10031

Charles Honorton
Psychophysical Research Laboratories, Inc.
301 College Road E.
Princeton, NJ 08540

Mind Science Foundation
Suite 215
102 West Rector Street
San Antonio, TX 78216

Gary Heseltine, M.D.
Science Unlimited Research Foundation
311 D Spencer Lane
San Antonio, TX 78201

Charles Tart, Ph.D.
Department of Psychology
University of California at Davis
Davis, CA 95616

H. E. Puthoff, Ph.D.
SRI International
Menlo Park, CA 94025

Rex Stanford, Ph.D.
Psychology Laboratory SB-15, Merillac
St. John's University
Grand Central and Utopia Parkways
Jamaica, NY 11439

Luthor Rudolph, Ph.D., and Robert Morris, Ph.D.
Syracuse University School of Computer and Information Science
313 Link Hall
Syracuse University
Syracuse, NY 15210

John F. Kennedy University
12 Altarinda Road
Orinda, CA 94563

McDonnell Laboratory for Psychical Research
Washington University
8631 Delmar Boulevard, Suite 8
St. Louis, MO 63124

Robert Jahn, Ph.D.
Princeton Engineering in Anomalies Research
School of Engineering/Applied Science
Engineering Quadrangle
Princeton University
Princeton, NJ 08544

Parapsychology Laboratory
University of Utrecht
Varkenmarkt 2
3511 BZ Utrecht
The Netherlands

Washington Research Center
3101 Washington Street
San Francisco, CA 94115

Edward Kelly, Ph.D.
Department of Electrical Engineering
Duke University
Durham, NC 27706

Institute für Grenzgebiete der Psychologie und Psychohygiene
Eichhalde 12
D7800 Freiburg 1 Dr.
West Germany

Carl Sargent, Ph.D.
Psychological Laboratory
Cambridge University
Cambridge CB2 3EB
United Kingdom

New Horizons Research Foundation
P.O. Box 427, Station F
Toronto, Ontario M4Y 2L8
Canada

Rhea White
Parapsychology Sources of Information Center
2 Plane Tree Lane
Dix Hills, NY 11746

The Society for Psychical Research
1 Adam and Eve Mews
London W8 6UG
England

Appendix D
Interview Questions for Parapsychologists

1. When and how did you first become interested in parapsychology?

2. How did you first become involved in research in parapsychology?

3. What effect did becoming socialized into the role of parapsychologist have on you? How has socialization into the role of parapsychologist affected you as a researcher?

4. How frequent and what types of interaction do you maintain with other parapsychologists?

5. How frequent and what types of interaction do you maintain with lay groups or the general public?

6. How frequent and what types of interaction do you maintain with the media?

7. What is your system of beliefs regarding psi, i.e., how strongly do you "believe in" psi?

8. What has been the effect of the research that you have conducted on your system of beliefs regarding psi?

9. Have you had any personal psychic experiences?

10. What has been the effect of these personal psychic experiences (if any) on your system of beliefs regarding psi?

11. Have you had any interaction with the Committee for the Scientific Investigation of Claims of the Paranormal?

12. How frequent and what type of interaction do you maintain with mainstream scientists?

13. Do you foresee parapsychology becoming a completely legitimate field?

14. In the future, what do you think the field of parapsychology will be like?

References

AAAS Files. "References in AAAS Minutes to Parapsychological Association." 1961–1979.

AAAS Minutes. Council on Affiliation, Nov. 20, 1961 (supplied by Ms. Catherine Borras, Assistant to the Executive Officer, AAAS).

Allison, P. D. "Social Aspects of Scientific Innovation: The Case of Parapsychology." Master's Thesis, University of Wisconsin, 1973.

Allison, P. D. "Experimental Parapsychology as a Rejected Science." Pp. 271–291 in *On the Margins of Science: The Social Construction of Rejected Knowledge*, Roy Wallis, ed. Hanley, England: J. H. Brookes, 1979.

American Society for Psychical Research. "Courses and Other Study Opportunities in Parapsychology," 1980, available through the American Society for Psychical Research, 5 West 73rd Street, New York, NY 10023.

Amick, D. J. "An Index of Scientific Elitism and the Scientist's Mission." *Science Studies*, 4 (1974), 1–16.

Ashby, R.W.S.N. "Verifiability Principle." In *The Encyclopedia of Philosophy*, Paul Edwards, ed. Vol. 8. New York: Macmillan, 1967.

Barber, Bernard. "Resistance by Scientists to Scientific Discovery." *Science*, 134 (Sept. 1961), 596–602.

Barnes, Barry. *Scientific Knowledge and Sociological Theory*. Boston: Routledge and Kegan Paul, 1974.

Barnes, S. B., and R.G.A. Dolby. "The Scientific Ethos: A Deviant Viewpoint." *European Journal of Sociology*, 11 (1970), 3–25.

Barry, James Dale. *Ball Lightning and Bead Lightning*. New York and London: Plenum Press, 1980.

Bartlett, Laile E. "What Do We Really Know About Psychic Phenomena?" *Reader's Digest*, Aug. 1977, 82–87.

Becker, Carl L. *The Heavenly City of the Eighteenth-Century Philosophers*. New Haven: Yale University Press, 1932.

Beloff, John. *New Directions in Parapsychology*. London: Elek Science, 1974.

Beloff, John, "Seven Evidential Experiments." *Zetetic Scholar*, 6 (1980), 91–94.

Bennett, Thomas L. *Introduction to Physiological Psychology*. Monterey, CA: Brooks/Cole, 1982.

Berkeley, G. A. "A Treatise Concerning the Principles of Human Knowledge." In *A New Theory of Vision and Other Select Philosophical Writings*. London: J. M. Dent and Sons, 1910 (originally published in 1710).

253

Berlitz, Charles. *The Bermuda Triangle.* New York: Avon, 1975.

Blackmore, S. J. "The Extent of Selective Reporting of ESP Ganzfeld Studies." *European Journal of Parapsychology,* 3 (Nov. 1980), 213–220.

Blom, J. G., and J. G. Pratt. "A Second Confirmatory ESP Experiment with Pavel Stepanek as a 'Borrowed' Subject." *Journal of the American Society for Psychical Research,* 63 (1969), 207–209.

Boring, E. G. "Paranormal Phenomena: Evidence, Specification, and Chance." In the Introduction to C.E.M. Hansel, *E.S.P.: A Scientific Evaluation.* New York: Charles Scribner's Sons, 1966.

Borras, Catherine (Assistant to the Executive Officer, AAAS). Personal letter, Dec. 14, 1981.

Bowers, John Z. "Reception of Acupuncture by the Scientific Community: From Scorn to a Degree of Interest." Pp. 91–104 in *The Reception of Unconventional Science,* Seymour H. Mauskopf, ed., Boulder, CO: Westview Press, 1979.

Brain/Mind Bulletin. "Founder Quits Anti-psi Committee, Cites 'Media Blitz.'" Dec. 19, 1977.

Braud, William G. "Studies of the Stimulus Specificity, Response Specificity, Process Specificity, and Task Specificity of the Behavioral Bioassay Phenomenon." Task Force on Field Initiated Research, National Institute of Education, Code 600, Project No. 10515F, Apr. 1973.

Braud, William. Personal communication, May 1979.

Braud, William G. "Liability and Inertia in Conformance Behavior." *Journal of the American Society for Psychical Research,* Vol. 74, no. 3 (1980), 297–318.

Braud, William. Private correspondence, Apr. 18, 1983.

Broad, C. D. "The Relevance of Psychical Research to Philosophy." In *Philosophy and Parapsychology,* J. Ludwig, ed. Buffalo, NY: Prometheus Books, 1978 (originally published in 1949).

Broad, William J. "Magician's Effort to Foil Scientists Raises Questions." *New York Times,* Feb. 15, 1983, Science Times section, p. C3.

Brown, G. S. "Statistical Significance in Psychical Research." *Nature,* 172 (1953), 154–156.

Brown, Richard H. *A Poetic for Sociology: Toward a Logic of Discovery for the Human Sciences.* New York: Cambridge University Press, 1977.

Brugmans, H. J. Report (in French) in the *Proceedings of the First International Congress of Psychical Research at Copenhagen,* 1922, pp. 396–408.

Burke, Kenneth. *The Philosophy of Literary Form.* New York: Random House, 1941.

Burtt, E. A. *The Metaphysical Foundations of Modern Physical Science: A Historical and Critical Essay.* London: Routledge and Kegan Paul, 1932.

Byrne, W. L., D. Samuel, E. L. Bennett, M. R. Rosenzweig, E. Wasserman, A. R. Wagner, R. Gardner, R. Galambos, B. D. Berger, D. L. Margules, R. L. Fenichel, L. Stein, J. A. Corson, H. E. Enesco, S. L. Chorover, C. E. Holt III, P. H. Schiller, L. Chiapetta, M. E. Jarvik, R. C. Leaf, J. D. Dutcher, Z. P. Horowitz, P. L. Carlson. "Memory Transfer." *Science,* 153 (1966), 658–659.

Camp, Burton, quoted by J. J. O'Neil. "In the Realm of Science: Extra-Sensory Perception Finds Champion in Mathematics If Not Psychology." *Herald Tribune,* Jan. 16, 1938; and in *Journal of Parapsychology* , 1, 305.

Carpenter, J. C. "The Differential Effect and Hidden Target Differences Consisting of Erotic and Neutral Stimuli." *Journal of the American Society for Psychical Research,* 65 (1971), 204–214.

Cerullo, John J. *The Secularization of the Soul.* Philadelphia, PA: Institute for the Study of Human Issues, 1982.

Charman, W. N. "Ball Lightning." *Physics Reports,* a review section of *Physics Letters,* Vol. 54, no. 4 (1979), 261–306.

CIBA Foundation Symposium on Extra-Sensory Perception. Boston: Little, Brown, 1956.

Collins, H. M. "The TEA Set: Tacit Knowledge and Scientific Networks." *Science Studies,* 4 (1974), 165–186.

Collins, H. M. "The Seven Sexes: A Study in the Sociology of a Phenomenon, or the Replication of Experiments in Physics." *Sociology,* 9 (May 1975), 205–224.

Collins, H. M. "Upon the Replication of Scientific Findings: A Discussion Illuminated from the Experiences of Researchers into Parapsychology." Paper presented at the First International Conference of the Society for Social Studies of Science, Cornell University, Nov. 1976.

Collins, H. M. "The Place of the Core-Set in Modern Science: Social Contingency with Methodological Propriety in Science." *History of Science,* 19 (1981), 6–19.

Collins, H. M. "The Metal Benders" (a book review). *Zetetic Scholar,* 9 (1982), 108–110.

Collins, H. M., and T. J. Pinch. "The Construction of the Paranormal: Nothing Unscientific Is Happening." Pp. 237–270 in *On the Margins of Science: The Social Construction of Rejected Knowledge,* Roy Wallis, ed. Hanley, England: J. H. Brookes, 1979.

Collins, H. M., and T. J. Pinch. *Frames of Meaning. The Social Construction of Extraordinary Science.* London, Boston, and Hanley: Routledge and Kegan Paul, 1982.

Collins, Randall. *The Credential Society.* New York: Academic Press, 1979.

Collins, Randall. *Sociological Insight. An Introduction to Non-Obvious Sociology.* New York: Oxford University Press, 1982.

Condon E. U. "UFOs I Have Loved and Lost." *Bulletin of the Atomic Scientists,* 25 (Dec. 1969), 6–8.

Coover, John Edgar. *Experiments in Psychical Research.* Stanford, CA: Stanford University Press, 1917.

Corless, William F. *Handbook of Unusual Natural Phenomena.* Glen Arm, MD: The Sourcebook Project, 1977.

Corless, William F. *Lightning, Auroras, Nocturnal Lights and Related Luminous Phenomena. A Catalog of Geophysical Anomalies.* Glen Arm, MD: The Sourcebook Project, 1982.

Crane, Diana. *Invisible Colleges: Diffusion of Knowledge in Scientific Communities.* Chicago: University of Chicago Press, 1972.

Currie, Elliot P. "Crimes without Criminals: Witchcraft and Its Control in Renaissance Europe." *Law and Society Review,* 3 (Oct. 1968), 7–28.

Davis, H. T. Quoted in the *Washington Evening Star,* Jan. 2, 1938, and in Mauskopf and McVaugh (1979).

Dean, E. Douglas. "The Parapsychological Association Becomes Affiliated with the American Association for the Advancement of Science. How It Was Done." Paper. Jan. 1, 1970.

Defense Intelligence Agency (author's name still classified). *Paraphysics R & D—Warsaw Pact (U).* Washington, D.C.: Defense Intelligence Agency, Mar. 30, 1978 (#DST-1810s-202-78).

Dentler, Robert A., and Kai T. Erikson. "The Function of Deviance in Groups." *Social Problems,* 7 (Fall 1959), 99–107.

d'Espagnat, Bernard. "The Quantum Theory and Reality." *Scientific American,* Vol. 241, no. 5 (1979), 158–181.

Diaconis, P. "Statistical Problems in ESP Research." *Science,* 201 (July 1978), 131–136.

Doherty, J. "Hot Feat: Firewalkers of the World." *Science Digest,* 90 (Aug. 1982), 66–71.

Dolby, R.G.A. "Reflections on Deviant Science." Pp. 9–47 in *On the Margins of Science: The Social Construction of Rejected Knowledge,* Roy Wallis, ed. Hanley, England: J. H. Brookes, 1979.

Dommeyer, R. C. "Parapsychology: Old Delusion or New Science?" *International Journal of Neuropsychiatry,* 2 (1966), 539–555.

Downey, K. J. "Sociology and the Modern Scientific Revolution." *Sociological Quarterly,* 8 (1967), 239.

Duane, T. D., and T. Behrendt. "Extrasensory Electroencephalographic Induction Between Identical Twins." *Science,* 150 (Oct. 1965), 367.

Duke, Marc. *Acupuncture.* New York: Pyramid House, 1972.

Dunne, Brenda J., and John P. Bisaha. "Precognitive Remote Viewing in the Chicago Area: A Replication of the Stanford Experiment." *Journal of Parapsychology,* 43 (Mar. 1979), 17–30.

Durant, Will, and Ariel Durant. *The Age of Voltaire.* New York: Simon and Schuster, 1965.

Durkheim, Emile. *The Rules of the Sociological Method.* Chicago: University of Chicago Press, 1938 (originally published in 1895).

Dyal, J. A. "Transfer of Behavioral Bias: Reality and Specificity." Pp. 219–264 in *Chemical Transfer of Learned Information,* E. J. Fjerdingstad, ed. Amsterdam: North Holland, 1971.

Ebon, Martin. *Psychic Warfare: Threat or Illusion.* New York: McGraw-Hill, 1983.

Ehrenwald, J. *Telepathy and Medical Psychology.* New York: W. W. Norton, 1948.

Eliade, Mircea. *Patanjali and Yoga,* translated by Charles Lam Markmann. New York: Funk and Wagnalls, 1969.

Erikson, Kai T. *Wayward Puritans.* New York: Wiley, 1966.

Evans, C. "Long Dream Ending." *New Scientist,* 41 (1969), 638–640.

Evans, C. "Parapsychology—What the Questionnaire Revealed." *New Scientist,* 57 (1973), 209.

Festinger, Leon. *A Theory of Cognitive Dissonance.* Evanston, IL: Row Peterson, 1957.

Festinger, L., H. W. Riechen, and S. Schachter. *When Prophecy Fails.* New York: Harper Torchbooks, 1956.

Feyerabend, Paul. "Against Method." *Minnesota Studies in the Philosophy of Science,* 4 (1970a).

Feyerabend, Paul. "Consolations for the Specialist." Pp. 197–230 in *Criticism and the Growth of Knowledge,* Imre Lakatos and Alan Musgrave, eds. Cambridge: Cambridge University Press, 1970b.

Fingarette, Herbert. *The Self in Transformation.* New York: Basic Books, 1963.

Frankel, Henry. "The Reception and Acceptance of Continental Drift Theory as a Rational Episode in the History of Science." Pp. 51–89 in *The Reception of Unconventional Science,* Seymour H. Mauskopf, ed. Boulder, CO: Westview Press, 1979.

Freedland, Nat. *The Occult Explosion.* New York: G. P. Putnam's Sons, 1972.

FRNM Bulletin, no. 10 (Autumn), 1968.

FRNM Bulletin, no. 12 (Spring), 1969.

Fuller, John C. *The Great Soul Trial.* New York: Macmillan, 1969.

Galilei, G. (The Assayer). In *The Controversy on the Comets of 1618,* S. Drake and C. D. O'Malley, ed. and trans. Philadelphia: University of Pennsylvania Press, 1960 (originally published in 1623).

Gallup, G. *The Gallup Poll, Public Opinion, 1978.* Wilmington, DE: Scholarly Research, Inc., 1979.

Gallup, George, with William Proctor. *Adventures in Immortality.* New York: McGraw-Hill, 1982.

Gardner, Martin. "Concerning an Effort to Demonstrate Extrasensory Perception by Machine." *Scientific American,* Vol. 233, no. 4 (1975), 114–118.

Gardner, Martin. "Science and the Citizen, Psi-Fi." *Scientific American,* Vol. 240, no. 4 (1979a), 84.

Gardner, Martin. "Quantum Theory and Quack Theory." *New York Review of Books,* 26 (May 17, 1979b), 39–41.

Gauld, A. *The Founders of Psychical Research.* London: Routledge and Kegan Paul, 1968.

Gauld, Alan, and A. D. Cornell. *Poltergeists.* Boston, MA: Routledge and Kegan Paul, 1979.

Gibson, H. B. *Hypnosis.* New York: Taplinger, 1980.

Gieryn, Thomas F., and Richard F. Hirsh. "Marginality and Innovation in Science." *Social Studies of Science,* 13 (1983), 87–106.

Goffman, E. *Stigma: Notes on the Management of Spoiled Identity.* Englewood Cliffs, NJ: Prentice-Hall, 1963.

Gould, S. J. "The Validation of Continental Drift." In *Ever Since Darwin: Reflections in Natural History.* New York: Norton, 1977.

Green, C. E. "Ecsomatic Experiences and Related Phenomena." *Journal of the Society for Psychical Research,* 44 (1967), 111–131.

Greene, John C. "The Kuhnian Paradigm and the Darwinian Revolution in Natural History." Pp. 297–320 in *Paradigms and Revolutions,* Gary Gutting, ed. Notre Dame, IN: University of Notre Dame Press, 1980.

Greenwell, J. Richard (Secretary, International Society of Cryptozoology). Personal correspondence, May 6, 1983.

Gregory, A. "Anatomy of a Fraud." *Annals of Science,* 34 (1977), 449–549.

Gregory, A. "Why Do Scientists Engage in Fraud?" *Parapsychology Review,* Vol. 11, no. 6 (1980), 1–6.

Griffith, Belver C., and Nicholas C. Mullins. "Coherent Social Groups in Scientific Change." *Science,* 177 (Sept. 1972), 959–964.

Gruenberger, Fred J. "A Measure for Crackpots." *Science,* 145 (Sept. 1964), 1413–1415.

Gurney, E., F.W.H. Myers, F. Fodmore. *Phantasm of the Living.* London: Trubner, 1886, 2 vols.

Gusfield, Joseph. "The Literary Rhetoric of Science: Comedy and Pathos in

Drinking Driver Research." *American Sociological Review,* 41 (1976), 16-34.

Hagstrom, Warren O. *The Scientific Community.* New York: Basic Books, 1965.

Hall, A. Rupert. "Merton Revisited: Of Science and Society in the Seventeenth Century." *History of Science,* 2 (1963), 3–6.

Hanlon, J. "Uri Geller and Science." *New Scientist,* Oct. 17, 1974, 170–185.

Hansel, C.E.M. "Experiments on Telepathy in Children." *British Journal of Statistical Psychology,* 13 (1960), 175–178.

Hansel, C.E.M. *ESP: A Scientific Evaluation.* New York: Charles Scribner's Sons, 1966.

Hansel, C.E.M. "A Critical Analysis of H. Schmidt's PK Experiments." *Skeptical Enquirer,* Vol. 5, no. 3 (Spring 1981), 26–33.

Hardin, C. L. "Tales From the Crypto." *Zetetic Scholar,* 10 (1982), 126–128.

Hare, R. *Experimental Investigation of the Spirit Manifestations.* 4th ed. New York: Partridge and Brittan, 1856.

Harley, T. A., and C. Sargent. "Two Studies of ESP in the Ganzfeld." Paper read to the 3rd International Conference of the Society for Psychical Research, Edinburgh, Scotland, Apr. 1979.

Hasted, John. *The Metal Benders.* London: Routledge and Kegan Paul, 1981.

Hastings, Arthur C. "Psychical Research." Background material prepared for "Changing Images of Man" Policy Research Report No. 4, Center for the Study of Social Policy, Stanford Research Institute, Menlo Park, CA, June 1973.

Hastings, Arthur C. "Report: Magicians, Magic, and Uri Geller." *Psychoenergetic Systems,* 2 (1977), 133–139.

Hayek, F. A. *The Counter-Revolution of Science: Studies on the Abuse of Reason.* Glencoe, IL: The Free Press, 1952.

Hebb, D. O. "The Role of Neurological Ideas in Psychology." *Journal of Personality,* 20 (1951), 39–55.

Heidelberger, Michael. "Some Intertheoretic Relations Between Ptolemean and Copernican Astronomy." Pp. 271–283 in *Paradigms and Revolutions,* Gary Gutting, ed. Notre Dame, IN: University of Notre Dame Press, 1980.

Hempel, Carl G. "Problems and Changes in the Empiricist Criterion of Meaning." *Revue Internationale de Philosophie,* 40 (1950), 41–63.

Heseltine, G. L., and J. H. Kirk. "Examination of a Majority Vote Technique." *Journal of Parapsychology,* Vol. 44, no. 2 (1980), 167–176.

Hoagland, H. "Editorial." *Science,* 163 (Feb. 1969), 625.

Hoffman, Ronald B. "Behavioral Modification in a Shape Discrimination Task via Brain Homogenates." Master's thesis, University of Houston, 1971.

Honorton, C. "Error Some Place." *Journal of Communication,* Vol. 25, no. 1 (1975), 103–116.

Honorton, C. "Psi and Internal Attention States." Pp. 435–472 in *Handbook of Parapsychology*, B. B. Wolman, ed. New York: Van Nostrand Reinhold, 1977.

Honorton, C. "Replicability, Experimenter Influence, and Parapsychology: An Empirical Context for the Study of Mind." Paper presented at the Annual Meeting of the American Association for the Advancement of Science, Washington, DC, Feb. 17, 1978.

Honorton, C., M. Ramsey, and C. Cabibbo. "Experimenter Effects in Extrasensory Perception." *Journal of the American Society for Psychical Research*, 69 (1975), 135–149.

Houdini, Harry. *Miracle Mongers and Their Methods: A Complete Exposé*. Buffalo, NY: Prometheus Books, 1981 (originally published in 1920).

Huberman, Jurgen. "Technology and Science as 'Ideology.' " Pp. 81–122 in *Toward a Rational Society*, Jurgen Huberman, ed. Boston: Beacon, 1971.

Hufford, David J. *The Terror That Comes in the Night*. Philadelphia: University of Pennsylvania Press, 1982.

Hume, David. *An Inquiry Concerning Human Understanding*, L. A. Selby-Bigge, 2nd ed. New York: Oxford University Press, 1967.

Humphrey, Betty M. "Introversion-Extroversion Ratings in Relation to Scores in ESP Tests." *Journal of Parapsychology*, 15 (1951), 252–262.

Huntington, E. V. "Exact Probabilities in Certain Card-Matching Problems." *Science*, 86 (Nov. 1937), 499–500.

Hyman, R. "Psychics and Scientists: 'Mind-Reach' and Remote Viewing." *Humanist* (May/June 1977), 16–20.

Hyman, R. "Further Comments on Schmidt's PK Experiments." *Skeptical Enquirer*, Vol. 5, no. 3 (1981), 34–40.

Journal of Parapsychology. "Glossary," Vol. 46, no. 1 (1982), 81.

Kanthamani, H., J. M. Haight, and J. E. Kennedy. "Personality and Spontaneous Experiences: An Exploratory Study." In *Research in Parapsychology, 1978*, W. G. Roll, ed. Metuchen, NJ: Scarecrow Press, 1979.

Kanthamani, H. (B. K.), and E. F. Kelly. "Awareness of Success in an Exceptional Subject." *Journal of Parapsychology*, Vol. 38, no. 4 (1974), 355–382.

Kanthamani, B. K., and K. Ramakrishna Rao. "Personality Characteristics of ESP Subjects. IV. Neurotizism and ESP." *Journal of Parapsychology*, Vol. 37, no. 1 (1973), 37–50.

Keil, H.H.J. "Pavel Stepanek and the Focusing Effect." *Research Letter of the Parapsychology Laboratory*, University of Utrecht, 8 (Oct. 1977), 22–40.

Kellogg, C. E. "New Evidence (?) for 'Extra-Sensory Perception.' " *Scientific Monthly*, 45 (Oct. 1937) 331–341.

Kelly, E. F., and B. K. Kanthamani. "A Subject's Efforts Towards Voluntary Control." *Journal of Parapsychology*, Vol. 36, no. 3 (1972), 185–197.

Kelly, E. F., H. (B. K.) Kanthamani, I. L. Child, and F. W. Young. "On the Relation Between Visual and ESP Confusion Structures in an Exceptional ESP Subject." *Journal of the American Society for Psychical Research*, 69 (1975), 1–32.

Kiang, T. "Sighted Hands: A Report on Experiments with 4 Chinese Children to Test Their Ability to See Color Pictures and Symbols with Their Hands." *Journal of the American Society for Psychical Research*, 51 (June 1982), 304–308.

King, M. D. "Reason, Tradition, and the Progressiveness of Science." *History and Theory*, Vol. 10, no. 1 (1971), 3–32.

King, Stephen. *Danse Macabre*. New York: Everest House, 1981.

Klotz, Irving M. "The N-Ray Affair." *Scientific American*, Vol. 242, no. 5 (1980), 168–174.

Kottler, M. J. "Alfred Russell Wallace, the Origin of Man and Spiritualism." *Isis*, 65 (1974), 145–172.

Krippner, Stanley. "Science as a Beauty Contest: Some Remarks on the 'Cryptoscience.' " *Zetetic Scholar*, 10 (1982), 129–130.

Kuhn, T. S. *The Structure of Scientific Revolutions*. Chicago: University of Chicago Press, 1962, 2nd ed. 1970a.

Kuhn, T. S. "Logic of Discovery or Psychology of Research?" Pp. 1–2 in *Criticism and the Growth of Knowledge*, Imre Lakatos and Alan Musgrave, eds. Cambridge: Cambridge University Press, 1970b.

Kuhn T. S. "Reflections on My Critics." Pp. 231–278 in *Criticism and the Growth of Knowledge*, Imre Lakatos and Alan Musgrave, eds. Cambridge: Cambridge University Press, 1970c.

Kuhn, T. S. *The Essential Tension*. Chicago: University of Chicago Press, 1977.

Kurtz, Paul. Personal conversation, Aug. 1979.

Langmuir, I. "Pathological Science." Colloquium given at the Knolls Research Laboratory, Dec. 18, 1953; transcribed and edited by R. Hall, General Electric Research and Development Center Report, 68-c-035, Apr. 1968, and cited by Zuckerman (1977:112).

Laudan, Larry. *Progress and Its Problems*. Berkeley and Los Angeles: University of California Press, 1977.

Laudan, Rachel. "The Recent Revolution in Geology and Kuhn's Theory of Scientific Change." Pp. 284–296 in *Paradigms and Revolutions*, Gary Gutting, ed. Notre Dame, IN: University of Notre Dame Press, 1980.

Lemert, E. M. *Social Pathology: A Systematic Approach to the Theory of Sociopathic Behavior*. New York: McGraw-Hill, 1951.

LeShan, L. *Toward a General Theory of the Paranormal.* Parapsychological Monographs no. 9. New York: Parapsychology Foundation, 1969.

LeShan, L. *The Medium, the Mystic, and the Physicist.* New York: Viking Press, 1974.

Locke, J. *An Essay Concerning Human Understanding.* New York: Dover Publications, 1959 (originally published in 1690).

MacKenzie, Brian, and S. Lynne MacKenzie. "Whence the Enchanted Boundary? Sources and Significance of the Parapsychological Tradition." *Journal of Parapsychology,* Vol. 44, no. 2 (1980), 123–166.

Marks, D., and R. Kammann. "Information Transmission in Remote Viewing Experiments." *Nature,* 274 (1978), 680–681.

Marks, David, and Richard Kammann. *Psychology of the Psychic.* Buffalo: Prometheus Books, 1980.

Marwick, B. "The Soal-Goldney Experiments with Basil Shackleton, New Evidence for Data Manipulation." *Proceedings of the Society for Psychical Research,* 56 (1979), 250–281.

Masterman, Margaret. "The Nature of a Paradigm." Pp. 59–89 in *Criticism and Growth of Knowledge,* Imre Lakatos and Alan Musgrave, eds. Cambridge: Cambridge University Press, 1970.

Mauskopf, Seymour H., and Michael McVaugh. "The Controversy over Statistics in Parapsychology, 1934–1938." Pp. 105–123 in *The Reception of Unconventional Science,* Seymour H. Mauskopf, ed. AAAS Selected Symposium Series, Boulder, CO: Westview Press, 1979.

Mauskopf, Seymour H., and Michael McVaugh. *Elusive Science: Origins of Experimental Psychical Research.* Baltimore: Johns Hopkins University Press, 1981.

McClenon, James. "An Investigation of a Haunting in Baltimore." Paper presented to the Southeastern Regional Parapsychological Association Conference, Winter Park, FL, Feb. 15, 1980.

McClenon, James. "A Continuing Investigation of a Haunting in Baltimore." Paper presented to the Southeastern Regional Parapsychological Association Conference, Duke University, Durham, NC, Feb. 13, 14, 1981a.

McClenon, James. "A Summary of an Investigation of a Haunting in Baltimore." *Theta, the Journal of the Psychical Research Foundation,* Vol. 9, no. 4 (1981b), 12–14.

McClenon, James. "A Skeptic/Believer Experiment Involving Psychic Influence of Response to a Questionnaire." Abstracted in the *Journal of Parapsychology,* Vol. 45, no. 3 (1981c), 266.

McClenon, James. "Deviant Science: The Case of Parapsychology." Doctoral dissertation, University of Maryland, 1981d.

McClenon, James. "A Survey of Elite Scientists: Their Attitudes Toward ESP and Parapsychology." *Journal of Parapsychology*, Vol. 46, no. 2 (1982), 127–152.

McConnell, J. V. "Memory Transfer through Cannibalism in Planarians." *Journal of Neuropsychiatry*, Vol. 3, suppl. 1 (1962), 42–48.

McConnell, J. V. "Worms and Things . . ." *Worm Runner's Digest*, Vol. 11, no. 1 (1969), 1–4.

McConnell, J. V., R. Jacobson, and D. P. Kimble. "The Effects of Regeneration upon Retention of a Conditioned Response in the Planarian." *Journal of Comparative and Physiological Psychology*, 52 (1959), 1–5.

McConnell, R. A. "The Motivations of Parapsychologists and Other Scientists." *Journal of the American Society for Psychical Research*, 69 (1975), 273–280.

McConnell, R. A. "The Resolution of Conflicting Beliefs about the ESP Evidence." *Journal of Parapsychology*, 41 (1977), 198–214.

McConnell, R. A., and T. K. Clark. "Training, Belief, and Mental Conflict within the Parapsychological Association." *Journal of Parapsychology*, Vol. 44, no. 3 (1980), 245–268.

McCready, William C., and Andrew M. Greeley. *The Ultimate Values of the American Population*. Vol. 23, Sage Library of Social Research. Beverly Hills, CA: Sage Publications, 1976.

McDaniel, Linda, and Catherine Borras. *Handbook, American Association for the Advancement of Science, 1979*. AAAS Publication 79-5. Washington, DC, 1979.

Mead, Margaret. Letter to Charles Tart, Oct. 9, 1975. From the files of Theodore Rockwell.

Mead, Margaret. Introduction to *Mind-Reach*, by Russell Targ and Harold Puthoff. New York: Dell, 1977.

Medhurst, R. G., K. M. Goldney, and M. R. Barrington. *Crookes and the Spirit World*. New York: Taplinger, 1972.

Merton, Robert. "Science and Technology in a Democratic Order." *Journal of Legal and Political Science*, 1 (Oct. 1942), 115–126.

Merton, Robert. *Social Theory and Social Structure*. New York: The Free Press, 1949; rev. ed., 1957; enlarged ed., 1968.

Merton, Robert K. *Science, Technology and Society in Seventeenth Century England*. New York: Harper and Row, 1970 (first published in 1938 as vol. IV, part 2, of *Osiris: Studies on the History of Philosophy of Science, and on the History of Learning and Culture*).

Merton, Robert K. *The Sociology of Science, Theoretical and Empirical Investigations*, Norman W. Storer, ed. Chicago: University of Chicago Press, 1973.

Millar, B. "The Observational Theories: A Primer." *European Journal of Parapsychology,* 2 (1978), 304–332.

Mitroff, Ian I. "Norms and Counternorms in a Select Group of the Apollo Moon Scientists: A Case Study of the Ambivalence of Scientists." *American Sociological Review,* 39 (Aug. 1974), 579–595.

Morris, Robert L. "Comments by Robert L. Morris." *Zetetic Scholar,* 6 (1980), 100.

Morris, R. L., W. G. Roll, J. Klein, and G. Wheeler. "EEG Patterns and ESP Results in Forced-Choice Experiments with Lalsingh Harribance." *Journal of the American Society for Psychical Research,* 66 (1972), 253–268.

Mosher, D. I. "The Development and Multitrait-Multimethod Matrix Analysis of Three Measures of Three Aspects of Guilt." *Journal of Consulting Psychology,* 30 (1966), 25–29.

Moss, S., and Butler, D. C. "The Scientific Credibility of ESP." California State University, Northridge (cited by Wagner and Monnet, 1979), n.d.

Mulkay, M. J. "Some Aspects of Cultural Growth in the Natural Sciences." *Social Research,* Vol. 36, no. 1 (1969), 22–52.

Mulkay, M. J. *The Social Process of Innovation.* London: Macmillan, 1972a.

Mulkay, M. J. "Conformity and Innovation in Science." In *The Sociology of Science,* Paul Halmos and Martin Albrow, eds. The Sociological Review Monograph, 18, Keele, England: University of Keele, 1972b.

Mulkay, M. J. "The Mediating Role of the Scientific Elite." *Social Studies of Science,* 6 (1976), 445–470.

Mulkay, M. J. *Science and the Sociology of Knowledge.* London: Allen and Unwin, 1979.

Murphy, G. *Challenge of Psychical Research.* New York: Harper, 1961.

Musso, J. R., and Mitra Granero. "An ESP Drawing Experiment with a High-Scoring Subject." *Journal of Parapsychology,* Vol. 37, no. 1 (1973), 13–36.

Nicol, J. Fraser. "Historical Background." Pp. 305–323 in the *Handbook of Parapsychology,* Benjamin B. Wolman, ed. New York: Van Nostrand Reinhold, 1977.

Overington, Michael A. "A Critical Celebration of Gusfield's *The Literary Rhetoric of Science.*" *American Sociological Review,* 42 (Feb. 1977), 170–173.

Overington, Michael A. "Doing What Comes Rationally: Some Development in Metatheory." *The American Sociologist,* Vol. 14, no. 1. (Feb. 1979), 2–11.

Palfreman, Jon. "Between Skepticism and Credulity: A Study of Victorian Scientific Attitudes to Modern Spiritualism." Pp. 201–236 in *On The Margins of Science: The Social Construction of Rejected Knowledge,* Roy Wallis, ed. Hanley, England: J. H. Brookes, 1979.

Palmer, John A. "Attitudes and Personality Traits in Experimental Research." Pp. 175–201 in the *Handbook of Parapsychology*, Benjamin B. Wolman, ed. New York: Van Nostrand Reinhold, 1977.

Palmer, John. "Extrasensory Perception: Research Findings." Pp. 59–243 in *Advances in Parapsychological Research, 2: Extrasensory Perception*, Stanley Krippner, ed. New York: Plenum, 1978.

Palmer, John. "A Community Mail Survey of Psychic Experiences." *Journal of the American Society for Psychical Research*, 73 (July 1979), 221–251.

Palmer, John. "Comments by John Palmer." *Zetetic Scholar*, 6 (1980), 106–107.

Parapsychological Association Council Resolution, 1979. From the files of Theodore Rockwell.

Parssinen, Terry M. "Professional Deviants and the History of Medicine: Medical Mesmerists in Victorian Britain." Pp. 103–120 in *On the Margins of Science: The Social Construction of Rejected Knowledge*, Roy Wallis, ed. Hanley, England: J. H. Brookes, 1979.

Pehek, J. O., H. J. Kyler, and D. L. Faust. "Image Modulation in Corona Discharge Photography." *Science*, 194 (Oct. 1976), 263–270.

Perelman, Chaim. *The New Rhetoric: A Treatise on Argumentation*. Notre Dame, IN: University of Notre Dame Press, 1969.

Phillips, David T. "Parapsychology at UCSB, a Proposal to the Executive Committee of the College of Letters and Science, University of California, Santa Barbara." Feb. 6, 1979.

Prabhavananda, S., and C. Isherwood. *How to Know God: The Yoga Aphorisms of Patanjali*. Hollywood, CA: Vedanta Press, 1953.

Prasad, J., and I. Stevenson. "A Survey of Spontaneous Psychical Experiences in School Children of Upper Pradesh, India." *International Journal of Parapsychology*, 10 (1968), 241–261.

Pratt, J. G. "The Homing Problem in Pigeons." *Journal of Parapsychology*, 17 (1953), 34–60.

Pratt, J. G. "Preliminary Experiments with a 'Borrowed' Outstanding ESP Subject." *Journal of the American Society for Psychical Research*, 42 (1964), 333–345.

Pratt, J. G. "A Decade of Research with a Selected ESP Subject: An Overview and Reappraisal of the Work with Pavel Stepanek." *Proceedings of the American Society for Psychical Research*, 30 (1973), 1–78. (See "The Findings as Evidence for ESP," pp. 24–29.)

Pratt, J. G. "Soviet Research in Parapsychology." Pp. 883–903 in the *Handbook of Parapsychology*, Benjamin B. Wolman, ed. New York: Van Nostrand Reinhold, 1977.

Pratt, J. G., and J. G. Blom. "A Confirmatory Experiment with a 'Borrowed' Outstanding ESP Subject." *Journal of the American Society for Psychical Research*, 42 (1964), 381–389.

Pratt, J. G., et al. "Identification of Concealed Randomized Objects through Acquired Response Habits of Stimulus and Word Association." *Nature*, 220 (Oct. 1968), 89–91.

Pratt, J. G., H.H.J. Keil, and I. Stevenson. "Three Experimenters' Tests of Pavel Stepanek During His 1968 Visit to Charlottesville." *Journal of the American Society for Psychical Research*, 64 (1970), 18–39.

Pratt, J., J. B. Rhine, B. M. Smith, C. E. Stuart, and J. A. Greenwood. *Extra Sensory Perception After Sixty Years*. New York: Henry Holt, 1940.

Price, Derek. *Little Science, Big Science*. New York: Columbia University Press, 1963.

Price, G. R. "Science and the Supernatural." *Science*, 122 (Aug. 1955), 359–367.

Price, G. R. "Apology to Rhine and Soal." *Science*, 175 (Jan. 1972), 359.

Puthoff, H. E. Personal communication, Aug. 1979.

Puthoff, H. E. "Documentation Report #1," Aug. 17, 1981(a).

Puthoff, H. E. "Addendum to Documentation Report #1 of 17 Aug. 1981." Letter from Zev Pressman, Sept. 24, 1981(b).

Puthoff, H. E., and R. Targ. "A Perceptual Channel for Information Transfer over Kilometer Distances: Historical Perspective and Recent Research." *Proceedings of the IEEE*, Vol. 64, no. 3 (Mar. 1976), 329–354.

Puthoff, H. E., and R. Targ. "Rebuttal of Criticism of Remote Viewing Experiments," *Nature*, 292 (July 1981), 388.

Puthoff, H. E., R. Targ, and C. T. Tart. "Resolution in Remote Viewing Studies: Mini-Targets." Brief presented at the 22nd Annual Parapsychological Association Convention, Moraga, CA, Aug. 15–18, 1979.

Randi, James. *Flim-Flam! The Truth about Unicorns, Parapsychology and Other Delusions*. New York: Lippincott and Crowell, 1980.

Rao, K. Ramakrishna. "The Scientific Credibility of ESP." *Perceptual and Motor Skills*, 49 (1979), 415–429.

Rao, K. Ramakrishna. "Comments by K. Ramakrishna Rao." *Zetetic Scholar*, 6 (1980), 107–109.

Rao, K. Ramakrishna. "Hume's Fallacy." *Journal of Parapsychology*, Vol. 45, no. 2 (1981), 147–152.

Rawcliffe, D. H. *Illusions and Delusions of the Supernatural and the Occult*. New York: Dover, 1959.

Rhine, J. B. *Extrasensory Perception*. (Reprint). Boston: Bruce Humphries, 1964 (originally published in 1934).

Rhine, J. B. *New Frontiers of the Mind.* New York: Farrar and Rinehart, 1937.

Rhine, J. B. Editorial, *FRNM Bulletin,* no. 7, 1967.

Rhine, J. B. "Some Guiding Concepts for Parapsychology." *Journal of Parapsychology,* Vol. 32, no. 3 (1968), 190–218.

Rhine, J. B. "News and Comments: Is Parapsychology Losing Its Way?" *Journal of Parapsychology,* Vol. 36, no. 2 (June 1972), 167–176.

Rhine, J. B. "News and Comments." *Journal of Parapsychology,* Vol. 37, no. 4 (1973), 351–366.

Rhine, J. B. "A New Case of Experimenter Unreliability." *Journal of Parapsychology,* 38 (1974), 215–225.

Rhine, J. B. Personal communication, May 1979.

Rhine, L. E. "Hallucinatory Psi Experiences I. An Introductory Survey." *Journal of Parapsychology,* 20 (1956), 233–256.

Rhine, L. E. "Research Methods with Spontaneous Cases." Pp. 59–80 in the *Handbook of Parapsychology,* Benjamin B. Wolman, ed. New York: Van Nostrand Reinhold, 1977.

Rhine, L. E. Personal communication, May 1979.

Richter, Maurice N., Jr. *Science as a Cultural Process.* Cambridge, MA: Schenkman, 1972.

Rockwell, Theodore, personal files, 3403 Woolsey Drive, Chevy Chase, MD 20815 (used with his permission).

Rockwell, Theodore. "*Science* Saga." Notes, 1978a.

Rockwell, Theodore. "Telephone conversation with R.C." Notes, Sept. 18, 1978b.

Rockwell, Theodore. "Notes." 1980.

Rockwell, W. Teed. "Inquiry Concerning Human Understanding." Paper, 1980.

Rogo, D. Scott. *Parapsychology: A Century of Inquiry.* New York: Dell, 1975.

Roll, William. "Poltergeists." Pp. 382–413 in *Handbook of Parapsychology,* Benjamin B. Wolman, ed. New York: Van Nostrand Reinhold, 1977.

Roll, W. G., and Judith Klein. "Further Forced Choice of ESP Experiments with Lalsingh Harribance." *Journal of the American Society for Psychical Research,* 66 (1972), 102–112.

Rosenthal, Robert. "Controversial Science, Crypto Science, and Taboo Science." *Zetetic Scholar,* 10 (1982), 103–104.

Rosenthal, Robert, and Donald B. Rubin. "International Expectancy Effects: The First 345 Studies." *Behavioral and Brain Sciences,* 3 (1978), 377–415.

Rostand, Jean. *Error and Deception in Science,* translated from the French by A. J. Pomerans. New York: Basic Books, 1960.

Runcorn, S. K., ed. *Continental Drift*. New York and London: Academic Press, 1962.

Ryzl, Milan. *Parapsychology: A Scientific Approach*. New York: Hawthorne, 1970.

Scarpitti, Frank R., and Paul T. McFarlane. *Deviance; Action, Reaction, Interaction*. Reading, MA: Addison-Wesley, 1975.

Schlitz, Marilyn, and Elmer Gruber. "Transcontinental Remote Viewing." *Journal of Parapsychology*, Vol. 44, no. 4 (Dec. 1980), 305–318.

Schmeidler, Gertrude. Form letter sent to people interested in working as a parapsychologist, n.d.

Schmeidler, Gertrude R. "Methods for Controlled Research on ESP and PK." Pp. 131–159 in *Handbook of Parapsychology*, Benjamin B. Wolman, ed. New York: Van Nostrand Reinhold, 1977.

Schmeidler, Gertrude R., and Michaelson Maher. "Judges' Responses to the Nonverbal Behavior of Psi-Conductive and Psi-Inhibitory Experimenters." *Journal of the American Society for Psychical Research*, Vol. 75, no. 3 (July 1981), 241–258.

Schmeidler, Gertrude, and R. A. McConnell. *ESP and Personality Patterns*. Westport, CN: Greenwood Press, 1973 (originally published, 1958).

Schmidt, H. "Quantum Processes Predicted?" *New Scientist*, 44 (1969), 114–115.

Schmidt, H. "PK Tests with a High-speed Random Number Generator." *Journal of Parapsychology*, 37 (1973), 105–118.

Schmidt, H. "A Logically Consistent Model of a World with Psi Interactions." Pp. 205–228 in *Quantum Physics and Parapsychology*, L. Oteri, ed. New York: Parapsychology Foundation, 1975a.

Schmidt, H. "Toward a Mathematical Theory of Psi." *Journal of the American Society for Psychical Research*, 69 (1975b), 301–319.

Schmidt, H. "Can an Effect Precede Its Cause? A Model of a Non-Causal World." *Foundation of Physics*, 8 (1978), 463–480.

Schmidt-Koenig, Klaus. *Avian Orientation and Navigation*. New York: Academic Press, 1979.

Schouten, S. A., and E. F. Kelly, et al. "On the Experiment of Brugmans, Heymans and Weinberg." *European Journal of Parapsychology*, 2 (1968), 247–290.

Science News, 112 (Aug. 20, 1977), 1.

Shapere, D. "The Structure of Scientific Revolutions." Review in *Philosophical Review*, 73 (1964), 363–394.

Shroyer, Trent. "Toward a Critical Theory for Advanced Industrial Society." *Recent Sociology*, no. 2, Hans Peter Dreitzel, ed. London: Macmillan, Collier-Macmillan, 1970.

Sidgwick, Henry. "Presidential Address." *Proceedings of the Society for Psychical Research*, 1, part 1 (1882).

Sidgwick, H. "Address to the Society for Psychical Research," Second Meeting, *Proceedings of the Society for Psychical Research*, 1 (1882–1883), 65–69.

Sidgwick, H., and Committee. "Report on the Census of Hallucinations." *Proceedings of the Society for Psychical Research*, 10 (1894), 25–422.

Singer, Barry, and Victor A. Benassi. "Occult Beliefs." *American Scientist*, Vol. 69, no. 1 (Jan.–Feb., 1981) 49–55.

Sklair, Leslie. "The Political Sociology of Science: A Critique of Current Orthodoxies." Pp. 43–60 in *The Sociology of Science*, Paul Halmos and Martin Albrow, eds. The Sociological Review Monograph, 18. Keele, England: University of Keele, 1972.

Society for Psychical Research. *Proceedings of the Society for Psychical Research*, 1 (1882).

Stanford, R. G. "An Experimentally Testable Model for Spontaneous Psi Events." *Journal of the American Society for Psychical Research*, 68 (1974), 34–57, 321–356.

Stanford, R. G. "Are Parapsychologists Paradigmless in Psiland?" Pp. 1–18 in *The Philosophy of Parapsychology*, B. Shapin and L. Coly, eds. New York: Parapsychology Foundation, 1977a.

Stanford, R. G. "Conceptual Frameworks of Contemporary Psi Research." Pp. 823–858 in the *Handbook of Parapsychology*, Benjamin B. Wolman, ed. New York: Van Nostrand Reinhold, 1977b.

Stanford, R. G. "Toward Reinterpreting Psi Events." *Journal of the American Society for Psychical Research*, 72 (1978), 197–214.

Stanford, R. G. "Comments by Rex G. Stanford." *Zetetic Scholar*, 6 (1980), 113–115.

Stanford, R. G. "Are We Shamans or Scientists?" *Journal of the American Society for Psychical Research*, 75 (Jan. 1981), 61–70.

Stern, B. E., and D. Lewis. *X-Rays*. Bath, England: Pitman Press, 1971.

Sterne, T. E. "The Solution of a Problem in Probability." *Science*, 86 (1937), 500–501.

Stevens, S. S. "The Market for Miracles." *Contemporary Psychology*, 12 (1967), 1–3.

Stevenson, Ian. "Reincarnation: Field Studies and Theoretical Issues." Pp. 631–663 in the *Handbook of Parapsychology*, Benjamin B. Wolman, ed. New York: Van Nostrand Reinhold, 1977.

Stevenson, Ian. "Cryptomnesia and Parapsychology." *Journal of the Society for Psychical Research*, 52 (Feb. 1983), 1–30.

Stuart, C. E., and J. A. Greenwood. "A Review of Criticism of the Mathematical Evaluation of ESP Data." *Journal of Parapsychology,* 1 (1937), 295–304.

Stump, J. P., W. G. Roll, and Muriel Roll. "Some Exploratory Forced Choice ESP Experiments with Lalsingh Harribance." *Journal of the Society for Psychical Research,* 64 (1970), 421–431.

Swann, I. *To Kiss Earth Good-bye.* New York: Hawthorne, 1975; New York: Dell, 1977.

Szasz, T. S. "A Critical Analysis of the Fundamental Concepts of Psychical Research." *Psychiatric Quarterly,* 31 (1957), 96–107.

Targ, Russell. "Precognition and Everyday Life: A Physical Model." Paper presented at the International Conference on Parapsychology, Amsterdam, 1972.

Targ, R., and H. Puthoff. "Information Transmission under Conditions of Sensory Shielding." *Nature,* 252 (Oct. 1974), 602–607.

Targ, R., and H. E. Puthoff. *Mind-Reach.* London: Jonathan Cape, 1977.

Tart, C. T. *Learning to Use Extrasensory Perception.* Chicago: University of Chicago Press, 1976.

Tart, C. T., Harold Puthoff, and Russell Targ. "Remote Viewing: An Examination of the Marks and Kammann Cueing Artifact Hypothesis." Brief presented at the 23rd Annual Parapsychological Association Convention, Reykjavik, Iceland, Aug. 13–16, 1980a.

Tart, C. T., H. E. Puthoff, and R. Targ. "Information Transmission in Remote Viewing Experiments." *Nature,* 284 (Mar. 1980b), 191.

Taylor, John. *Superminds.* New York: Viking Press, 1975.

Taylor, John. *Science and the Supernatural.* New York: E. P. Dutton, 1980.

Terry, J. C., and C. Honorton. "Psi Information Retrieval in the Ganzfeld: Two Confirmatory Studies." *Journal of the American Society for Psychical Research,* 70 (1976), 207–219.

Thalbourne, Michael A. "Extroversion and the Sheep–Goat Variable: A Conceptual Replication." *Journal of the American Society for Psychical Research,* 75 (1981), 105–119.

Theta, The Journal of the Psychical Research Foundation, Vol. 8, no. 3 (Summer 1980).

Thompson, R., and J. V. McConnell. "Classical Conditioning in the Planarian, *Dugesia dorotocephala.*" *Journal of Comparative and Physiological Psychology,* Vol. 48, no. 1 (1955), 65–68.

Thouless, R. H. *Experimental Psychical Research.* Baltimore: Penguin, 1963.

Tietze, T. R. *Margery.* New York: Harper and Row, 1973.

Timmerman, John P. (Chairman, Associates Education and Business Office, Center for UFO Studies). Personal correspondence, Dec. 10, 1982.

Touimin, S. E. "Does the Distinction Between Normal and Revolutionary Science Hold Water?" Pp. 197–230 in *Criticism and Growth of Knowledge*, Imre Lakatos and Alan Musgrave, eds. Cambridge: Cambridge University Press, 1970.

Travis, G.D.L. "On the Construction of Creativity: The 'Memory Transfer' Phenomenon and the Importance of Being Earnest." Pp. 165–193 in *The Social Process of Scientific Investigation*, Karin D. Knorr, Roger Krohn, and Richard Whitley, eds. Boston: D. Reidel, 1980.

Travis, G.D.L. "Replicating Replication? Aspect of the Social Construction of Learning in Planarian Worms." *Social Studies of Science*, Vol. 11, no. 1 (1981), 11–32.

Truzzi, Marcello. "Editorial: On Psuedo-sciences and Proto-sciences." *The Zetetic*, Vol. 1, no. 2 (Spring–Summer 1977), 3–8.

Truzzi, Marcello. "On the Extraordinary: An Attempt at Clarification." *Zetetic Scholar*, 1 (1978), 11–14.

Truzzi, Marcello. "Editorial." *Zetetic Scholar*, 6 (1980), 3.

Vasiliev, Leonid. *Experiments in Mental Suggestion*. Church Crookham, England: Institute for the Study of Mental Images, 1963.

Velikovsky, Immanuel. *Worlds in Collison*. Garden City, NY: Doubleday, 1950.

Voegelin, Eric. "The Origins of Scientism." *Social Research*, 15 (1948), 462–494.

Wagner, M. W., and Mary Monnet. "Attitudes of College Professors Toward Extra-Sensory Perception." *Zetetic Scholar*, 5 (1979), 7–16.

Walker, E. H. "Foundations of Paraphysical and Parapsychological Phenomena." Pp. 1–53 in *Quantum Physics and Parapsychology*, L. Oteri, ed. New York: Parapsychology Foundation, 1975.

Walker, Jearl. "Drops of Water Dance on a Hot Skillet and the Experimenter Walks on Hot Coals." *Scientific American*, Vol. 237, no. 2 (1977), 126–131.

Warner, L. "A Second Survey of Psychological Opinion on ESP." *Journal of Parapsychology*, 16 (1952), 284–295.

Warner, L., and C. C. Clark. "A Survey of Psychological Opinion on ESP." *Journal of Parapsychology*, 2 (1938), 296–301.

Weber, Max. "Science as a Vocation." Pp. 569–589 in *The Sociology of Science*, Bernard Barber and Walter Hirsch, eds. New York: Free Press of Glencoe, 1962.

Wegener, A. *The Origin of Continents and Oceans*, trans. John Biram, from the 4th (1924) German ed. New York: Dover, 1966.

Westrum, Ron. "Science and Social Intelligence about Anomalies: The Case of Meteorites." Paper presented at the meetings of the American Sociological Association, Chicago, IL, Oct. 1977a.

Westrum, Ron. "Science and Social Intelligence about Anomalies: The Case of UFO's." *Social Studies of Science*, Vol. 7, no. 3 (1977b).

Westrum, Ron. "Crypto-Science and Social Intelligence about Anomalies." *Zetetic Scholar,* 10 (1982), 89–102.

Wheeler, John. "Drive the Pseudos Out of the Workshop of Science." *New York Review of Books,* Apr. 13, 1979a.

Wheeler, J. A. "Parapsychology—A Correction." *Science,* 205 (July 1979b), 144.

White, John. "Second Thoughts: The New Disciples of Scientism." *Human Behavior,* Feb. 1979, 70–73.

White, Rhea. *Parapsychology: Sources of Information.* Metuchen, NJ: Scarecrow Press, 1973.

White, Rhea A. "The Influence of the Experimenter Motivation, Attitudes and Methods of Handling Subjects in Psi Test Results." Pp. 273–304 in the *Handbook of Parapsychology,* Benjamin B. Wolman, ed. New York: Van Nostrand Reinhold, 1977.

White, Rhea A. "On the Genesis of Research Hypotheses in Parapsychology." Paper presented to the 22nd Annual Parapsychological Association, Moraga, CA, 1979.

White, Rhea. Personal letter, Dec. 1982.

Whiteman, J.H.M. "Parapsychology and Physics." Pp. 730–756 in the *Handbook of Parapsychology,* Benjamin B. Wolman, ed. New York: Van Nostrand Reinhold, 1977.

Whitley, Richard D. "Black Boxism and the Sociology of Science: A Discussion of the Major Developments in the Field." Pp. 61–98 in *The Sociology of Science,* Paul Halmos and Martin Albrow, eds. The Sociological Review Monograph, 18. Keele, England: University of Keele, 1972.

Whyte, William H., Jr. *The Organization Man.* New York: Simon and Schuster, 1956.

Willoughby, R. R., to J. B. Rhine, Aug. 1, 1934. Rhine Papers, Department of Manuscripts, Perkins Library, Duke University, Durham, North Carolina; also quoted by Mauskopf and McVaugh (1979:109).

Wilson, Colin. *The Occult.* New York: Random House, 1973.

Winkelman, Michael. "Science and Parapsychology: An Ideological Revolution." Paper presented to the 22nd Annual Meeting of the Parapsychological Association, Moraga, CA, 1979.

Wolfe, Bernard, and Raymond Rosenthal. *Hypnotism Comes of Age.* New York: Bobbs-Merrill, 1948.

Wolman, B. B., ed. *Handbook of Parapsychology.* New York: Van Nostrand Reinhold, 1977.

Wood, Robert C. "The Rise of an Apolitical Elite." Pp. 41–72 in *Scientists and National Policy Making,* Robert Gilpin and Christopher Wright, eds. New York: Columbia University Press, 1964.

Wortz, E. C., Jeff Eerkens, et al. "Novel Biophysical Information Transfer Mechanisms." Jan. 14, 1976, Doc. #76-13197; CIA contract #XG 4208 (54-20)75S.

Wright, Christopher. "Scientists and the Establishment of Science Affairs." Pp. 257–302 in *Scientists and National Policy Making*, Robert Gilpin and Christopher Wright, eds. New York: Columbia University Press, 1964.

Young, Gay. "Parapsychology: Alternative World View." Paper presented to the Southern Sociological Society, Louisville, KY, Apr. 8–11, 1981.

Zimmerman, Howard. Personal letter, Dec. 27, 1982.

Zimmerman, Howard. Files of the Executive Secretary of the Parapsychological Association.

Zorab, G. "Parapsychological Developments in the Netherlands." *European Journal of Parapsychology*, 1976, pp. 57–82 (see pp. 64–67).

Zuckerman, Harriet. "Deviant Behavior and Social Control in Science." Pp. 87–138 in *Deviance and Social Change*, Edward Sagarin, ed. Beverly Hills, CA: Sage Publications, 1977.

Zusne, Leonard, and Warren H. Jones. *Anomalistic Psychology*. Hillsdale, NJ: Lawrence Erlbaum Associates, 1982.

Index